A WORLD BANK COUNTRY STUDY

China

Between Plan and Market

The World Bank
Washington, D.C.

Copyright © 1990
The International Bank for Reconstruction
and Development/THE WORLD BANK
1818 H Street, N.W.
Washington, D.C. 20433, U.S.A.

World Bank Country Studies are among the many reports originally prepared for internal use as part of the continuing analysis by the Bank of the economic and related conditions of its developing member countries and of its dialogues with the governments. Some of the reports are published in this series with the least possible delay for the use of governments and the academic, business and financial, and development communities. The typescript of this paper therefore has not been prepared in accordance with the procedures appropriate to formal printed texts, and the World Bank accepts no responsibility for errors.

The World Bank does not guarantee the accuracy of the data included in this publication and accepts no responsibility whatsoever for any consequence of their use. Any maps that accompany the text have been prepared solely for the convenience of readers; the designations and presentation of material in them do not imply the expression of any opinion whatsoever on the part of the World Bank, its affiliates, or its Board or member countries concerning the legal status of any country, territory, city, or area or of the authorities thereof or concerning the delimitation of its boundaries or its national affiliation.

The complete backlist of publications from the World Bank is shown in the annual *Index of Publications,* which contains an alphabetical title list (with full ordering information) and indexes of subjects, authors, and countries and regions. The latest edition is available free of charge from the Publications Sales Unit, Department F, The World Bank, 1818 H Street, N.W., Washington, D.C. 20433, U.S.A., or from Publications, The World Bank, 66, avenue d'Iéna, 75116 Paris, France.

ISSN: 0253-2123

Library of Congress Cataloging-in-Publication Data

```
World Bank.
    China : between plan and market / World Bank.
       p.   cm. -- (A World Bank country study)
    ISBN 0-8213-1671-0
    1. China--Economic policy--1976-  2. Economic stabilization-
  -China. 3. China--Economic conditions--1976-   I. Title.
  II. Series.
  HC427.92.W67   1990
  338.951--dc20
                                              90-47320
                                                  CIP
```

This Report was prepared by a mission which visited Beijing, Shanghai and Guangzhou in November 1989. The mission was comprised of Shahid Yusuf (Mission Leader), Peter Harrold (AS3CH), Anthony Pellechio (AS3CO), Barry Naughton and Adrian Wood (Consultants). Tejaswi Raparla (AS3CO) participated in the mission work in Washington. The Report was revised following discussions with the Chinese authorities in April 1990. Statistics for the first half of 1990 were updated in Juy 1990 prior to publication.

This Report examines developments in the late 1988 and 1989 and reviews medium-term policies. Detailed information on China's reforms through 1988 can be found in a report, titled Macroeconomic Stability and Industrial Growth under Decentralized Socialism, published in July 1990.

CURRENCY EQUIVALENTS

The Chinese currency is called Renminbi (RMB).
It is denominated in Yuan (Y). Each Yuan is
1 Yuan = 10 jiao = 100 fen

Calendar 1989

US$1.00 = Y 3.72
Y 1.00 = US$0.27

January 1990

US$1.00 = Y 4.72
Y 1.00 = US$0.21

FISCAL YEAR

January 1 - December 31

WEIGHTS AND MEASURES

Metric System

LIST OF ACRONYMS

BIC	-	Bank for International Settlements
FDC	-	Foreign Direct Investment
FEAC	-	Foreign Exchange Adjustment Center
FTC	-	Foreign Trade Corporation
GATT	-	General Agreement for Trade and Tariffs
LIBOR	-	London Interbank Offer Rate
MOFERT	-	Ministry of Foreign Economic Relations and Trade
OECD	-	Organization for Economic Cooperation and Development
OEM	-	Original Equipment Manufacturers
PBC	-	People's Bank of China
PCBC	-	People's Construction Bank of China
RCC	-	Rural Credit Cooperative
SAEC	-	State Administration for Exchange Control
SEZs	-	Special Economic Zones
SPC	-	State Planning Commission
TIC	-	Trust and Investment Corporation
TVEs	-	Township and Village Enterprises

ABSTRACT

The focus of this report is on economic trends in China since June 1989, the government's policy intentions, likely prospects and creditworthiness in the medium term. China's economy has been subject to cycles of increasing amplitude since the start of the reform program in the late seventies. The third cycle culminated in the inflationary crisis of 1988 which induced the authorities to introduce deflationary measures. These were tightened still further following the Tiananmen Incident. The report briefly describes the economic pressures that surfaced during 1988-89. It details the various steps announced by the government between September 1989 and June 1990 for gradually reflating the economy while maintaining price stability. Finally, the report analyzes future proposals for reforms being advanced by the authorities. It provides a series of suggestions in the areas of price, industrial, and trade reforms calling for change on a wider scale over the medium term which makes full use of the window of opportunity created by favorable price trends in 1989-90 and the consensus on a firm macropolicy stance.

Table of Contents

Executive Summary

Introduction

i.   The purpose of this report is to review recent economic developments, including the progress of the medium-term (1989-91) stabilization program being implemented by the authorities since late 1988, and to discuss options for China's future development strategy. The report also analyzes the economic reforms initiated in late 1978.

Background

ii.   Over the last decade, China's GDP growth rate has averaged 9.5 percent per annum. Investment was high throughout (averaging 31 percent of GDP during the early 1980s and 38 percent of GDP since 1985) and was matched by a strong savings performance, which contained the need for external borrowing. Industrial modernization increased the competitiveness of China's manufactures in the international market and merchandise exports grew from $18.3 billion in 1980 to $52.5 billion in 1989. China's share of international trade rose from 0.97 percent to 1.7 percent during the same period. The average incomes of the 800 million rural population more than doubled and absolute poverty receded nationwide. In 1988, some 13 percent of rural households fell below the poverty line, compared with 17 percent in 1981. Infant and child mortality declined, the rate of population growth was slowed and universal education of five years was achieved.

iii.   Economic system and management reforms introduced incrementally after a period of regional experimentation have played a major role in these achievements. They have served to magnify the growth impulse derived from China's high rate of capital accumulation based on domestic savings. The major areas of reform can be summarized as follows:

- farmers and nonagricultural (industrial, commercial, transport) enterprises now have greater freedom to determine the composition and pricing of output, to retain profits and decide on the disposition of retained earnings;

- administrative decentralization has transferred more of the authority to plan and manage economic activity from the central government to provincial and local bodies, better informed about the local situation and strongly motivated to promote development;

- central control over the economy has been scaled back by reducing the number of commodities and the volume of production subject to mandatory plan targets, and the share of key products distributed through state controlled channels;

- although China remains an economy where public ownership is dominant, the government has permitted other forms of ownership (e.g., private, cooperative, foreign joint venture, etc.) and supported these with the necessary regulations and constitutional amendments.

- resources previously annexed by the state have been transferred to enterprises and rural producers and this, together with a degree of fiscal decentralization, has given provincial authorities more discretion in taxation and expenditures;

- product markets have been created, first in the rural areas and then extended to the urban sector, which allow producers to trade their above plan output at freely determined prices;

- financial reforms have dismantled the old monobanking system and increased the variety of financial institutions, as well as the volume and scope of financial transactions and instruments. The pronounced shift away from budgetary support of investment has reinforced the importance of the financial sector in mobilizing and allocating resources;

- external trade, now equivalent to over a quarter of GDP, has opened up the economy significantly, and, in parallel, there has been greater readiness to seek direct foreign investment in a range of manufacturing and service industries. The creation of several Special Economic Zones, with adequate infrastructure, legislation governing foreign investment and the steady elaboration of laws defining the rights of overseas businesses operating in China, have helped attract a large volume of foreign capital.

iv.   The attempts at transforming such a complex economy in fairly short span of time have inevitably resulted in macroeconomic as well as institutional imbalances. During the course of the 1980s, China experienced three cycles in economic activity of increasing severity. This instability, which appears to be associated with the transition from a centrally planned system to one where plan and market are more evenly balanced, has at least three sources. First, the lag between administrative decentralization and the creation of an institutionalized capacity for macromanagement, gave rise to excessive monetary expansion that stoked inflation. Second, multiple pricing, that has evolved with the emergence of free markets alongside the planned system, leads, at times, to additional distortions; it reinforces the propensity towards negotiating prices, taxes, and input allocations; the possibilities for corruption multiply; and enterprises are sheltered from the full force of competition by bureaucratic connections, that provide intermediate goods on terms guaranteeing high returns. Third, because of slow progress towards nationally integrated and competitive markets that would supplement the now attenuated planning mechanism as a source of discipline, decentralized industrial management has permitted provincial bureaucracies to push ahead with unsustainable rates of expansion. Only a fraction of enterprises, almost exclusively in the township and village enterprise (TVE) sector, are financially autonomous. As yet China has been unable to enforce financial accountability on the state and collective enterprises. Closely related to this is the problems posed by the exit of firms through bankruptcy. Closure of state or collectively owned enterprises has been resisted because it leads to unemployment and a loss of productive assets. As a consequence, the effects of market forces to rationalize capacity or achieve efficient resource allocation has so far been blunted. A social security system and some separation of ownership from management, that could dissuade local authorities from becoming too involved in the operations of the enterprise sector would ameliorate these difficulties. However, the development of national welfare system and of an institution such as joint stock ownership is a slow process. Trials have been conducted but full scale operation is still some years away.

Economic Developments in 1988/89

v.   It was against this background of partial reforms that demand pressures became pronounced in the first half of 1988, pushing the economy to the limits of its productive capacity. When, under these overheated conditions, the authorities announced in June 1988, plans for a major price reform to be implemented in 1989, inflation worsened as consumers switched in some panic from financial into real assets. Prices that had been rising at annualized rates of 10-15 percent in early 1988 soared to rates approaching 80 percent, on an annualized basis, by August. Faced with this crisis, the government postponed further price liberalization and, in late 1988, adopted a series of stabilization measures.

vi.   First, the authorities introduced administrative guidelines to reduce state investment in 1989 by 20 percent and to cancel or defer a large number of projects in low priority sectors such as services, office construction and processing industries. By the end of 1988, 14,000 construction projects with a planned investment of almost Y 50 billion had been cancelled. While this amounted to only 4 percent of the total volume of construction then in progress, the impact of the controls on investment became more apparent in early 1989. The value of new projects begun in 1989 declined by 80 percent compared to the previous year.

vii.   Second, a contractionary monetary policy, relying principally on the administrative allocation of credit, was imposed. The Central Bank set a target of 15 percent for the growth of credit in 1989 and began stringently monitoring changes in credit supply on a weekly basis. Conventional monetary instruments reinforced credit controls. Reserve ratios were raised from 12 percent to 13 percent for banks, up to 30 percent for nonbank institutions; rediscount policies were tightened; the redeposit obligations of specialized banks increased; and both deposit as well as lending rates were pushed up by 4 percent and 3 percent respectively, with savings deposits of three years and more being indexed.

viii.   Third, direct controls on prices and marketing were stiffened beginning in late 1988. Numerous regulations, generally ignored during recent years, were applied, albeit with varying degrees of effectiveness in different cities and regions of the country; and local governments were required to notify the central authorities whenever they raised prices for a range of daily necessities and certain raw materials. Finally, the credit squeeze was used to leverage incomes policies with the result that the wage bill of the urban formal sector remained unchanged until the last quarter of 1989, when some wage increases were permitted.

ix.   These measures have reduced the rate of inflation significantly, from an annualized rate of 26 percent in December 1988 to less than 1 percent (on a monthly annualized basis) in the first quarter of 1990. They have checked the growth of labor earnings and, for the time being at least, alleviated cost push pressures. In addition, the steps taken plus curbs on imports of consumer goods have reversed the trade imbalance. After rising in the first two quarters, the trade deficit stabilized at about $6.7 billion in the third quarter of 1989 and a quickening of exports lowered the deficit to $6.6 billion by the year's end. Exports rose 15.4 percent in the first half of 1990, while imports were 17.7 percent lower. As a result, China registered a trade surplus of $4.54 billion. There was a marked slackening in the rate of industrial growth throughout 1989, which became negative in the last quarter. By the first quarter of 1990, industrial output had regained lost ground and was at about the same level as a year earlier. It rose more rapidly in the second quarter and, for the first six months of 1990, registered a growth of 2.2 percent. Urban unemployment worsened somewhat, rising to 2.7 percent by the end of 1989. Initially, much of the shock was absorbed by the large transient population of rural migrants, many of whom have returned to the countryside. But the persistence of slow growth in the first half of 1990 pushed the unemployment rate to over 3.5 percent.

x. The imbalances that developed in 1987/88 and the stabilization measures that have been applied during 1988-90 have brought into sharper focus both the strengths and weaknesses of China's economy. At this juncture, it appears that the latent dynamism of its productive sectors will enable the economy to continue growing during the 1990s at rates (once the contractionary policy is eased) that would be considered very respectable in most other countries. Neither the resource needs for investment nor the prerequisites for external borrowing, are likely to become major constraints.

Economic Consequences of the Events of June 1989

xi. The apparent short-term implications of the events of June 1989 are a somewhat slower growth rate; smaller trade and current deficits; greater unemployment; the possibility that certain reforms will be postponed for a longer period of time than was apparent in May 1989; partial withdrawal of investors from OECD countries; a fall in tourist traffic from Western countries which has also forced a rescheduling of various hotel loans; and greatly reduced access to the international capital market, which is now compelling China to seek trade and current account surpluses to manage its external transactions. However, there are signs that some of the adverse developments in the period immediately following the events of June 1989 are being reversed: tourist arrivals are on the rise; there is renewed interest on the part of foreign investors; and industrial activity is starting to pick up.

The Fifth Plenum of the Thirteenth Party Congress and Medium-Term Plans

xii. In November 1989, the Fifth Plenum of the Thirteenth Party Congress declared the government's intention to concentrate during the next two years on stabilization; on restoring growth; and on correcting deficiencies that have become apparent in reform of macromanagement and pricing.

xiii. The Fifth Plenum's call for some augmentation of the center's authority, particularly in selected areas of macroeconomic management, is a prudent one and could enlarge the role of indirect instruments, that can be employed more flexibly than administrative measures. The decision to abolish dual pricing for major items such as transport and petroleum and move towards a unified price system, will also be a positive step, provided that it leads to a more basic liberalization of prices rather than a return to administered prices and central allocation. However, although the Fifth Plenum identified the two major areas of reform, it was not explicit about their content, phasing or direction as considerable uncertainty persisted at that time regarding the degree to which macrostability had been regained. Now that inflation has been reduced, the most urgent task facing the government is to prepare an agenda of actions that will establish a sound basis: for strengthening macroeconomic policies and institutions to prevent a recurrence of demand and price pressures; and for advancing towards the next stage of price and market liberalization.

xiv.   The modernization of China's institutions for macromanagement will require initiatives in the areas of fiscal, monetary and exchange rate policies. For example, budgetary discipline could be enhanced if all current and capital expenditures are matched by clearly defined sources of funds. The focus of monetary control could be shifted more towards controlling base money using reserve ratios, rediscount rates, and open market operations. Interest rates might be used more extensively to regulate aggregate demand within the context of meaningful budget constraints on enterprises. As financial markets are broadened, there may also be greater opportunity for open market operations. Finally, there still is considerable room for introducing market forces into the allocation of foreign exchange.

xv.   As long as the authorities are able to sustain a macropolicy that will keep inflation at bay, it would be important, during 1990, to resume the selective decontrol of prices. In mid-1989, procurement prices for grain were adjusted, followed by railway and airline fares in the fourth quarter, and freight tariffs in March 1990. As the severity of deflation has brought market prices of several commodities, such as rubber and cement, very close to state fixed prices, decontrol of some of these could be relatively painless. During the course of 1990, the government intends raising the procurement prices of sugar, cotton and oilseeds. Parallel to price reform, it is equally necessary to proceed with a gradual dismantling of quantitative allocation. In 1989, the list of commodities distributed by the state was augmented slightly and the share of coal output passing though state channels is to be raised. While the chaotic market conditions of 1988 might have made the enhancement of quantitative controls unavoidable, with the return of normalcy, the justification for such measures is less obvious.

Economic Prospects and Creditworthiness

xvi.   To avoid a worsening of open unemployment (disguised unemployment is of course far greater), the government has begun injecting more credit into the economy while remaining within its tight annual credit ceiling of Y 180 billion. Instead of releasing most of the credit in the second half of the year, in conformity with past pattern, more has been provided at an earlier stage so as to pull the economy out of the doldrums. As production accelerates by the third quarter (once inventories begin to be run down), it might be possible to achieve 3-4 percent growth for the year as a whole. This assumes that the austere macroeconomic policy is kept in place. The delayed effects of devaluation and proposed price adjustments could result in inflation of as

II. MACROECONOMIC DEVELOPMENTS 1988-90

Stabilization Measures of 1988/89

2.1   The Government's stabilization program sought to remedy problems in four areas:

(a) Monetary Policy. Monetary growth was reduced so as to reinforce administrative directives aimed at cutting investment and to ease the pressure of consumer demand. A tightening of the money supply was also seen as a way of enforcing incomes policies applied with redoubled force to bring the increase in employee earnings closer to trends in industrial productivity.

(b) Investment Expansion. Spending on fixed capital had climbed to nearly Y 449 billion (32.4 percent of GDP in 1988), far in excess of plan targets, which called for fixed investment of Y 330 billion (23.8 percent of GDP of 1988). The government decided to bring state investment down by Y 50 billion in 1989 and to cancel or defer a large number of projects in nonpriority sectors, for example, services, office construction and processing industries.

(c) Price Expectations. The authorities moved to allay the fears of the urban public by making clear its intention to discontinue price reforms until such time as inflation had been curbed and to use price regulation and consumer subsidies more forcefully to flatten price trends.

(d) Savings. To reverse the depletion of savings balances and the shift to real assets, the interest on three year savings deposits was indexed to the retail price index. This was instituted in September 1988 and did much to stem panic buying.

2.2   These measures were implemented through 1989 and into 1990 so as to "improve the economic environment". Details of the policies, and an assessment of their efficacy is discussed below.

(i) Monetary Policy

2.3   Interest Rate Policy. To reverse the flight from financial assets, interest rates on deposits were raised by 1 percent with effect from September 1, 1988. This was followed by the already noted introduction of price-index-linked interest rates on deposits of three years or longer. The next step was to increase all deposit rates by 3 percent and all lending rates by 2 percent in February 1989. However, as the rate of inflation declined through 1989 and into the first quarter of 1990, indexed savings deposits, while still significant, have become relatively less important in this regard. Correspondingly, the increases in ordinary deposit and lending rates, which were initially modest in the face of double digit inflation, have become significant as inflation has dropped to levels of less than 1 percent on an annualized basis. For the first time since 1984, real, long-term interest rates are positive by a significant margin and in March 1990 the government attempted to moderate the growing interest burden on enterprises through a 1.26 percent reduction in rates.

<u>Table 2.1</u>: INTEREST RATES, 1987-89
(%)

	1987	1988 Sep 1	1989 Feb 1
<u>Deposits Rates for Individuals</u>			
Six months	6.12	6.48	9.00
One year	7.20	8.64	11.34
Three years	8.28	9.72	13.14/a
Eight years	10.44	12.42	17.64
<u>Lending Rates</u>			
Working capital	7.92	9.00	11.34
Fixed assets:			
1-3 years	8.64	9.90	12.78
3-5 years	9.36	10.80	14.40
5-10 years	10.08	13.32	19.26

/a Indexation introduced in September 10,1988 added a mark-up (or subsidy rate) to the base deposit rates. These subsidy rates were:

4th Quarter 1989	7.28 percent
1th Quarter 1989	16.13 percent
2nd Quarter 1989	14.13 percent
3rd Quarter 1989	13.64 percent
4th Quarter 1989	8.36 percent

Source: People's Bank of China.

2.4   <u>Credit Policy</u>. For 1989, the credit target was set at Y 160 billion, a 15 percent increase over the 1988 level.1/ Furthermore, to minimize slippages that had marred monetary management during 1984-88, the People's Bank placed more emphasis on tried and tested credit ceilings. The compulsory and binding nature of detailed quotas was underlined through repeated affirmations of national policy. They were no longer to be treated as points of reference, but a prime instrument of credit control. Banks were assigned explicit sectoral priorities and issued separate quotas for fixed investment lending and total lending. Provincial quotas were firmly established, and provincial branches of the People's Bank were made responsible for controlling the total allocation of credit by the specialized banks, so that their local branches could not use head office (or their own) funds for lending that would exceed total local lending limits. Finally, quarterly credit quotas were promulgated and strictly enforced.

2.5   These regulations, along with new rules requiring all PBC branches to report on a monthly basis to the head office, helped lower the rate of monetary increase in 1989. In the first quarter, broad money grew by 18.3 percent, falling to 13.5 percent in the third quarter (see Chart 2.1 and Table A6.1). Of the Y 160 billion in credit planned for 1989, Y 60 billion was allocated for the period through September, in accordance with past seasonal

---

1/ The subceilings were Y 110 billion for working capital, Y 23-28 billion for fixed assets with the balance going to agriculture and the TVEs.

patterns of demand. In the final quarter, a further Y 125 billion was disbursed, Y 25 billion above the target, in response to signs of severe liquidity shortages (and M2 grew by 18.3 percent).

2.6   Beginning in September 1989, the central bank began to inject liquidity into the system on a gradual basis. Injections of credit, frequently targeted to specific sectors, were made gradually to brake the decline in aggregate demand and assure adequate fund availability for agricultural procurement. Thus, in practice, credit was being managed not only on a quarterly, but on a monthly basis, which has greatly strengthened the macroeconomic leverage exerted by the central government. At the same time, this calls for a high standard of information about the economy, and the elaboration of a full set of macroeconomic indicators. Such an approach in an overall contractionary environment has placed enterprises on a "lean" credit diet and forced them to orient production decisions to credit availability. Rather than providing credit directly to industry, a significant proportion is being funneled through commercial and foreign trade corporations, whose purchasing activity increases effective demand to the industrial sector. (There have been some exceptions in the case of large state-run factories.) By creating, at least in part, a demand-driven environment for state-run factories, it counters the impact of "soft" budget constraints.

2.7   The effects of credit quotas have been reinforced by indirect instruments of credit control. Redeposit requirements and a tightening of PBC's rediscounting policy have been effectively used to manage reserve money, as is apparent from the absence of substantial excess reserves. These actions have contributed to the enforcement of credit ceilings because they prevent banks from drawing upon large excess reserves to manipulate lending and thereby meet credit requirements on reporting dates. In the last quarter of 1988, reserve ratios were raised from 12 to 13 percent. At the same time, Y 5 billion of deposits by the Rural Credit Cooperatives (RCCs) in the specialized banks were immobilized, effectively increasing the required reserves of the RCCs. As bank reserves had been depleted by the withdrawal of deposits, the effect on credit supply was unusually severe at a time when demand was at a peak because of the winter harvest. Many farmers had to be paid with IOUs and enterprises holding small liquid balances were subjected to considerable hardship. In addition, reserve ratios of 30 percent were fixed for nonbank financial institutions (trust and investment companies or TICs), and some enterprise bank accounts were reportedly frozen in February 1989 on the initiative of the authorities in certain provinces.

2.8   Banks are thus subject to a dual control system. They must still base lending on fund availability as determined by the deposit base, reserve requirements and central bank rediscounting. But the authorities have carried out a policy of tightening fund availability beneath the credit quotas, so that central bank policy is brought into line with credit quotas and serves to reinforce them. However, this has been achieved through a series of mostly ad hoc measures. On the formal reserve ratio equal to 13 percent of deposits, the central bank has superimposed a requirement that most provinces maintain excess reserves of 5-7 percent. Only a few provinces, which were already managing with low levels of excess reserves, have been exempted. In addition, the national specialized banks now require that branches maintain reserves of about 2 percent to facilitate remittances. Hence, different branch banks in different regions may now face informal but nevertheless binding reserve

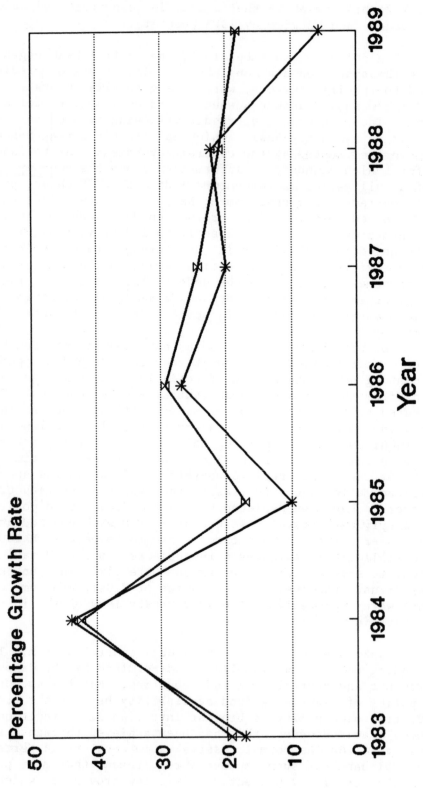

Chart 2.1:

GROWTH RATES OF M1 AND M2

(4 th Quarter to 4 th Quarter)

requirements ranging from 13 percent to 22 percent of their deposits. From the standpoint of the local banks, it is the availability of funds that most directly determines their decision-making. But seen from a national level, it appears that fund availability is adjusted to conform with the quotas set on a case by case regional or sectoral basis.

2.9   It was always the intention of government that this should be a selective credit tightening. In particular, given the government's analysis that excessive growth of processing industries had been a major source of excess demand, it was intended that lending to rural industry should not increase (in nominal terms) in 1989. Restrictions were placed on lending to Township and Village Enterprises (TVEs) from the state banking system but similar limits on lending by RCCs were not as rigidly enforced. (see Tables A6.6 and A6.7).

2.10   Rural enterprises also have access to funds from informal credit markets which, by all accounts, have grown rapidly in recent years, particularly in rural areas. While no aggregate estimates are available, it appears that credit from the informal market is only slightly less important than state and cooperative financial institutions for rural enterprises in the major coastal provinces. In 1988, of the total fixed investment carried out by rural collective organizations (63 percent of this was for industry), funding came from the following sources: 32 percent from state and cooperative financial institutions; 41 percent from retained funds of the organizations; and 27 percent from "other" sources, which refers predominantly to informal credit market transactions. While bank credit to TVEs for fixed investment is indeed being reduced, these funds amount to only one sixth of total funding sources.

2.11   The government has moved to limit the access to informal credit by TVEs, but no attempt is being made to close these markets. Rural enterprises are forbidden to raise capital publicly until the province in which they are located has fully subscribed its compulsory allotment of government bonds (State Council Document No. 21). However, provinces may permit uninterrupted access to informal markets for TVEs by guaranteeing the subscription of Treasury bonds, and provinces such as Jiangsu and Zhejiang, with the largest concentrations of rural enterprises, have done so. In addition, it is unclear whether the government has the capability or desire to actually choke off informal credit markets. Finally, it should be noted that TVEs are extremely important as a source of revenue to county and township officials. These officials will do their utmost to protect TVE development.

2.12   The result of these offsetting tendencies was a slowing of TVE growth rates to 12.7 percent in 1989, compared with rates of over 30 percent for the past several years.2/ These are higher than the growth rate of state industry (3.7 percent), but it should be noted that price deflation techniques used to compute real growth rates are extremely poor in the TVE sector, and the reported increase could well be smaller in real terms. In the first quarter of 1990, a worsening of the industrial recession and mounting unemployment has

---

2/ Communique on the Statistics of 1989 Economic and Social Development, State Statistical Bureau, February 20, 1990, p. 3.

induced the authorities to moderate their position somewhat and raise the supply of credit to TVEs.

Table 2.2: CREDIT AVAILABILITY
(Y billion)

	1987 Dec	1988 Jun	1988 Dec	1989 Jun	1989 Sep
Total Loans Excluding RCCs /a	884.2	935.9	1,023.9	1,045.0	1,082.3
Industrial	221.2	241.3	260.4	275.5	289.4
Commercial	350.0	343.0	409.5	406.5	420.4
Fixed investment	111.9	120.3	138.7	139.0	143.3
Agriculture	65.4	78.5	77.9	82.3	83.6
RCC loans to TVEs	32.9	46.3	45.6	51.2	53.7

/a Loans by the specialized banks and the universal banks.

Source: People's Bank of China.

(ii) Investment Policies

2.13   At first, investment policy was aimed at curtailing certain nonproductive construction projects. Shortly thereafter, localities were instructed to prepare an inventory of all projects being implemented. New administrative limits were promulgated embracing the totality of capital expenditure, including private and rural collective investment, that had previously been outside planned control. Each locality and ministry was directed to cancel a certain proportion of their projects under construction, especially those in light manufacturing, so that resources could be diverted to energy, transportation and the raw materials sectors.a/

2.14   The number of projects actually eliminated was not great. By the close of 1988, over 14,000 construction projects had been cancelled, with a planned investment of almost Y 50 billion, but this amounted to only 4 percent of the total volume of construction in progress. The significance of the administrative controls became more apparent at the beginning of 1989, as the value of new projects begun declined by 80 percent compared to the previous year. Total reductions in the budgeted scope of construction eventually amounted to about Y 80 billion, or roughly 7 percent of the total budgeted value of all construction projects.b/

2.15   During 1989, state-owned capital construction projects numbered 123,000, some 43,000 less than in the preceding year. Preliminary estimates for 1989 indicate that fixed investment amounted to Y 400 billion, which represents an 11 percent reduction over 1988.3/ Several priority sectors increased their share of total investment. State investment in energy overall grew by 5.3 percent, of which investment in coal was 13.3 percent higher while petroleum received 9.5 percent more. Transportation and communications investment, after declining in the first quarter, revived rapidly in the third

---

3/ Communique on Statistics, op. cit., 1990.

a/ Lettered footnotes are to be found in Annex II.

quarter and posted an increase of 2.8 percent over 1988.4/ In all these cases, however, the growth rates of nominal investment imply decreases in real investment, assuming average rates of inflation of producer goods. There is little doubt that these dramatic changes in the level and structure of invest-ment were brought about overwhelmingly by direct imposition of administrative controls.

(iii)   Price Policies and Developments

2.16   Direct controls on prices and marketing began to be enforced with renewed determination in late 1988. Price inspectors fanned out to different cities, finding numerous regulations to enforce, which had been generally ignored during the era of liberalization.a/ Regulation of consumer prices is relatively decentralized and the degree to which control was intensified has varied across cities. Tables A12.2-A12.4 offer a glimpse of price dispersion. Local supplies and impediments to interprovincial transport had a hand in price movements. Tianjin was able to hold inflation well below the average in 1988, because administrative regulation is more pervasive. At the other extreme, Guangzhou, which hews to a more liberal line, was considerably above the average, as was Chengdu. After the disturbances in June 1989, the Sichuan authorities were remarkably effective in bringing down the rate of price increase. Guangzhou registered above average rates and Tianjin remained the city with the least inflation in the group.

2.17   The focus of price control efforts after September 1988 was on the range of essential food items, which have traditionally attracted government concern and subsidies. It is estimated that about 20 percent of urban consumer spending is covered by this category. Many of these commodities had already been subject to price controls of varying degrees of effectiveness before September 1988, but the trend had been towards greater liberalization. In some cases--such as staple grains--price controls had never been lifted. In other cases, particularly fresh vegetables, fixed price supply had basic-ally been abandoned, but was quickly reinstated. The effect of price controls and renewed subsidization on the inflation rate has been most apparent in the case of fresh vegetables. At the height of the inflation in August-September 1988, the price of vegetables was 48 percent over that a year previously which accounted for nearly 7 percentage points of the total 30 percent inflation rate estimated for that period. However, the prices of vegetables stabilized almost immediately, and in August 1989, they were only 0.3 percent higher than in the year previous, which cut the overall inflation rate by almost 7 percent (see Table A12.2).5/

4/   Additions to production capacity in 1989 included 24.95 million tons of coal; 9.02 million kW of electricity; 1.70 million tons of oil; 760 million m^3 of natural gas; 318 km of double-track railways and 229 km of electrified railways; and 48.85 million tons of cargo handling capability in ports. Communique on Statistics, op. cit., 1990, p. 6.

5/   The increase in the (urban) prices of fresh vegetables for 1989 as a whole was 2.1 percent. The rate of change in December 1989 over the previous year was -13.8 percent. Communique on Statistics, op. cit., 1990, p. 8.

2.18   There are great differences between regions in the effectiveness of
price controls. In Harbin, 383 categories of consumer goods are now subject
to strict price controls, whereas only 6-7 basic goods are controlled in some
parts of southern China. This depends largely on the policy goals of local
authorities, their administrative capacity to regulate prices and the fiscal
resources at their disposal from which to finance price subsidies. However,
local governments are now required to notify the central government whenever
they permit price increases for a range of daily necessities and certain raw
materials. Clearly, this is intended to pressure local governments into holding the line on price increases, and it lessens price flexibility. Intensified price supervision was applied to that portion of producers' goods mar-
keted directly by enterprises as well, with the establishment of upper limits
on prices and restrictions on the marketing of certain commodities. Most
indications are that these controls were relatively ineffective until after
excess demand for these commodities had been quenched.

Table 2.3: PRICE TRENDS, 1987-89
(corresponding month in previous year: 100)

		Living costs	Retail prices	Free market goods
1987:	June	107.8	107.8	120.1
	December	108.9	109.1	120.8
1988:	March	111.3	111.6	128.8
	June	116.3	116.5	122.4
	September	126.4	125.4	137.3
	December	127.9	126.7	130.6
1989:	March	127.1	126.3	119.2
	June	122.8	121.5	115.0
	September	111.5	111.4	103.3
	December	n.a.	106.4	93.4

Source: State Statistical Bureau: Monthly Bulletin of Statistics.

(iv)   Wages and Consumption

2.19   The total urban wage bill of the formal sector stagnated in nominal
terms through the middle of 1989. It amounted to Y 19.9 billion in October
1988, and except for large year-end bonuses, did not substantially increase
till the last quarter of 1989, when the authorities acted on a decision taken
in late 1988 to adjust the wage structure. For 1989 as a whole, total earnings including bonuses, rose by 14 percent, with much of this coming from
relatively generous year end bonus payments (23.6 percent greater than in
1988). At the same time, the cutback in investment has resulted in several
million casual laborers leaving the cities. While these workers may find
employment in the rural areas, their incomes will undoubtedly decline. Third,
and finally, sales of consumer goods to organizations (primarily enterprises)
which account for over 10 percent of consumer goods sales have been subjected
to intensified control, and these declined 5.6 percent in nominal terms
between August 1988 and August 1989, or about 19 percent in real terms. Urban
per capita incomes were 11.6 percent higher in nominal terms by the end of
1989, although in real terms, they were down by nearly 5 percent over 1988.

2.20   This decline in real incomes would, by itself, reduce real household expenditures even if the propensity to consume remained unchanged. In fact, a number of additional factors have depressed the latter:

(a)   Expectations about the future have shifted. Government economic policy now emphasizes slower growth and strict restraint on consumption and household income. In this context, households are revising downwards their expectations of future income growth, and correspondingly adjusting their long-term consumption plans. The government has also become critical of conspicuous consumption, thereby inducing households to reconsider purchases of high-quality goods.

(b)   Households built up stocks of consumer durables during the "panic buying" of 1988. These stocks are above equilibrium levels, allowing buyers to postpone purchases.

(c)   Relative prices have been manipulated by the government to favor financial saving and discourage the accumulation of durables. Very high taxes on certain consumer durables were enacted in 1989. The tax on color televisions, for example, was set at Y 600-900, and on automobiles at Y 30,000. Such punitive taxes caused prices to more than double.6/ Simultaneously, indexing of savings deposits has greatly enhanced the desirability of financial savings.

2.21   For these reasons, household purchases of consumer goods declined more rapidly than household income. In fact, retail sales of consumer goods fell by 7.6 percent in real terms during 1989, although the amount of sales denominated in nominal terms grew by 8.9 percent to Y 810 billion.

(v)   Output Trends

2.22   Reducing "excessive" growth was one of the principal aims of stabilization efforts. It was the overheated economy that was perceived as being responsible for inflation. At the same time, the government's intention--paralleling its credit policies--was that the decline in output should be selective. Growth in processing industries was to be restrained allowing output of basic industries, energy and grain to catch up.

2.23   To a significant degree, this target was achieved in 1989. GNP had grown by 11.2 percent in 1988, but by only 3.9 percent in 1989. Moreover, the ratio of the industrial to the agricultural output growth rate had been 6.5 in 1988 (20.7 percent/3.2 percent), and this ratio fell to 2.5 (8.3 percent/3.3 percent). Some success was also achieved in moving towards the perceived balance desired, as the growth rates of both light and heavy industry were more or less the same. The basic industries did not fall as far behind as in the

---

6/   By November, deflationary measures had largely extinguished the demand for cars. Inventories accumulated and production slowed virtually to a halt at the Volkswagen plant in Shanghai and the Peugeot factory outside Guangzhou, "Running on Empty", China Trade Report, January 1990. In early 1990, the government has attempted to revive the industry by providing various state organizations the funds to purchase cars.

past, although output growth for energy, steel, cement and timber were still below average growth rates. It should also be noted that output of "big item" consumer durables fell dramatically, notably color TVs (-9.6 percent), washing machines (-21 percent) and refrigerators (-12.6 percent). Thus, there continued to be a strong disparity in growth rates classified by ownership, and despite attempts at a skewed credit policy (see para. 2.9), output of SOEs only grew by 3.7 percent, while TVEs grew by 12.7 percent. Output of the private enterprises grew by 24 percent, even though some 2 million private enterprises (about 14 percent of the total) are estimated to have disappeared in 1989.

Table 2.4: OUTPUT AND EXPENDITURE TRENDS

	1987	1988	1989 est.
Real GNP	10.6	11.2	3.9
Industrial output	14.2	17.7	8.3
Of which: State-owned enterprises	11.3	12.6	3.7
TVEs	42.5	33.4	12.7
Agricultural output	4.8	3.2	3.3
Gross domestic investment/GDP	39.2	38.9	36.5

Source: State Statistical Bureau: "Communique on the Statistics of 1989".

(vi) Fiscal Policy

2.24   Fiscal policy was relatively neutral during 1989, in that increased spending on subsidies was offset by a modest increment in taxes. A broadening of the tax base compensated for the difficulties experienced by recession-hit industries in meeting their tax obligations. During the first half of 1989, profit of in-budget industrial enterprises fell 12 percent, or 4.1 billion yuan. All of this decline was in the profit of central government factories, and the change is largely due to the increased losses in coal and petroleum alluded to above. Local enterprises profits barely increased, growing 1.7 percent. Remittance of profit to the budget decreased by 4.3 billion yuan, so the budget bore the entire burden of decreased profitability.7/ Tax collection from individual enterprises and peddlers was stepped up, including more determined collection of new taxes legislated in 1988 and 1989. Revenue from industrial and commercial taxes increased by 19.3 percent in 1989 or Y 30.4 billion. Tax arrears and taxation of the private sector were important sources.8/ These raised revenues from the individual and private enterprise sectors to around 12 billion yuan, up 35-40 percent from last year. New consumption taxes contributed about 4 billion yuan, and miscellaneous taxes on banquets, local products and land conversion an additional one billion yuan. By far the largest source of increased revenues in 1989 was the levy on

---

7/ Digest of Industrial Economics Management, 1989, No. 9, p. 5.

8/ "Tax Men Collect Extra 8.7 Billion", China Daily, January 23, 1990. It should be noted that these measures are not a way of stabilizing or even raising the tax/GNP ratio. For that, it will be necessary to depend on indirect taxes and the taxes levied on state enterprises.

extrabudgetary funds.9/   In past years, 15 percent of extrabudgetary funds have been drawn back into the budget, rising in 1989 to 25 percent.   The additional 10 percent was projected to raise about 12 billion yuan in the course of the year.   Thus, new taxes in 1989 are estimated to have brought in about 20 billion yuan, or a little over 1 percent of GNP.   These approximately offset the slow growth of budgetary revenues from industry caused by contractionary policies, but the ratio of budgetary revenue to GNP will not increase.

Table 2.5: FISCAL TRENDS
(as % of GNP)

	1987	1988	1989	
			Budget	Estimate/a
Total revenue	22.6	20.4	19.0	19.2
Tax	(20.4)	(18.3)	(16.6)	(16.8)
Nontax	(2.2)	(2.1)	(2.4)	(2.4)
Total expenditure	24.8	22.9	20.8	21.2
Subsidies	(5.9)	(5.4)	(5.6)	(6.1)
Capital	(6.8)	(5.8)	(4.7)	(4.7)
Overall deficit (-)	-2.2	-2.5	-1.8	-2.0
Foreign financing	0.6	0.8	0.7	0.7
Domestic financing:				
Bank	0.6	0.6	-	0.3
Nonbanks	1.0	1.1	1.1	1.0

/a See Table A7.10.

Source: IMF.

(vii) Trade

2.25   By the end of 1987, a strong export performance was bringing the merchandise trade account closer to balance. As exports maintained a growth of nearly 20 percent in the first half of 1988, the government began relaxing import controls to accommodate rising demand. The spike in consumer spending in the third quarter of 1988 resulted in an abrupt reversal in trends. Exports actually declined in that quarter while imports rose by 12 percent so that a trade deficit of $0.5 billion in the second quarter widened to one of $2.3 billion three months later. The strength of internal demand, rising prices and shortages of raw material dampened export growth through the middle of 1989. In sharp contrast to earlier years, overseas sales increased by a mere 7 percent. Meanwhile, imports were rising at an annual rate of 20 percent.

2.26   Although the government moved quickly to staunch spending, the flow of imports was not interrupted, in the interests of demand management.

9/ Extrabudgetary funds can be defined as state-owned financial resources mobilized by line ministries from various units and local governments, which are not subject to state budgetary allocation. They mainly include (a) local surtaxes; (b) various special funds such as for energy, afforestation and road maintenance; and (c) state enterprises' retained depreciation funds, as well as those for bonuses and welfare.

Imports rose by 34 percent in the fourth quarter and the trade deficit for 1988 amounted to $7.7 billion. While the slowing of the economy diminished the strength of import demand in the first half of 1989, the trade balance remained substantially in deficit. For the twelve-month period ending in June 1989, the trade deficit reached $12.3 billion or 4.3 percent of GDP. By then, the economy had cooled, consumer demand and industrial production were slowing and depleted inventories of raw materials as well as finished products were being replenished. At that point, the authorities reversed their position on trade, imports were tightly restricted and export industries provided with the credit supplies and raw materials needed to boost their flagging performance. These incentives, plus a drying of opportunities on the domestic market, revived export sales, which grew by 18 percent in the third quarter of 1989 over the same quarter in the previous year, whereas imports rose by just 3.8 percent. The trade deficit narrowed to $0.7 billion and as the pattern continued into the final quarter, it dropped to $0.1 billion.10/

<u>Table 2.6</u>: TRADE PATTERN 1987-89
(US$ billion)

Year	Exports	Imports	Balance
1987	39.4	43.2	-3.8
1988	47.5	55.2	-7.7
1989	52.5	59.1	-6.6
1988 Q1	8.8	9.5	-0.7
Q2	12.1	12.6	-0.5
Q3	11.9	14.2	-2.3
Q4	14.8	19.0	-4.2
1989 Q1	9.7	11.6	-1.9
Q2	12.6	16.5	-3.9
Q3	14.0	14.7	-0.7
Q4	16.2	16.3	-0.1
1990 Q1	10.8	9.9	0.8

Source: China's Customs Statistics.

Assessing Stabilization in 1989

2.27   The success of stabilization can be measured against several yard-sticks. For instance: (i) how quickly were inflationary pressures controlled; (ii) were inflationary expectations significantly modified; (iii) was it possible to prevent inertial wage-price forces from taking hold; (iv) what was the cost in terms of reduced and/or negative growth rates and unemployment; (v) how large a BOP deficit resulted; (vi) what were the effects on investment levels and savings performance; lastly (vii) was the economy's

---

10/ China's earnings from tourism rose from $1.8 billion (4.2 percent of exports GNFS) in 1987 to $2.2 billion in 1988. In 1989 they declined by almost 20 percent to $1.81 billion (3.4 percent of exports) but appear to be recovering in 1990. The Asian Games, scheduled for September 1990 in Beijing, should provide an additional late-season boost.

growth potential impaired and has stabilization improved the prospects for continued rapid growth without inflation.

2.28   Now that preliminary macroeconomic results for 1989 are in, it is possible to advance some tentative judgments regarding the efficacy of the initial measures employed. In December 1988, the urban cost of living was increasing at an annual average rate of 26 percent. Fourteen months later in February 1990, it had declined to under one percent, having fallen sharply to single digit rates by mid-year. Although the actual increase in the retail price index for calendar 1989 was 17.8 percent (as against 18.5 percent a year earlier) and urban living costs grew by 16.3 percent compared to 20.7 percent in 1988, this was an exceedingly swift reversal of the trends that had appeared in late 1987. Administrative controls and deflationary actions not only arrested the price spiral, but they have also been able to check the growth in labor earnings and, for the moment at least, to alleviate cost push.d/ Expectations that introduce a strong inertial element into wage demands may also have been prevented from taking root by the speed with which inflation has been brought close to historical rates of under 5 percent per annum.

2.29   Under the influence of the contractionary regimen, industrial expansion slackened steadily throughout 1989, with the rate becoming negative in the last quarter. Even though agriculture grew by 3.3 percent, the modest--by Chinese standards--6.8 percent increase in industrial output (excluding TVEs) and negative growth of services, brought GNP growth down to 3.9 percent. As a result, many of the symptoms of overheating such as severe shortages of energy and industrial supplies have tended to dissipate. Urban employment worsened somewhat, rising from 2.1 percent to 2.7 percent,11/ but much of the shock was absorbed by the transient population of recent migrants, some of whom have returned to farming.12/ Socialist employment practices have enabled workers in the formal sector to retain their jobs 13/ and the soft budget constraint (i.e. the weakness of financial discipline and the ability to obtain administrative support for the financing of deficits) has allowed most state and collective enterprises to weather the storm.

2.30   After rising in the first two quarters, the trade deficit was stabilized at about $6.65 billion in the third quarter of 1989 and improved export performance nudged it to $6.5 billion by the year's end. China has thus

---

11/ The urban workforce in 1989 numbered 137.4 million, a 1.32 million increase over 1988.

12/ Officials conducting China's latest census have reported a floating population of between 60 and 80 million people, some 30 million of which may have gravitated to the urban areas. The New China News Agency announced in early February 1990 that about 10 million recent migrants to the cities had returned to the rural hinterland.

13/ As long as a cyclical downswing is expected to be of a short duration, even firms in market economies will retain their workers either because they are honoring implicit contracts, or because they want to minimize the costs of hiring and firing.

managed to cope with its macroeconomic difficulties while holding the BOP current account deficit down to about 1.0 percent of GDP or $4.3 billion. A significant proportion of this has been financed by drawing upon reserves so that net external borrowing was minimized. Total external indebtedness rose from $42 billion in 1988 to $43.9 billion in 1989.14/

2.31   One of the most unfortunate effects of contraction can be the damage it does to investment incentives. China has managed, by and large, to avoid this. Investment as a ratio of GNP was close to 38.9 percent in 1988. It declined in 1989 but remained at a respectable 36.0 percent and seems poised to recover once macropolicies become less contractionary. Likewise, savings have shown considerable resilience. A weakening in the latter part of 1988 has been succeeded by significant buoyancy in 1989. There is little to suggest that growth would not climb back to a 6-7 percent level within a year, if the restraints on investment and consumption were relaxed. In fact, the sixteen months breathing space has resulted in a ballooning of inventories and allowed the government to divert more resources to the bottleneck sectors through intensified targeting begun in June 1989.15/ Constraints of energy, steel and other materials should be less troublesome in the future.

2.32   Whether the desirable growth rate can be attained with low rates of price increase will depend in the medium term on the coordinated use of fiscal, monetary and incomes policies. Unlike many other developing countries confronted with problems of inflation and adjustment, China's budget deficit to GNP has changed little over the last four years in spite of a decline in the tax/GNP ratio. The deficit rose from 2 percent of GNP in 1986 to 2.5 percent of GNP in 1988 but dipped back to 2.3 percent in 1989 (see Tables A7.5 and A7.10). Given China's high rate of household and enterprise saving (see Tables A1.1 and A1.9), the budget shortfall can be covered through the issue of bonds without much risk of investment being crowded out (see Chapter 3). Since 1988, the government has been attempting to finance the entire deficit through foreign borrowing and bond issues so as to minimize its borrowing from the People's Bank. Because an adequate volume of bonds could not be placed, some recourse to PBC funding has been necessary--about Y 7.9 billion in 1988 and Y 5 billion in 1989.

2.33   It has taken the People's Bank of China nearly four years, since its designation as a central bank in 1984, to gain a measure of control over credit expansion and deflect the demands of local government authorities on its provincial branches. Earlier episodes of credit tightening in 1985, 1986

14/ This is a World Bank staff estimate--medium- and long-term (MLT) $35.1 billion and short-term (ST) $8.8 billion. The official figures announced on May 4, 1990 were: total DOD $41.3 billion, of which MLT $37.0 billion and ST $4.3 billion. In past years, the discrepancy between Chinese official debt statistics and World Bank estimates is traceable to the classification and evaluation of short-term debt (see footnote 8, Chapter 5).

15/ The State Statistical Bureau estimates that the level of inventories was Y 600 billion at the end of 1989 as against Y 450 billion a year earlier.

and 1987 could not be sustained in the face of provincial opposition. But the procedures now being applied appear to be effective and the People's Bank is in a position to regulate the money supply when there is a policy consensus at the highest levels of the government.

2.34   Administrative decentralization and rising enterprise autonomy has appreciably weakened the effectiveness of incomes policy but, when used in conjunction with monetary and fiscal policy, it is still capable of producing results. Incomes policies can be applied with considerable force because the Party remains influential in the workplace and, within limits, can moderate wage demands; many of the larger enterprises must still obtain the approval of supervisory agencies before they can proceed with annual wage adjustments; both wage hikes as well as bonuses are subject to penal taxation when they exceed a certain percentage.e/

2.35   One aspect of stabilization policies that could have implications for the longer term is the significant reliance on administrative means. No doubt the situation at the end of 1988 was very serious, indirect levers were insuf- ficiently developed and in China's "planned market" economy, administrative instruments could be very potent. This is particularly so with regard to credit policy and investment controls, and was recognized explicitly in the World Bank's last Country Economic Memorandum (1989).

2.36   Such reliance on direct control measures has been more widespread and of longer duration than might be desirable. Moreover, their apparent effec- tiveness in the short term may discourage the authorities from proceeding with the difficult but necessary actions required to strengthen longer-term macro- economic management through institutional reforms. The longer these are put off, the more difficult they become. For example, the use of price controls on basic commodities may prevent price rises in the short term, but they fur- ther distort the price system, and make the eventual price adjustment required even greater. Similarly, the use of direct controls over lending decisions by banks may have helped in the short term to direct more resources to bottleneck sectors, but has further reduced the autonomy of institutions. Now that the economy is in the trough of the cycle, administrative controls which were use- ful as an emergency measure, should at least partially, be displaced by shift- ing more of the burden of control onto indirect economic levers. In this fashion, the government would strengthen market based policy instruments and enhance its ability to minimize future fluctuations in economic activity.

2.37   The second negative aspect of the stabilization program has thus been the severity of the recession induced, and the consequent difficulties in the microeconomic situation. Enterprises were slow to accept the determination of the authorities to enforce deflation, and maintained production levels for some months above the current level of demand. As a consequence, excess stocks of both raw materials and finished goods have accumulated, tying up large amounts of finance, and causing cash-flow problems for such factories. These have also led to high levels of inter-enterprise arrears, and arrears in interest and principal payments to banks approaching Y 100 billion (6 percent of GNP). Third, many urban factories have been forced to send workers home for several months, while maintaining basic wages. None of these are surpris- ing, nor are they severe by Western standards, but by not permitting the hardest-hit enterprises to close their doors, three problems have arisen;

first, the effect of the squeeze is very widespread, and nearly all enter-
prises--even the good ones--end up with cash-flow problems; second, keeping
debt ridden enterprises afloat consumes disproportionate amounts of credit,
and total productivity thus tends to decline more than is necessary; and third
the necessary restructuring of capacity is put off. How to revive the economy
from this sluggishness without restarting inflation is one of the main issues
confronting the government at the present time.

2.38   The administrative measures used also affected the financial system
and the patterns of provincial growth and interprovincial relationships. During the first three quarters of 1989, interest rate policy tended to undermine
the profitability of the banking system, because the indexation of savings
deposits was combined with only modest increases in lending rates. This
resulted in negative spreads that have lowered the profitability of the banks.
Budgetary revenues were reduced as the banking system has contributed substantial funds to the budget in recent years. Moreover, increases in deposit
rates not matched by adjustments in lending rates were especially onerous for
Rural Credit Cooperatives, which already operate as financially independent
entities. In 1987, 5 percent of Rural Credit Cooperatives operated at a loss,
while in 1988, this increased to over 30 percent, and total losses amounted to
400 million yuan. As inflation has continued declining through early 1990,
these problems have tended to become much less acute.

2.39   The manner in which administrative controls were applied to the banking system has also interfered with the developing interbank market, which
could serve as a very effective vehicle for exerting Central Bank control.f/
Under current circumstances, few bank branches would be willing to lend funds
to another branch, as they would have to reveal to their supervisors that they
have "excess" funds which might then be subject to informal blockage. Indeed,
the only instance in which an interbank transaction would now occur volunta-
rily would be if one bank had a binding lending limit but excess funds, and
located a branch with a slack lending limit but insufficient funds, an
unlikely event. Hence, the interbank market has shrunk substantially. For
example, last year Guangdong province enjoyed a net inflow of capital of 2-3
billion yuan (including the interbank market and direct investment from other
provinces), but this inflow ceased in 1989 and was replaced by a small outflow
as other provinces liquidated their interests in Guangdong. Further development of an interbank market is an indispensable part of the creation of a
modern banking network in China.16/

2.40   While lending limits differentiate clearly between different sectors
and ownership forms, they seem to be relatively uniform across geographical
areas irrespective of its growth rate giving each province a roughly equal
percentage growth of credit. The two outliers are Shanghai and Jiangsu. The
largest percentage growth of credit in the first three quarters of 1989 (10.9
percent) went to Shanghai, the provincial level unit with the slowest industrial growth since 1982; while the lowest credit growth (0.4 percent) went to

---

16/ Gross interbank transactions rose from Y 30 billion in 1986 to Y 520
    billion in 1988. In the first half of 1989, the level of transactions
    was Y 140 billion, 70 percent of what it was in 1988.

Jiangsu, the province with the second fastest industrial growth since 1982. The pattern is linked to the relative output shares of state and collective or private ownership in output in these provinces: State ownership and the share of favored basic industries is dominant in Shanghai, and substantially less important in Jiangsu.17/ Overall there is a significant negative correlation between growth of credit in 1989 and growth performance of the preceding six years. The policy of equal percentage increases in credit will, if continued, limit the growth of more efficient provinces without necessarily improving the performance of less efficient provinces.

2.41   Finally, the strict application of administrative controls over capital flows disrupts interprovincial development efforts. These arrangements are often based on investment by one province in another in return for guaranteed supplies. Without the assurance that either control over funds or control over the resulting output can be maintained, such cooperation will inevitably decline. There is some evidence of it happening already. Investment from Zhejiang province in other provinces peaked at Y 85 million in 1986. It then declined to Y 52 million in 1987 and Y 31 million in 1988. A conference in March 1988 promoted some 300 cooperative investment projects in China's inland Third Front regions,18/ but in the subsequent year and a half, virtually none of the projects have been undertaken by coastal provinces. In a similar fashion, the intensified control over regulated prices and emphasis on subsidizing crucial commodities interferes with interprovincial trade flows. As localities are increasingly responsible for price subsidies, they will resist the "export" of subsidized products, in order to limit the benefits of public subsidization to the local citizenry. Meanwhile, local governments might easily use the current stress on planned management of commodities as a rationale in their efforts to expand control of subsidized goods.

Economic Consequences of the Events of June 1989

2.42   The most immediate economic effect of the events of June 1989 was on tourist arrivals and earnings from tourism. The former declined by 23 percent in 1989 to 24.5 million with income falling to $1.86 billion (20 percent less than in the preceding year). The number of tourist arrivals began to pick up in the first half of 1990, but are still below the levels of early 1989. Hotel occupancy rates in Beijing and Shanghai were in the 60 to 70 percent range during January-March 1990, which is 50 percent higher compared to October-December 1989. Applications from foreign investors, which had been on a rising curve, were also affected and, in fact, are estimated to have declined by 75 percent after June 1989. This did not influence disbursements

---

17/ Shanghai weathered 1989 with less pain because the PBC branch was able to allocate credit quotas more evenly over the course of the year, providing 33 percent of the total during the January-September period as against 12 percent for the nation as a whole and in Jiangsu.

18/ The Third Front program of the sixties and early seventies attempted to build a heavy industry base in China's interior provinces, so as to enhance their autonomy and strengthen the country's defense posture. See China: CEM, 1989, op. cit, Vol. 2, Chapter 8.

flowing from past investment decisions (which rose by 4 percent to $3.3 billion).

2.43   The June event essentially closed off China's access to medium- and long-term borrowing from the international market and no more than $400 million were raised in the second half of the year.g/ Particularly affected was the access to bilateral concessional flows. Trade financing, however, was not interrupted. Because the Chinese were unable to tap external sources for capital--or were dissuaded from doing so by substantially higher interest margins--they were forced to run down exchange reserves. These declined from about $19 billion in May 1989 to a low of $15 billion in August before recovering to $18.5 billion by end-December 1989. In addition, import controls were hardened in the third and fourth quarters, which quickly reversed the upward trend that was emerging in the first half of 1989.

2.44   Monetary policy had been tightened in the first half of 1989 and both the growth rate of output as well as the increase in prices was slowing by the middle of the year. The events of June 1989, by disrupting industrial production, accelerated the decline, so that by the fourth quarter, industry was registering negative growth. The government also strengthened its grip on controlled prices and slowed inflation even further.

2.45   In sum, the consequences of the policies that authorities have adopted since June 1989 are a slower growth rate; smaller trade and current deficits; greater unemployment; the possibility that certain reforms will be postponed for a longer period of time than was apparent in May 1989; partial withdrawal of investors from OECD countries; a fall in tourist traffic, which has also forced a rescheduling of various hotel loans; and reduced access to the international capital market, which is now compelling China to seek trade and current account surpluses to manage its external transactions. However, these are signs that some of the adverse developments in the period immediately following the events of June 1989 are being reversed: tourist traffic is on the rise; exchange reserves are increasing rapidly; industrial production has begun quickening; and more investment applications have started flowing in since early 1990.

The Fifth Plenum's Economic Program

2.46   The future course of stabilization policy and options for reform were debated during the Fifth Plenary Session of the Thirteenth Central Committee in November 1989 which was the first occasion on which the authorities turned their attention fully to economic matters after the events of June 1989. Moreover, it was already clear by this time that the three main targets of the "improvement" program--lower inflation, lower industrial growth, higher grain output--had been achieved. This Plenum adopted the "Decision on Further Improving the Economic Environment, Straightening Out the Economic Order, and Deepening the Reforms" on November 9, 1989, and it is this decision that shaped the government's economic statements to the National People's Congress in April 1990 and is expected to influence economic policy until the end of 1991.

2.47   The program emerging from the Fifth Plenum session has three components related to: (i) macroeconomic stability; (ii) growth; and (iii) reform. The primary macroeconomic objective, already partially achieved, is single digit inflation. Although prices were increasing at an annual average rate of 6-7 percent in the second half of 1989, the government believes that excess demand has not been eliminated and could once again drive up prices if controls were relaxed. The demand management strategy being adopted calls for: (i) a regulation of the money supply in line with the desired growth rate; (ii) a slower increase in consumption; (iii) holding fixed investment in 1990 and 1991 at about the level of 1989 in nominal terms; and (iv) an erasing of the budget deficit by 1991.

2.48   Given these austere macroeconomic intentions during the stabilization period, the growth rate being sought is a suitably modest 5-6 percent per annum. Much of this is expected to be derived from a diversion of investible resources to agriculture, primary industries, transport infrastructure and energy. The external sector is also seen as a more significant source of growth than in the recent past. Export diversification towards products with a higher value added will be the guiding aim, although China will continue to capitalize on its strength in processing and assembly industries. The drive for a trade surplus will also be supplemented by measures to discourage the import of luxury consumer items.

2.49   The Fifth Plenum recognized that the "improvement and rectification" program "does not mean to hold up or even relinquish the reform effort".19/ However, China's efforts are directed towards the striking of a better balance between plan and market. Public ownership is to remain dominant but a plurality of ownership forms are being sought in the interests of modernization. The Plenum concentrated on "stabilizing, enriching, readjusting and improving the reform measures introduced over the past few years," rather than on the elaboration of major reform initiatives.

2.50   Therefore, the main reform goals of the Plenum were:

    (a)   to restore some of the center's managerial powers while retaining the major benefits of the decentralization to provinces and enterprises; and

    (b)   to establish a framework for macroeconomic control which promotes a stable development of the economy.

To achieve them, the Plenum identified broad reform priorities in seven areas:

    (a)   Enterprise Contract Responsibility System. This was to be maintained as the centerpiece of industrial reforms. The responsibility of the factory director for the management of the enterprise and the meeting of contractual targets was confirmed, and it was stated that the factory director would confer with the Party Secretary in the enterprise in making decisions.

    (b)   Fiscal Contract System. The main change to this system is that in the short term some provinces would be asked to give more to the

---

19/   "Decision on Further Improving the Economic Environment, Straightening Out the Economic Order, and Deepening the Reforms," Article 33.

center, and the center's grants to the localities would be reduced. (This policy was implemented in the 1990 budget.)[20]

(c) Financial System Reform. This reform emphasized the strengthening of the central bank, especially in control of currency issue and authority over its branch network in the provinces. On banking reform, the Plenum emphasized the need for banks to lend in conformity with the government's industrial policy and credit plan, and cautioned against extending too much autonomy to banks in case that again leads to an excess supply of credit.

(d) Foreign Trade Contract System. Again, the essential benefits of the system were recognized, but it was considered that decentralization of trading rights and foreign exchange retention had gone too far and needed to be corrected.

(e) Materials Management System. The proportion of certain "important" materials subject to state-unified allocation was to be raised "appropriately".

(f) Price Reform. The reform of the price structure "should be carried out step by step ... by focusing on the prices of some commodities at a given time on the principle of a strict control of the general price level". Some price control powers would be recentralized while "relaxation of control of the prices of certain commodities will be continued".

(g) Planning System Reform. The Plenum envisaged "appropriately enlarging the scope and proportion of products covered by mandatory plans." This was to extend to the investment system, and "power to examine and approve construction projects already delegated to lower levels will be taken back by authorities at higher levels".

2.51   Steps to raise the performance of agriculture was the remaining item on the reform agenda. The Party Committee did not specify in any detail what will be done, but indicated that it was critically important to maintain the growth of grain and other foodstuffs through investment in infrastructure, water control, drainage, soil conservation and the provision of inputs such as fertilizer and plastic sheeting. In the 1990 National Economic and Social Development Plan it was indicated that "guidance planning will be resumed for acreage devoted to certain major items of farm produce". Although the Plenum tended to stress the role of planning, this is more a recognition of the remaining shortcomings in the instruments of macromanagement than a change in attitudes towards the desirability of reform (paras. 6.6-6.8).

---

[20] The 1990 budget has revenues sent by localities to the center rising by 10.8 percent, but funds distributed to the localities growing by only 3.3 percent. Moreover, funds raised directly by the center are projected to increase by 22.7 percent, while those gathered by provinces are projected to rise only 3.8 percent.

Third Session of the Seventh National People's Congress

2.52   The agenda of the Fifth Plenum was the point of departure for the Third Session of the National People's Congress which took place in Beijing March 20-April 5, 1990. This was the opportunity for the government to state the operational implications of the agenda discussed at the earlier political forum. As such, the 1990 Budget and Social and Economic Development Plan hold few surprises, but indicate how some of the Fifth Plenum's guidelines will be implemented.

2.53   In the 1990 development plan, the Government is aiming for 5 percent GNP growth, with industrial output rising by 6 percent, and agriculture expanding 4 percent. In the industrial sector, TVEs are projected to increase at 15 percent, well above the average. The GNP growth rate also implies a strong recovery of the services sector after its decline in 1989. In agriculture, the Government is targeting a 1.2 percent growth in grain (to 412.5 million tons), a 16.1 percent increase in cotton, a 15.4 percent increase in oilseeds, and a 10.5 percent increase in sugar output. To achieve the latter the Government announced that prices for these three crops would be raised.

2.54   Although GNP is projected to expand, the target for fixed investment is Y 410 billion, an increase of only 2.5 percent, and if this is the outcome it will most likely register a further real decline.21/ The growth of non-state investment will be higher than state investment, and within the state-owned sector, investment in technical transformation projects will increase more rapidly than capital construction. Foreign trade could register a surplus in 1990, following the devaluation and given the low initial level of demand, but clearly the achievement of the GNP growth target will require a higher level of real consumption. This may be one of the intentions behind the drop in interest rates of 1.26 basis points, along with the desire to "reduce the burden on enterprises". The Government also announced a slight relaxation of the credit policy stance. In the original credit plan, industrial and commercial credit in the first half of the year was going to be Y 30 billion, compared to Y 12 billion last year. It was raised to Y 55 billion in early 1990, although it was stated that this did not represent any net increase in the credit plan for the year as a whole, but merely a readjustment of the timing of the credit program. Finally taxes on certain consumer items, such as TV sets, are being scaled down.

2.55   There was little in the way of specific information with regard to reform. Some agricultural prices, freight charges (freight tariffs on waterways and railways were adjusted on March 15, 1990) and prices of crude oil, will be adjusted, although, in most cases the amounts have yet to be determined. The price of coal will remain unchanged in 1990. The Prime Minister, in his address to the NPC, emphasized the role of the "open areas" in attracting foreign direct investment (para. 3.56) as well as the need to continue to proceed with reforms in housing and social security.

21/ It should be noted that the Chinese data relate to fixed investment only, and that investment in stocks rose rapidly in 1989. As these stocks can be expected to be run down somewhat in 1990 if demand picks up, the decline in investment in 1990 will be even larger.

2.56   In his speech, the Prime Minister also referred to measures that would strengthen the role of planning, at least during the period of rectification and improvement. For instance a few "more key and scarce materials will be distributed solely by the state" and the government is prepared to fix ceiling prices on the above plan sales of these items if the need arises. Similarly, the Government will resume control of investment approvals exceeding Y 30 million (para. 4.9). The Budget speech, delivered at the same session of the NPC, expressed the government's intention of moving ahead with experiments in reforms in the areas of separating taxes from enterprises contracts, and to try out alternative forms of tax sharing between the central government and the provinces. Certain revenues would be transferred to the center, including 80 percent of the proceeds from an investment regulatory tax, that is to be introduced in the future. On the expenditure side, the most notable features were that enterprises subsidies are budgeted to rise by 9.6 percent to Y 66 billion (16.5 percent of total expenditures),22/ and price subsidies are set to rise by 9.5 percent to Y 41 billion. This increases the pressure on the authorities to seek price adjustments that will lessen the burden of subsidies on the fiscal system (para. 3.40).

2.57   By most counts, this first phase of stabilization, spanning the fifteen months from late 1988 through the end of 1989, must be judged a qualified success. It has surpassed what might reasonably be expected from such a program in the context of a large and complex economy. Specifically, inflation has been reduced significantly without the economy's growth potential being impaired and without some of the attendant liabilities associated with a severe deflationary shock in other countries; for example: an enlarged debt burden, capital flight or debilitating industrial strife.

2.58   These immediate gains must, however, be weighed against the concerns listed (in paras. 2.35-2.41) as well as some others. For example, the frequency of economic cycles, their amplitude and the disruption they cause is one worry. Approximately four years separated the first two cycles; the third followed hard on the heels of the second. Another concern is that the virulence of the urban public's reaction against price increases, corruption and widening income differentials, might lead to an indefinite postponement of reforms, which are needed if China is to surmount the current difficulties and proceed towards its developmental goals.

22/ While this is an increase of 9.6 percent on last year's actual
     expenditure, it represents a 26 percent increase on last year's budget,
     which had a 15 percent overrun on this item.

2.59   With price stability having been largely restored, the authorities now have an opportunity to move forward with reforms. Some price increases were introduced in October 1989 and March 1990. More should follow with the attention being focused on agricultural commodities, industrial raw materials and industrial products. Institutional changes and strengthening of the financial market should be pursued so as to make indirect instruments the primary means of macromanagement. And it would be highly advantageous to resume, on a wider scale, experiments in the private trading of leases for agricultural land, as a prelude to the emergence of full-fledged land markets.

III. GROWTH AND EQUITY

3.1   As indicated in Chapter 1, past trends and the opportunities created by China's relative technological backwardness strongly endorse the continuation of rapid growth. Per capita GDP rose annually by 7.5 percent during the eighties and a doubling of the national product remains a realistic target for the year 2000. Although total factor productivity changed little in the two decades preceding the reform era, it is estimated to have risen by between 3 percent and 5 percent per annum during 1980-85.a/ Whether China can realize its economic ambitions over the next ten years with only a limited recourse to foreign capital, rests on the skillful application of macro and sectoral policies. This chapter will summarize some of the issues and policy options in two areas: (a) growth and (b) distributional equity. Chapter 4 will examine policies influencing efficiency; and Chapter 5 will delve into trade, and external borrowing and creditworthiness.

A. Determinants of Growth

3.2   Reform owed its widening acceptability in the eighties to the growth and productivity gains that came with it. A further improvement in living standards will remain the basis of its appeal during this decade. Industry was responsible for about 50 percent of the growth between 1980-85, rising to 86 percent in the latter part of the decade. The contribution of agriculture was large in the earlier years, but some preliminary research (see Table A1.7) suggests that the rate of GNP growth rather than economic reforms is what exerts a greater influence on technical efficiency and hence on factor productivity.b/ Growth has many determinants, major as well as minor. In the Chinese context, three are likely to dominate: (a) the volume and allocation of investible resources; (b) the strategy towards bottleneck sectors; and (c) technological advances.

(a) Investment

3.3   The pace of capital accumulation in China far exceeds the level of most low and middle-income countries including other centrally planned economies. Between 1980 and 1989, investment as a ratio to GDP averaged 34.3 percent. High rates of investment drive economic expansion, directly by augmenting productive capacity and indirectly by introducing new technology embodied in capital goods. About one third of the variance in growth rates in a sample of 112 countries is explained by investment spending.c/ While the quantum of capital accumulated is one factor, of equal importance is the pattern of investment across various sectors and regions. A concentration of investment in industry and the adequate provision of infrastructure favor growth. In China, the scale of investment and its implications for growth will be decisively influenced by (i) future composition of leading industries; (ii) inter-sectoral resource transfers and agricultural development; and (iii) the government's ability to at least sustain the level of fiscal resources currently at its disposal and use a portion of these for the purposes of developing physical and social infrastructure.

3.4   (i) Industrial Strategy: Future Leading Subsectors. The allocation of capital across the various manufacturing subsectors will have important

---

a/ Lettered footnotes are to be found in Annex II.

implications for trend growth rates. Compared to other developing countries, China's industrial base is both more diversified and accounts for a larger share of GDP--46.1 percent in 1988 (Table A1.1). Machinery is by far the most prominent subsector, with a 28 percent share, followed by textiles and clothing (18 percent), chemicals (12 percent) and metallurgy (8 percent) (Table A9.5). For a developing country, this is an atypical composition and it resembles instead the industrial landscape of Eastern Europe. It bears the imprint of a development strategy whose principal aim has been to create a heavy manufacturing base that would minimize external dependence and satisfy the demands of a large military establishment. For these reasons, machinery and metallurgical industries acquired the leading role. They have kept their lead through all the changes that have transformed China in the eighties. For a few years, in the early part of the decade, heavy industry's share was exceeded by light manufacturing, but since 1986, producer goods industries have regained their dominance (Table A9.2). The weight of machinery and metallurgy in industrial product is responsible, in part, for the high energy and steel intensity of Chinese economy (Table A14.1). Because these industries have remained relatively sheltered from external competition, they have tended to be technologically backward, saddled with obsolete capacity and their levels of productivity do not, on average, bear comparison with foreign manufacturers. Over the years, machinery and metal industries have acquired powerful bureaucratic patrons that have ensured sufficient funding and raw material even in lean times.d/ And the strong interaction between these two subsectors as well as between them and energy producers has maintained demand at a high pitch.

3.5   In effect, China's capacity in these areas may be overbuilt from the perspective of emerging demand patterns and from the perspective of a dynamic industrial strategy for the nineties. The acute problems encountered by some of the engineering enterprises as demand slowed in 1989, underscores the mismatch between need and availability. Heavy industry absorbs far too much capital, provides below-average returns, and its appetite for energy is one of the root causes of chronic shortages. By targeting machinery and metal industries for promotion, China will starve more deserving sectors of capital, perpetuate an artificial shortage of investment funds in a situation of resource availability few countries can rival, and limit its growth potential.

3.6   Future growth calls for some fresh thinking about industrial policy and the reshaping of engineering and basic materials industries to meet the demands that will emanate from industry's new leaders. The implications of China's current industrial development pattern for environmental problems of water and air pollution also need to be addressed; namely poor energy efficiency, reliance on coal, and the water-intensive nature of China's often outdated industrial processes, which is a major factor contributing to water shortages and pollution in most of the industrialized provinces.1/

3.7   By way of illustration, it might be noted that the strongest econo- mies on the international stage, whether developing or industrialized, display certain structural similarities.e/ In each of them, the leading sectors, with the most numerous linkages, the ones that are setting the technological pace and generating the most employment--direct as well as indirect--are drawn from a small group: transport industries and consumer electronics. These two, especially the automobile and aircraft industries, support not just the machine tool, metallurgical and electronics industries but, through forward linkages, a host of service suppliers as well. Growth of these industries and the technological demands they have placed on their suppliers, is perhaps the single most important source of technical progress and productivity increase in the core industries of the modern economy: basic metals, engineering, chemicals, and electronic components. In recent years, the manner in which the leading sectors have evolved their product strategies, has profoundly

---

1/ Few countries are so dependent on coal as is China. Unlike most countries, electric power generation is not the largest coal consumer. Industrial use of coal is currently much greater. There has been strong growth of coal consumption in the household sector, caused both by urban population growth and increasing coal use in rural areas. Many of the environmental problems in China are related to its heavy and dispersed coal use, for example in industry and households. They occur at every stage of the coal chain: mining and disposal of mine waste, coal washing, transport and handling, processing or combustion, and ultimately ash disposal. Water pollution occurs both in mining regions and in dense urban areas, caused by problems in disposing of coal mining and processing wastes and the coal ash remaining after combustion. In many large cities in China, ambient concentrations of particulates and sulfur dioxide in the air are at very high levels. The concentration of particulates is the most serious problem; it is largely related to the extensive use of coal, the high ash content of some coals (20-30 percent) and often incomplete combustion because of poor matching of coal qualities to boiler designs. The average sulfur content of coal is relatively low (in the range of 1.2-1.7 percent), but the extent of coal use means sulfur emissions are growing; moreover, there are some regions using very high-sulfur coal. The prospects of continued increasing coal use are sobering for their environmental implications and underline the need for better policies and more resources for investments to conserve coal and mitigate its environmental effects. An effective environmental strategy will involve a mixture of pricing incentives, mandatory policies and resources to improve the quality of the coal supply, to raise the efficiency of the large boiler population, to improve the technical efficiency of combustion controls, and to develop better options for household coal use. In addition, greater resources must be committed to fuller exploration and development of cleaner fuels.

influenced the substitution of other metals, plastics and composites for steel; has lowered energy intensity; and has enlarged the role of electronic components.

3.8   China stands at the crossroads. It can continue for several years to build production capacity in the heavy industry sector with the frequently obsolescent equipment emerging from its engineering enterprises. The input-output relationships would keep the various constituents of the sector employed. But, in time, the country would be faced with the dilemma that Eastern Europe and the Soviet Union will have to resolve: too much antiquated capacity in the wrong places.

3.9   Selecting the leading players for the future industrial strategy is a matter of such complexity that it might be left largely to market forces. For instance, a decision on the automobile industry cannot be taken in isolation from decisions that impinge upon steel production, electronics, petroleum production and refining, infrastructure building, urban development, trade policy, the provision of supporting services and environmental policy, to name just the most obvious.f/ The ramifications are vast but the question cannot be sidestepped. China needs to refine and implement industrial policies announced in March 1989.g/ It needs, in addition, to define a long-term vision that guides the investment process and forces rival ministries each, pushing their own projects, to coordinate their plans with reference to an agreed scenario. The Eighth Five Year Plan, to be introduced in 1991, offers an opportunity for a fresh approach to strategy, which also more fully internalizes the potential inherent in market guidance.

3.10   At one level the scale of investment holds out the hope that China can sustain the growth trends of the recent past. However, the quantum of investment alone is not enough. Unless resources are being put to sound industrial uses and the future of manufacturing linked to dynamic subsectors, the future of growth is not assured. If industry is to receive its due share of capital in the Eighth Plan period, selecting appropriate, forward-looking policies becomes doubly important for growth objectives are to be met.

3.11   (ii) Intersectoral Transfers and Agricultural Development. Although the level of aggregate savings is unlikely to be a constraint on growth, the intersectoral distribution of resources could affect the pace of industrialization. China is clearly concerned about food security and seeks a fairly high degree of self-sufficiency.h/ As urbanization is bound to continue encroaching upon the arable acreage, raising output will call for substantial investment, which will divert resources from other uses where the returns are generally higher.

3.12   The beginning of China's reforms and early successes were in the rural sector, whose minimal linkages with the rest of the economy made it easier to introduce as well as manage the process of change. Starting with the poorest regions of the country, reform entailed a progressive diminution of communal agriculture and greater reliance on production contracts with individual households. In 1979, prices paid for both quota and above quota purchase of crops by the State were raised by 20 percent and 50 percent respectively. At the same time, costs of inputs were cut by 10-15 percent. Permission to sell surplus grain and produce on free rural markets added to farmers' incentives. Gradually, during the early eighties, the stress on grain output was moderated and farmers were given the autonomy to rationalize land use.i/

3.13   Heavy investment in water management and land reclamation, using labor mobilized through the communes, had steadily enlarged productive potential since the sixties,j/ while the increasing availability of high quality fertilizer from 13 new fertilizer complexes purchased in the mid-seventies, also helped to shift outward the production possibility frontier.k/ By the close of the 1970s, China's agriculture was poised for growth. Reforms provided the needed spur and pushed grain harvests from 283 million tons in 1977 to 407 million in 1984.

3.14   The dramatic increase in grain availability in the early eighties convinced planners that China's food supply problems were under control. Attention shifted to the fiscal costs of food subsidies arising from the state's commitment to acquire, at fairly high prices, all the grain farmers wished to sell above the quota. Worsening rural underemployment was a another concern. A second round of reforms in 1985/86, in effect, reduced grain price supports; raised the cost of items such as diesel and fertilizer; widened farmer's choices with regard to cropping patterns; cut state investment in agriculture; and gave further incentives to rural township and village enterprises, so that off-farm employment would be enlarged.l/

3.15   Rural industrialization which had begun gathering momentum in the early eighties, accelerated and by 1988 had absorbed 67 million workers. But as price incentives were reduced, grain production slackened, forcing China to import between 9 and 15 million tons of grain per annum during 1986-89. The declining attractiveness of mainline agriculture induced peasants to put more of their savings into industry or housing construction. State investment, which might have stimulated local effort, also began drying up (Table A13.8).

3.16   Clearly the benefits of past investment in land and infrastructure as well as fertilizer capacity have been fully exploited. If China is to prudently limit its net purchases of coarse grains, and wheat on the international market, production incentives will need to be restored and backed by the needed investment.m/ This is recognized in the program approved by the Fifth Plenum of the Thirteenth Central Party Committee (paras. 2.46 and 2.51).

3.17   A productive, commercially oriented, agriculture that will generate growth rates sufficient to meet China's targets for the nineties will make large demands on investible resources. Between 1955 and 1985, manipulating the rural-urban terms of trade allowed the state to transfer an estimated 600 to 800 billion yuan to other sectors.n/. These flows continue although the amounts involved are now quite small. Agricultural modernization is likely to call for significant net transfers to agriculture by way of (i) higher prices for grain and other products; (ii) expenditure on water management, especially in the poorer provinces; and (iii) investment in manufacturing capacity to provide agriculture with fertilizer, pesticides and machinery.2/ As modern agriculture is energy-intensive,o/ it will also absorb increasing amounts of China's fuel supplies, either directly for the running of machinery or indirectly through inputs such as fertilizer.3/

3.18   These measures will call for some redirection of budgetary resources, in the medium-term, towards the rural sector at the expense of urban consumers and state enterprises. As in most advanced countries, the costs will be borne primarily by industry and over a period of time, major industrial adjustments will be necessary to accommodate the transfers. From the perspective of growth, the higher agricultural ICORs and energy intensities are likely, on balance, to slow the increase of GDP. To the extent that China is willing to draw on the international market and finance imports of foodstuffs through the sale of manufactures, the scale of resource transfers and the associated growth effects could be decreased. But the choices p/ are constrained by

---

2/ The increase in fertilizer use fell from 8.9 percent per annum in 1978-84 to 3.7 percent per annum in 1984-87, in spite of large imports. In future China will need to spend heavily on this subsector. Investment will also be required on transportation and storage facilities to cut losses in threshing, drying, storage and handling, currently estimated at 25 million tons per year.

3/ The challenge to agriculture in the 1990s and beyond is to only to provide food for the world's most populous nation, but also to achieve that level of production with less environmental damage than is apparent today. This will require attention to technology in three main areas: those that reduce the environmental burden of pesticides and fertilizers (for example, integrated pest control which includes a wide range of techniques--chemical pest control, mechanical manipulation of the soil and many biological strategies--to control pests while minimizing the environmental burden of chemicals and frequent passages of tillage and pest control machinery through fields), those that reduce the demand for irrigation water (for example, lasers can be used to guide machines that level the field precisely making it possible to flood them quickly and uniformly; trickle or drip irrigation systems; and new techniques to reduce salinization problems from traditional irrigation systems by cycling wastewater back into the farm's irrigation system) and those that continue to improve crop production per hectare (for example, multiple cropping which includes crop rotation, intercropping with trees and annual crops sharing the same fields, overseeding legumes into cereals and also double-cropping--growing two or more crops simultaneously in a single field). Creating the policies and institutions that will induce farmers to adopt new technologies and management practices may be the most difficult and challenging task. In this regard, property rights to farmland and reduced subsidies for water and fertilizer may be of prime importance.

effects could be decreased. But the choices p/ are constrained by China's
very size.4/

3.19   (iii) Fiscal Revenues. The third item on the list of factors that
will influence investment is the fiscal resources at the disposal of the
government. China's budgetary revenues were equal to 36 percent of GNP in
1978, far above the level of low income countries. By 1988 the revenue to GNP
ratio had declined to 20 percent.5/ This change is closely linked to the
sectoral incidence of taxation.q/ China relies overwhelmingly on taxes from
the industrial sector, and the direct tax burden on other sectors is quite
modest. In 1978, industrial revenues accounted for 75 percent of budgetary
revenues (state industrial profits and taxes accounted for 69 percent of total
state enterprise profits and taxes).r/ Industrial prices were kept at high
levels while those of agricultural products and other raw materials were much
lower. This price differential--called the "scissors gap" by socialist econ-
omists--earned handsome profits for industry, which were then gathered up by
the budget. The weight of direct taxes on agriculture was extremely modest,
but the rural sector indirectly bore much of the burden of supporting state
financed industrialization. This began changing in the late seventies when
reforms shifted the terms of trade in favor of agriculture, shrinking the
"scissors gap". Inevitably, the ability of the government to rely on industrial profits to fund government programs was weakened. Ordinarily, the
concentration of the tax burden on industry should have resulted in a high
elasticity of fiscal revenue, as industry has grown substantially faster than
GNP. However, because of the systematic shift of the terms of trade against
industry, this has not occurred.

Table 3.1:   EVOLUTION OF BUDGETARY REVENUES
(Percent of GNP)

	1978	1988
Total Revenues	36.4	19.8
(of which: Subsidies)	(5.2)	(5.4)
Extrabudgetary Revenues	9.7	16.8
Budgetary Plus Extrabudgetary Revenues	46.1	36.6

Source: Ministry of Finance.

3.20   Net industrial output grew 184 percent in real terms between 1978 and
1988, compared to a 142 percent real increase in net material product, but in
current prices, industry's share of net material product declined during the
period from 49.4 percent to 46.2 percent. These numbers together imply a 20
percent deterioration in the terms of trade against industry. The same shift

4/   These choices are analyzed in a forthcoming study by the World Bank
entitled Managing Agricultural Transition, June 1990. China and India
are the countries which will most profoundly influence the cereals
deficit of developing countries (and hence market prices) through the
year 2000.

5/   The ratio of current revenue to GNP for all low-income countries in
1986 was 15.4 percent and 21.4 percent for lower middle-income
countries, World Development Report, 1988, World Bank, 1988, p. 268.

in the terms of trade during 1978-88 is reflected in the net/gross output ratio in industry which fell from 35.1 percent to 30 percent. Within industry, the tax base is concentrated on state-run and large-scale collective industry whose net output value declined from 37.9 percent of GNP in 1978 to 30.7 percent in 1988. Again this was a function of relative price changes, as the sector's real growth was slightly faster than GNP overall.

3.21   A change in the distribution of net income resulting from enterprise reform further diminished the revenue potential of industry. Wages, benefits and interest payments have increased their shares, while that of profits and taxes in net output declined. Finally, with reform came programs of profit retention, which reduced the proportion of profits and taxes remitted to the central authorities. These changes are summarized in Table 3.2.

Table 3.2: NET OUTPUT TO BUDGETARY REVENUES FROM INDUSTRY

	(1) NVIO/GNP	(2) (p+t)/NVIO	(3) R/(p+t)	(4) R/GNP (1)x(2)x(3)
1978	0.379	0.67	0.98	0.249
1988	0.307	0.53	0.58	0.094

NVIO = Net output value of independent accounting industrial enterprises, township level and above.
p+t = Profit and tax of those enterprises.
R = Remittances of profit plus tax payments of those enterprises (estimated).

3.22   The mutually reinforcing changes in the distribution of net industrial output account for a decline in budgetary revenues equal to 15.5 percentage points of GNP, compared to a total decline in budgetary revenues of 16.6 percentage points of GNP. Direct tax burdens on other sectors being light, the increase in their shares in net output has contributed little to revenues. The decline in the ratio of net industrial output to GNP has pushed revenues down by 4.7 percent of GNP; that of the share of profit and tax in net output value caused revenues to fall by an additional 5.2 percent of GNP;

and the lower proportion of remittances accounted for the final 5.6 percent of
GNP reduction in revenues.6/

3.23   The extent to which taxes and remittances have diminished is related
to the tax reforms introduced in stages between 1980 and 1986. These reforms
were in response to complaints regarding excessive fiscal centralization, the
involvement of the central ministries in the budgetary decisions of local
governments and the annual ad hoc changes in rates of revenue sharing.s/ They
substantially increased the autonomy of provinces in determining expenditures
and pegged center-local revenue sharing arrangements to contracts negotiated
with each province on a three-year cycle. In the context of these new tax
rules, the government also moved to raise the share of revenues directly paid
to the central authorities so as to safeguard its fiscal situation.

3.24   While fiscal contracting spurred provincial expenditures they did not
have the expected positive effect on provincial tax effort, especially in the
richer coastal provinces with high rates of economic growth such as Jiangsu,
Heilongjiang and Shanghai. In 1978, 17 provinces ran budget surpluses and
spent 52 percent of the revenues collected. Ten years later, just eight provinces were in surplus and they were spending two-thirds of what they
raised.t/ Only three provinces, Zhejiang, Jiangsu and Hubei showed budgetary
surpluses in 1987 that were above those registered in the late seventies.

3.25   Partially compensating for the weakening revenue performance of the
provinces was the greater independence attained by the center in the sphere of
tax collection. Local governments gathered 79 percent of total revenues in
1981 but only 62 percent in 1988 (see Table 3.3). At the start of the decade,
58 percent of central government expenditures were funded by transfers from
the provinces, falling to 16 percent in 1985. From 1986, the center began
making a net transfer to local governments. The amounts have become steadily
larger since and represent a significant transfer of funds from surplus to
deficit provinces and is an important facet of the government's regional
policy.u/

6/   A different perspective on the evolution of fiscal receipts is provided
by examining changes in budgetary and extrabudgetary funds which
together have declined by 9.5 percent of GNP. This change reflects the
first two factors given in Table 3.2, the declining share of net
industrial output and the increased share of labor and interest in net
output. In addition, there is a shift of 7.1 percent of GNP from
budgetary to extrabudgetary funds. This corresponds appropriately to
the diminished share of budgetary revenues in total tax and profit,
because by far the largest component of extrabudgetary funds are
enterprise retained funds. (Retained earnings accounted for 80 percent
of the increase in extrabudgetary funds between 1978 and 1988.) These
resources are used largely for fixed investment, the responsibility for
which has been shifted from the budget to enterprise-level and other
decentralized funding sources. As this analysis makes clear, fiscal
revenues are lower because the responsibility for various kinds of
outlays has been reapportioned.

Table 3.3: CENTER-PROVINCIAL REVENUES AND EXPENDITURES
(billion yuan)

	Sum of provincial revenues and percent of total revenues	Consolidated national revenues	Sum of provincial expenditures and percent of total expenditures	Consolidated national expenditures
1981	86.15 (79%)	108.96	50.89 (46%)	111.50
1985	117.72 (63%)	186.64	103.62 (56%)	184.48
1988	160.64 (62%)	258.78	164.34 (62%)	266.83

Sources: 1988 data is from 1989 Economic Yearbook. 1981-85 data is from China Fiscal Statistics, 1950-85.

3.26   Changed relative prices, enterprise reforms and fiscal decentralization have greatly altered the fiscal picture. Whether this shrinkage of budgetary resources has any major developmental or macroeconomic consequences can only be gauged by examining the trends in expenditure.

3.27   Total Expenditures. Lower revenues have been matched by a reduced budgetary outlay in three areas. Capital expenditures (capital construction, renovation of existing assets, and new product expenditures) fell from 14.4 percent of GNP in 1978 to 5.4 percent in 1988. Allocations for working capital (primarily the finance of initial inventories for new enterprises) amounted to 1.9 percent of GNP in 1978, but for only 0.1 percent of GNP in 1988. Third, military spending has declined from 4.7 percent of GNP in 1978 to only 1.6 percent in 1988 (Table A7.6).7/ These three components together account for a reduction in budgetary outlays from 21 percent to 7.1 percent of GNP, or a net reduction of 12.9 percentage points. Current civilian expenditure, net of subsidies, declined quite modestly from 10.4 percent to 9.3 percent of GNP. Among current expenses, the share of health and education grew from 3.1 percent of GNP to 3.4 percent of GNP and subsidies rose slightly from 5.2 percent of GNP to 5.4 percent of GNP.

3.28   By 1987, overall spending by local governments exceeded central government expenditures by 23 percent, and were budgeted to exceed them by 50 percent in 1989. Because all of the budget deficit is accounted for at the central level, the difference is greater on the revenue side: local government revenues in 1989 are budgeted at 70 percent more than central government revenues. It is possible to apportion budgetary expenditures to central and local government levels according to three broad categories: capital (fixed investment only); current; and subsidies. These figures are provided in Table

---

7/ Budgeted expenditure on defense increased by 15 percent in 1990, but as a percent of budgetary outlay it has risen marginally from 8.3 percent in 1989 to 8.4 percent in 1990 (Table A7.10). Of course, not all expenditures on the defense establishment are included in this category. R&D and military pensions, for example, appear under other headings.

- 44 -

A7.7. As nearly all military expenses are borne by the central government, local governments account for 75-80 percent of current civilian expenditures. Similarly, they were responsible for 73 percent of all subsidies in 1989, a substantial increase over past years. By contrast, the central government carried out two-thirds of capital outlay in 1987, and its budgeted share rose to 72 percent in 1989. Nearly 40 percent of central government spending in the late 1980s was on investment, while local government capital expenditures were only 18 percent of total outlay in 1987, declining to 10 percent in the 1989 budget. Thus, by the late 1980s, the division of responsibilities between the central and local government levels was such that the central government had primary responsibility for capital spending and defense, while local government undertook most of the current civilian expenditure and subsidies.

3.29   Capital Outlay. Besides shouldering the expenditure on fixed investment financed from the budget, the central government also has a fixed investment plan which determines a major proportion of such investment in the economy. By contrast, local government investment from budgetary funds is modest. While decentralized investment as a whole is quite substantial, most of this is in the domain of enterprises and households, and the role of local government investment funding and local investment plans is correspondingly limited. Because of this relationship, the dramatic decline in budgetary funding of fixed investment, documented above, primarily reflects the changed role of the central budget in the economy.

3.30   It is possible to quantify the changing relationship between the central government investment plan and central government financing of investment so as to derive the central government borrowing requirements for its investment plan. In 1978, 31.2 billion yuan of completed investment (9.0 percent of GNP) was undertaken as part of the central plan, while the budget included 44.4 billion yuan for fixed investment purposes 8/ (see Table A7.8). Assuming that the division of responsibility over budgetary outlays for such fixed investment was the same in 1978 as in 1987/88, the central government investment plan corresponds almost exactly to central government outlay for fixed investment. In other words, in 1978, not only was the budget balanced (in that fiscal revenues equaled expenditures), but in addition the central government investment plan was fully funded from the budget.

8/   It should be noted that the juxtaposition of these figures is not exact. Investment refers to investment actually carried out (bricks laid and machines installed), while the budgetary figures refer to funds allocated. Budgetary allocations thus reflect both the setting aside of funds not yet expended, and the purchase of materials and equipment not yet installed. In a growing economy, allocations will generally be larger than the equivalent amount of investment actually completed in a given year. The calculation in Table A7.8 is based on the investment actually completed in a given year, and on the assumption that the ratio between funding and completed investment is the same for central and local governments. In addition, Table A7.8 understates the central government funding requirements to the extent that funding is also required for the preparatory stages of investment.

3.31   Completed investment within the central plan amounted to 104.1 billion yuan (7.5 percent of GNP, down slightly from 1978) in 1988, while funding
from budgetary sources was only 47 billion. Of budgetary expenditures for
fixed investment, the central government accounted for 68 percent; if the same
proportions applied to completed investment funded from the budget, the
central government accounted for 32 billion yuan, or only 2.3 percent of GNP.
In order to complete its investment plan, the central government had an additional funding requirement equal to 5.2 percent of GNP. Table A7.8 shows the
evolution of this funding requirement. From 1978 through 1981/82, while
central government funding of investment diminished, the central investment
plan also declined as a proportion of GNP. From 1983, however, the central
investment plan expanded as a proportion of GNP, while central government
funding continued to slip. The result has been a substantial increase in the
central government borrowing for investment by state enterprises, which is
financed through the banking system and the profits of the People's Bank of
China.

3.32   Subsidies. Total subsidies in 1981 are estimated at 9 percent of
GNP, and the urban food subsidy alone was 6 percent of GNP.9/ Subsequently,

---

9/ Chinese statistics on subsidies are divided in price subsidies and
    subsidies to loss-making enterprises, and are complete from 1986. The
    category of price subsidies is well-defined, and has been included in
    budgetary expenditures and revenues since 1986. However, the category
    of subsidies to loss-making enterprises is very heterogeneous;
    moreover, it has never been included in budgetary outlays in Chinese
    statistics. In practice, subsidies to loss-making enterprises include
    primarily enterprises in the commercial, industrial and foreign trade
    sectors, although loss-making enterprises can be found to some degree
    in every sector. Most crucially, subsidies to urban food supplies are
    included both in price subsidies and in subsidies to loss-making
    enterprises. Although practice is not entirely uniform across
    provinces, the most common pattern is that the central government
    provides a fixed amount of "price subsidy" that covers the differences
    between purchases of grain at the relatively low quota price and sales
    to the urban population at even lower prices. In addition to quota
    purchases, local governments also procure grain at higher above-quota
    prices, and the additional losses incurred in selling this grain to the
    urban population are considered to be "enterprise losses" borne by the
    local government on a separate account. In the above discussion,
    subsidies refers to the aggregate of price subsidies and subsidies to
    loss-making enterprises. Precise breakdowns of aggregate subsidies are
    not available, but those going to urban food supplies are by far the
    largest single portion, accounting for perhaps 60 percent of the total
    volume of subsidies.

       In 1978, subsidies to loss-making factories were quite
    significant, amounting to more than 1 percent of GNP. Subsidies to
    commerce (predominantly urban food supplies) were already important,
    amounting to more than 2 percent of GNP. In the following years,
    industrial subsidies were reduced, primarily by closing inefficient
    small industries, while commercial subsidies skyrocketed. The total
    subsidy burden reached its zenith in 1981, because of extensive
    commercial subsidization combined with temporarily inflated industrial
    losses caused by a short-term retrenchment program.

with economic growth and reform of nonstaple food prices, total subsidies declined significantly. From 1986 through 1988 they have remained in the range of 5 to 6 percent of GNP, with urban food subsidies amounting to about 4 percent of GNP. Urban food subsidies were brought down through 1985, but in subsequent years have stubbornly resisted further reduction. Moreover, there are preliminary indications of an increase in urban food subsidies in 1989. Subsidies for command plan imports and mandatory exports comprise a second major category.

3.33   Subsidies to industry are much smaller overall than subsidies to the commercial sector, and probably a little smaller than foreign trade subsidies. Industrial subsidies were lowered by the mid-1980s, but have tended to rise in the latter half of the 1980s. From 0.56 percent of GNP in 1986, industrial subsidies crept up to 0.59 percent in 1988, and are estimated to surpass 1 percent of GNP in 1989. About a fifth of all state enterprises incurred defi-cits in 1989. Industrial losses are overwhelmingly concentrated in energy and raw material industries (see Table A7.9). Coal and petroleum, accounted for half of all industrial losses. In coal, attempts to restrain costs through the contract responsibility system, that allows mines to keep all of any cost reduction, has failed to solve the problem. In each successive year from 1985 through 1988, losses exceeded the contracted figure, and in 1988 losses were more than double the contracted figure. For 1989, they are estimated at 6 billion yuan, almost twice those of 1988. In petroleum, extraction costs have been increasing at annual rates of 15 percent for several years, while output prices have remained unchanged. As a result, this sector, which was once a major contributor of revenues to the budget, now makes virtually no net finan-cial contribution. Profit has been reduced by a billion yuan annually, and losses over 1 billion were incurred for the first time in 1988. Losses for 1989 are estimated at 2-3 billion. Because they are concentrated in primary energy production, industrial losses are borne primarily by the central gov-ernment, which manages the large-scale energy producers. The burden is thus quite different from that of commercial subsidies, most of which are now managed by local governments.v/

3.34   Implications of Budgetary Developments. From this overview a number of points can be distilled. Raising the tax/GNP ratio would involve partially reversing some of the reforms introduced and its redistributive effects would be widely resisted.w/ Having just emerged from one long drawn-out campaign of tax reform, the attractions for the center of immediately embarking on another are far from obvious. Repeated tax changes interfere with decision-making for the longer term because they generate expectations of further reforms to come. The advantages of increasing as distinct from stabilizing the ratio around 20-21 percent of GNP, must be carefully scrutinized in the context of future expenditure needs. A significantly higher level of taxation would blunt incentives and rob the economy of some of its dynamism. A number of studies have found that heavier taxation, by diminishing incentives, and reducing the marginal productivity of labor as well as capital, is associated with sluggish economic performance.x/ With a savings rate approaching 36 percent of GDP, financing the deficit in a noninflationary manner should not pose serious problems over the medium term.

3.35   In the majority of developing and industrialized economies, resources are transferred from the household sector to government.y/ There are instances when such transfers have resulted in some crowding out of other claims on these resources and have generated inflationary pressures. Large household savings diminish the likelihood of this happening. For example Japan, Italy and Malaysia have all incurred significant fiscal deficits in the eighties. However, the government's efforts at financing, generally through the issue of bonds, have caused minimal macroeconomic stress because these countries have household savings rates that are among the world's highest.10/

3.36   Longer-run efforts at narrowing the fiscal gap in China might approach the problem from the side of expenditures by reducing subsidies or administrative costs, for instance. Furthermore, there is no compelling reason to finance a bigger share of infrastructure investment through the budget. In most other countries where the supply of financial savings is abundant, it would be more appropriate use the capital markets to finance and discipline most types of spending on infrastructure. From a small beginning in 1981, bond sales, principally by the state, are on the rise. A broadening and deepening of the bond market would multiply the options for making good budgetary shortfalls and financing projects that currently rely on banks or

---

10/	Average fiscal deficit, % of GNP, 1979-84	Average household savings rate as % of GNP, 1979-84
Japan	4.5	16.5
Italy	13.08 (1981-84)	19.0
Malaysia	15.2 (1980-84)	15.2 (1980-84)

Source: Japan: Facing Economic Maturity, by E. J. Lincoln, Brookings Institution, 1988, pp. 76-77, 93; World Bank, Economic and Social Data Base.

the public purse.11/ There remain certain types of expenditures such as education,12/ health and funding for development in the poorer provinces, which may require the direct fiscal support of the government but, except for these, it is not desirable that the state should seek to enlarge its budgetary presence in investment after having deliberately withdrawn just a few years ago.

3.37   Stabilizing the ratio of revenues to GNP does have definite attractions because it would facilitate long-term planning of expenditures and help sustain interprovincial resource flows. To achieve this, a revenue elasticity, higher than what has been attained in recent years is essential. Three avenues might be explored. First, there are extensions of the VAT so as to augment its revenue generating capacity.z/ Higher rates and broader coverage would provide the revenues streams needed by the state. Refinements of the

---

11/ Placement of Treasury bonds was begun in 1981 and has grown since. To increase their initially limited attractiveness for individuals and enterprises, the principal holders, maturities were shortened after 1985 from nine years to five years and to two years in 1988. Coupon rates were raised and when inflation accelerated, rates were indexed. Active trading of bonds was permitted and their use as collateral was allowed for the purposes of enterprise borrowing. The menu of offerings was lengthened after 1987 with the sale of key construction bonds by the MOF; key enterprise bonds of PCBC and capital construction bonds by the State Planning Commission. Because of the maturity structure of recent flotations, MOF is faced with having to refinance an average of 22 billion yuan worth of bonds per annum during 1990-92. This will be in addition to the financing of any deficits the government might incur. The refinancing amount is equivalent to about 1 percent of GNP. At a time when other investment spending is likely to be low and only a handful of state agencies are active in the bond market, refinancing ought not to be a major hurdle, especially given the powers of mandatory placement. But for the 1990 fiscal year, the government has decided to minimize its efforts at raising funds through bond placement and instead will not redeem bonds held by banks, enterprises and government institutions that will be maturing in the course of the year. Future financing needs could be facilitated by requiring (i) specialized banks to hold a portion of their excess cash requirement in the form of treasury bonds; (ii) achieving a balance of maturities; (iii) strengthening the secondary market for government debt; and (iv) tailoring these instruments so that they suit the preferences of households. These and other proposals are discussed at length in China: Financial Sector Review, World Bank, June 29, 1990, Report No. 8415-CHA.

12/ Although China allots a smaller percentage of the GDP to education than other developing countries in equivalent income brackets (2.2 percent as against an average of 3.0 percent in 1986) high teacher-student ratios, underused facilities, inefficient use of funds and low teacher salaries, all suggest that much more output can be obtained without additional budgetary commitments. There remains a problem in the very poor districts, but that calls for targeted expenditures covering all services, not just education.

enterprise contracting system, which separate tax payments from other remittances and loan servicing, would also strengthen the center's finances. This
has been experimented with in Chungching and will now be extended to several
other cities. Second, problems of evasion and compliance could be lessened by
improving the capabilities of the central tax administration. Effective
auditing, firmly enforced penalties for nonpayment, a system for reviewing and
adjudicating appeals, and inducements to tax payers to maintain accurate
accounts, would diminish the hemorrhage that afflicts China's tax network.aa/

3.38   Third, rather than attempting to recentralize much more, the center
should encourage the provincial authorities to redouble their efforts to raise
revenue. Perhaps the greatest disincentive to tax effort is the fear that any
sizable gains will be appropriated by the center through special levies or
through borrowing. A province whose performance is above par also runs the
risk of having to surrender more resources when its three year tax contract is
renewed. Surplus provinces have responded to the uncertainty by allowing
their tax revenues to stagnate while, in certain cases, enlarging their control over extrabudgetary resources.

3.39   This has created a vicious cycle. The slow growth of revenues from
the surplus provinces forces the center to employ ad hoc tactics that sharpen
the suspicions of provincial governments regarding the center's intention and
result in even more expenditure and even less tax effort. A firm commitment
to tax contracts (if contracting is retained over the medium term) which
restores mutual trust, and greater reliance by the center on broad-based taxes
with the requisite elasticity, may be the route to stronger tax effort in the
provinces. The government is currently considering various schemes for tax-
sharing. Over the longer term, these will help resolve many of the existing
difficulties.

3.40   In sum, major new tax initiatives, as distinct from a refinement and
strengthening of existing arrangements, may be neither desirable nor feasible.
Stabilizing revenues in the short run and a modest increase over the medium
term might best be sought through the changes in contracting referred to
above. By adopting a low-key approach that works through many small initiatives, including the improvement of tax administration, the government is less
likely to provoke resistance.ab/ Improving the efficiency of the tax system
might well take precedence over efforts to substantially enlarge the fiscal
resources at the center's disposal or strain the economic consensus. These
themes are echoed in the 1990 budget which calls for a reasonable adjustment
of business tax rates, somewhat higher contributions by localities to the
center; and the imposition of an investment regulatory tax if spending shows
signs of rising too rapidly. However, higher outlay on subsidies is likely to
prevent a narrowing of the deficit. It is expected to remain at close to 2.3
percent of GNP, but it is an objective the government must continue pursuing
over the medium run. (see Table A7.10).

(b) Bottleneck Sectors

3.41   Both the Sixth as well as the Seventh Five-Year Plans sought to raise
national product annually by 7.5 percent. This served to determine the level
of investment in long-gestation projects to supply the economy with energy,

steel, timber, cement, petrochemicals and transport capacity to mention only
the most important inputs. Actual growth rates exceeded the target by an
average of 2.5 percent per annum between 1980 and 1988 and investment levels
were far above those built into the Plan. More significantly, during cyclical
peaks, GDP increased by an average of 12 percent per annum. It is scarcely
surprising that industry has complained about shortages. These complaints
take on a particular urgency, when growth accelerates and the pinch of constraints, together with the associated pressure on prices, are felt most
severely. Surprisingly, these bottlenecks, that have been widely noted in
other socialist countries ac/ as well, have not been linked with the failure
of macroeconomic policy to restrain demand but are blamed instead on inadequate investment. Every few years, the government has been moved to try and
shift more resources into the bottleneck sectors only to be caught short when
the next surge in growth, by triggering capacity expansion in the processing
industries, pierces planned ceilings for basic industries and infrastructure.

3.42   While there is no doubt that industry and consumers had to cope with
troublesome energy, material and transport constraints in 1987/88, production
trends and investment shares for the "bottleneck sectors" belie some of the
concerns that have been expressed. It is not apparent that administrative
intervention by the state should be redoubled, so as to divert more resources
from other uses to these sectors or to restrain consumption in the interests
of even higher growth rates for heavy industry. First, from Table A9.2, it
can be seen that over the past four years, heavy industry has either kept
abreast or grown somewhat faster than light industry. Second, again at the
aggregate level, the share of energy in capital construction has risen substantially since 1985 and is almost a quarter of the total (Table A13.7).
Third, disaggregated data on capital construction for state enterprises indicates, that metallurgical, power, petroleum and chemical industries have
increased their shares since 1985. Coal and machine-building have suffered an
erosion, but in the former case it has been counterbalanced by collective
investment. Fourth, production statistics show that growth rates during
1986-88 have ranged between 2.8 percent and 3.4 percent for coal, crude oil
and natural gas. Rates for rolled steel, cement, railway freight cars and
electricity were between 6.6 percent and 9.5 percent, while building materials, machinery and chemicals rose by between 13.6 percent and 18 percent
(Table A9.4).

3.43   Coal and petroleum are the two critical commodities that seem to have
lagged behind. In the case of petroleum, production has stagnated in spite of
heavy expenditures because China's major fields, Daqing and Shengli, have
entered late maturity and new finds have failed to keep production on earlier
trends.ad/ In 1989 coal production passed a billion tons.ae/ This in itself
was a considerable achievement in view of the difficulties both the US and the
USSR have encountered in pushing production to that level.af/ Although the
Chinese have invested heavily in commissioning new mechanized coal faces,ag/
it would be unrealistic to expect growth rates much above 3-4 percent per
annum. Instead of trying to raise output, improving the quality of coal
through appropriate washing techniques, concentrating production in a smaller

number of mines and, most importantly, conserving the use of fuel, are worthier goals.ah/ Returns on energy-saving efforts can be extremely high.ai/

3.44   At growth rates of 6-7 percent per annum, it may not be necessary to increase coal's share of investible resources, especially if more can be done to conserve energy. China has pushed the energy consumption/GDP ratio down from 1.5 in 1978 to 1.0 in 1988, a decline of over 27 percent. This is still almost twice the OECD average for 1987 (see Table A14.1).aj/ The scope for additional savings is large, for instance, in the steel industry, where the coke rate (kg of coke/ton of pig iron) is 550, whereas in Japan the rate for modern plants is 400-450.ak/ Indirectly, coal consumption could also be reduced by conserving on electricity use. More efficient lighting, sophisticated electronic controls for industrial processes, motors incorporating the latest electronic advances, could yield enormous energy savings.al/ Not only is there substantial room for conserving fuels, but also China's high rates of investment make possible a rapid renewal of industrial and transport equipment.

3.45   Steel is another industry where significant capacity expansion needs to be viewed with caution. China produced 61.2 million tons in 1989 (48.6 million tons of rolled steel), only a fifth of which was suitable for the manufacture of modern machinery, autos and consumer durables. Imports of rolled steel made up the shortfall. During 1986-89, these have averaged 12 million tons per annum, mostly from Japan. Increasing the ratio of quality steel is definitely a matter of some urgency. But how far China should go in enlarging its steel capacity and whether steel should gain resources at the expense of another sector, needs deeper analysis. In most advanced countries, steel is a sunset industry because the change in the pattern of final demand and the substitution of other materials for steel are steadily reducing its importance. There is no indication that these inexorable trends will be reversed. In which case, the aim should be to tailor steel capacity to long-run steady state needs and to meet a hump in demand for building infrastructure or other purposes from imports.

3.46   Temporary sectoral imbalances, that result in bottlenecks, are inevitable in an economy developing at a high speed. Every country voices these complaints. In spite of such hindrances, China has grown at 10 percent per annum through much of the eighties and industrial capacity utilization has averaged 70 percent to 75 percent, which is probably reasonable, as the sector is saddled with much outdated and inefficient equipment. These rates suggest that the imbalances are by no means crippling and, except in years of extraordinary growth, constraints are "normal".

3.47   Marginal changes in investment allocation are surely desirable, for instance to transport, where investment as a ratio to GNP (1.5 percent during 1980-88) has lagged behind such comparators as the USSR 2.8 percent of GNP, 1980-87) and India (2.1 percent of GNP, 1980-87). But it is not obvious that a major effort to redirect resources towards metallurgical industries, heavy machinery and energy are necessary. Such a move, by draining funds from other uses, and consumption, could perpetuate China's dependence on its backward heavy industries and drag down the growth rate.

(c) Technological Advances

3.48   Technological progress closely rivals capital as a determinant of
growth. In fact, it is difficult to separate the contribution of one from
that of the other, as investment is one of the principal vehicles for introducing new technology. China's deficiencies in many spheres of technology
means that there is a large backlog to be exploited. By absorbing this knowledge, China can magnify the expansionary effects of capital accumulation. In
its pursuit of modernization, the country enjoys certain conspicuous advantages. After three decades of breakneck industrialization, there is a sizable
pool of skilled labor. Engineering talent is abundant, and especially in the
defense sector, of a high order. Many of China's senior policymakers are
engineers with careers in heavy industry and deeply committed to technological
advancement. Having developed a broad industrial base, mostly through their
own efforts, the Chinese are also well along the learning curve in areas such
as basic research, design and plant engineering. There is a fund of experience which makes it easier to assimilate new ideas. Last but not least, the
sophistication of the science establishment and specialized engineering facilities is fully up to the task of devising advanced, customized technologies.

3.49   Rising productivity in the eighties, the diversification of manufactured exports and qualitative evidence of technological gains in a broad range
of fields, all suggest that China is benefiting from the traffic in ideas and
an active player in the market for technology. Nevertheless, given the scale
of opportunities, the extent to which China has profited from an infusion of
new technology and the degree to which it has been able to enlarge the share
of productivity in GDP growth, does not compare too favorably with East Asia's
leading economies. A more systematic technology policy would allow modernization to pick up speed in the nineties and, more importantly, it would lessen
the costs of development in terms of resources.

3.50   Acquiring technology and harnessing it to industrial purposes
requires a many-pronged approach. For instance, the import of capital equipment and associated technical assistance from suppliers is a channel that
China is now using. The importance of skilled workers, technicians and scien-
tists is recognized and the authorities are working to create the institutional framework that, suitably primed with resources, will provide industry
with the human capital it needs.13/ Technological trends are now oriented
towards the saving of energy and materials through the intensive use of information rather than the displacement of labor by capital. Generating information calls for trained workers, which the educational system is being groomed
to produce. Bit by bit, the barriers between China's vertical ministerial
hierarchies are being chipped away. Horizontal contacts between enterprises
drawn from different subsectors are multiplying as are the links between
enterprises, research institutes and universities. Defense industries, backed
by the sector's elaborate scientific infrastructure, are producing for the
civilian market.am/ All of these tendencies facilitate the flow of ideas and

13/ Fully utilizing the trained manpower now available calls for greater
     job mobility, an area where China lags badly. About a third of the
     country's scientists still lack suitable work.

will make possible, eventually, the interindustrial coordination of effort that is becoming the hallmark of an enlightened industrial strategy.

3.51   Education, cooperative R&D, a more commercial bent to the scientific pursuits of universities and research establishments, will raise the tempo of technological progress over the long run. In the medium term, China can enlarge its technology gains by heightened efforts in five areas.

   (a)   Uniform industrial standards and protocols would add to quality, performance, utilization and scale economies in a range of industries, most notably electronics.an/

   (b)   Korean and Japanese experience suggests that determined efforts at gaining close familiarity with all aspects of a particular industrial process steepens the learning curve.ao/ In steel, petrochemicals and electronics, buying equipment is one step. Exposing significant numbers of the staff, who will be working with the machinery, to the best operating practices in use abroad is essential to obtain the most from the new capital goods. Otherwise, lessons must be acquired through trial and error, which constrains productivity. The reluctance to invest in disembodied knowledge has a cost in terms of breakdowns, low utilization rates and impaired quality. A deliberate policy is needed to encourage enterprises to actively seek the transfer of experience through training, when purchasing major pieces of equipment.

   (c)   Much information is available freely through scientific, government and trade publications, conferences and factory visits. But to gather and utilize these technological leads necessitates a systematic effort at scanning written materials, attending seminars, working at overseas institutes and touring factories.ap/ This requires a sizable budget and staff to collect, screen and disseminate within the local industrial establishment. Although China's attempts at scanning have increased, it is vital that recent developments do not result in a resurgence of the insular attitudes which can only lead back to technological stagnancy.

   (d)   Low product quality is a shortcoming that inflicts major costs on the economy. Oversized equipment used in underground mining, for instance, raises costs. Equipment breakdowns necessitating frequent repair and entailing loss of output; machinery that does not operate to specifications and the difficulty in correcting malfunctions because of poor design, are some of the consequences of inattention to quality. Technological upgrading not only relates to the introduction of more advanced products and processes, but also the refinement of existing products so that they are cheaper to produce, give better performance and are relatively trouble-free.

   (e)   Foreign direct investment has been the source of new technology for a number of East and Southeast Asian nations, including China. Its effects are felt initially by the export sector but over time, the knowledge and skills acquired diffuse through the entire economy. It is likely that China's export performance through the mid-nineties will continue to be influenced powerfully by foreign investment. Hence, policies that assure the flow of overseas capital and the technology it brings contribute importantly to the growth process. This point is treated at greater length below.

3.52   Direct Foreign Investment. The pledged value of foreign investment was $9 billion in 1984. By end-1989, 20,000 projects worth nearly $34 billion had been approved with $15.4 billion of investment actually in place. Hotels and service industries have attracted a third of the funds actually disbursed. Oil exploration and electricity generation, together with assembly-type industries, are other areas in which foreign investors have evinced strong interest. Commitments in 1989 totaled $5.6 billion, a 5.6 percent increase over the previous year. Actual disbursements amounted to $3.3 billion, a 4 percent improvement over 1988. However, there was a drop in applications, particularly after the events of June 1989, which if it persists, could affect the flow of capital 2-3 years in the future. Anecdotal evidence points to some revival of foreign entrepreneurial interest in the coastal provinces since the beginning of 1990, but the number of projects approved during the first half of 1990 decreased by 8 percent to 2,784 and the contracted amount was $2.35 billion, or 22 percent less than in 1989.

3.53   Foreign investment has plummeted in the past as well--in 1979 and again in 1986--but in each case growth was soon resumed. However, in the earlier years, investors were drawn by the desire to establish business connections with China so as to gain eventual access to its vast domestic market. Others came because large profits were to be made by servicing tourists flocking to China. Still others invested because their competitors had decided to do so. Investors have learned some lessons; their earlier enthusiasm has been tempered and the events of mid-1989 have sharpened fears of future political instability, that is a fundamental consideration with foreign companies. Small firms based in Hong Kong and Macau (China), that have been establishing contractual joint ventures averaging $1 million per investment in southern China, are unlikely to be discouraged. Language, proximity, labor costs, social ties with producing villages and an understanding of the bureaucratic ropes, draw them to China. Other Southeast Asian countries seem far less inviting and language is a formidable barrier for the small producer.

3.54   The larger investors from East Asia as well as the industrial countries, who have other choices and are being attracted by opportunities in East Europe, might need more encouragement than is currently provided by China's favorable tax laws. There are several areas which merit attention. In many of them, the government has been prepared to yield a little in the past, but it is far from having satisfied foreign investors. For example, time-consuming negotiations precede the signing of a contract and central government agencies can add another epicycle by entering discussions at an advanced stage. On the average, a joint-venture contract can take two years to negotiate.

3.55   Foreign direct investment (FDI) is conducted in a competitive environment, where production costs are decisive. Basic wages in China are low but bonuses and subsidies can double the outlay. Land use fees, costs of energy and of infrastructure can be high aq/ and are subject to arbitrary escalation. Chinese partners to a joint venture are reluctant to assume risks and have a tendency to enter into agreement with several foreign parties bidding for the same project.ar/ Even after a contract has been signed, its performance can be affected by the existence or promulgation of rules and internal guidelines unknown to the foreign partner. Furthermore, because legislation concerning FDI has a fairly short history, there remain gaps that can complicate the enforcement of contracts. As courts are relatively inexperienced and their independence has yet to be defined with any precision, contractual uncertainty can be troublesome.as/

3.56   To revive foreign investment, the government took a major step in April 1990, which involves leasing land in the "open cities" and Special Economic Zones for up to 70 years. Among the most recent actions in this regard was the decision to proceed with the Yangpu harbor project in Hainan Province, involving a long lease to the Hong Kong subsidiary of a major Japanese corporation. The central government is also supporting the development of Shanghai's Pudong district as an "open economic zone". A similar project was launched in 1989 with the leasing of a tract of land in Tianjin to the MGM Corporation of the United States for the development of an industrial park oriented towards high-technology enterprises. A related move, currently under review, is to allow foreign banks to establish branches in selected cities and compete with domestic banks for local business.at/

3.57   A modification of the law on Sino-foreign equity joint ventures, announced on April 4, 1990, affecting nine of the articles, should also be welcome news for foreign investors. The changes introduced allow foreign partners to chair the board of directors; protect equity joint ventures against expropriation by the state; and abolish fixed periods for income tax exemption.

B. Distributional Equity

3.58   One of China's achievements over the decades preceding 1980 has been the equitable manner in which the fruits of progress have been distributed. In decentralizing the economy and mixing in market forces with planning, government took a step away from its earlier position and embraced a modicum of inequality for the sake of rapid modernization. For much of the eighties this was accepted, especially in the rural areas, with considerable enthusiasm. As per capita incomes were rising by over 8 percent per annum in real terms, and provincial growth rates tightly clustered together, the modest deviations from earlier standards of distribution caused little discontent. People saw a few of their neighbors doing conspicuously better and took that as a sign that, in future, their own condition would improve even more rapidly.au/

3.59   A greater sensitivity to inequality became apparent when reforms spread to the cities in the mid-eighties. A large segment of the urban populace, possibly a third, is on fixed incomes. Many of them belong to the urban elite--government employees, Party cadres, university teachers and their students. These groups had long occupied the pinnacles of status and incomes.

Their earnings began falling behind those of industrial and construction workers; of people who flocked to the expanding services sector; and of the farmers in the periurban areas who supplied produce to the burgeoning free
markets.

3.60   These emerging differentials did not arouse serious resentment in
1985/86 because, in the reform milieu, they were viewed as legitimate gains.
A widening of the gap in 1987/88 was less acceptable av/ as the dispersion of
incomes became associated with rising inflation and the spread of corrupt
practices, which arrived with the decentralized administration of dual price
regimes.aw/

3.61   There is little evidence of a serious shift in inter- or intraprovincial income distribution. In fact, the growth performance of the poorer provinces has been close to the average (Chart 3.1). Intraprovincial rural distribution has been altered marginally, although data are scarce.ax/ Township
and village enterprises have enriched some of the more entrepreneurial peasants, but at the same time rural industry has provided off-farm employment
for poorer households, bringing them nearer the mean. China entered the
reform era with Gini coefficients in the 0.26-0.28 range. A steep reduction
in the number of people living in poverty may have reduced the dispersion in
incomes (see Chapter 1, para. 1.1). Offsetting this trend is the emergence of
the new rich among specialized farmers living near the cities, industrial
entrepreneurs, distributors and those responsible for developing the country's
nascent service sector businesses. Overall, the gains have been evenly distributed. That said, it is evident that intraurban shifts, even though they
involve relative deprivation for a minority, have led to mounting alienation
and a feeling that a long-standing social compact is endangered. The uneasi-
ness extends to urban workers whose incomes have risen both relatively and
absolutely. This privileged group that has long enjoyed tenurial status, is
now threatened by the spread of contract employment and competition from
migrants that have found their way to cities. By end-1989, about 11.75 million workers of an urban workforce numbering 137.4 million were on contract
with state-owned factories and some 20 million or more temporary migrants had
found jobs, mostly in construction and services. A more flexible labor market
that accommodates much greater geographical and interfirm mobility could
result in a restructuring of urban wages. Quite possibly, the wages of
unskilled and semiskilled workers might fall and skill differentials widen.
Fewer labor market rigidities would be a net plus for economic growth but
their distributional consequences may not be negligible.

3.62   Rapid growth in the eighties has raised living standards across the
board. At the same time, reforms have led to a reshuffling of income shares,
particularly in the urban areas. Fixed-income groups have lost in relative
terms. Industrial labor, although it has been richly rewarded, is worried
over the changing intersectoral terms of trade, migration to the cities and
the gradual elimination of tenurial status. In a society used to a rigid
income hierarchy and narrow income differentials, the shock administered by
reforms has been deeply unsettling. Higher real incomes have not been able to
banish growing concerns over relative standing and some twisting of the income
distribution, however modest it may have been.

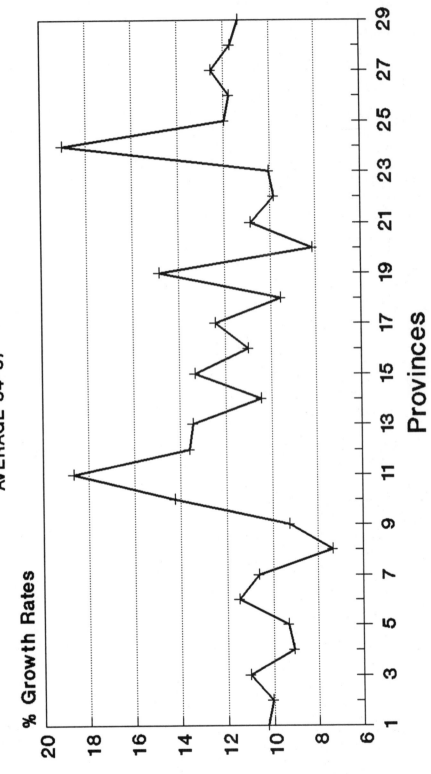

Chart 3.1:

PROVINCIAL OUTPUT GROWTH

AVERAGE 84-87

—+— National Income

See Annex Table 1.8 for Province names.

3.63   If future growth is linked with reforms that will enlarge the role of the market, alter relative prices and introduce fluidity into the income shares of individual groups, then it is likely to face considerable opposition from the very people whose welfare it is supposed to enhance. Reforms will, therefore, have to balance growth with equity, which may constrain the flexibility of product and factor markets and limit the options for institutional reform (Chapter 4).

3.64   Resource mobilization, technology and industrial strategy may be the prime movers, but growth will only follow the planned trajectory if the emerging distribution conforms to the people's notion of fairness. Perceptions have begun changing, more can be done to modify people's outlook with regard to tenured employment, job mobility and income differentials for instance. It may be a slow process and permit less growth than the economy is capable of.

IV. REFORMS AND ECONOMIC EFFICIENCY

4.1   The quest for noninflationary growth is tightly interrelated with reforms calculated to promote efficiency. Virtually all socialist countries have now learned that central planning of a complex economy will be unable to achieve either allocative efficiency or the full utilization of resources. For these purposes the market is conspicuously more effective.

4.2   Alongside decentralization, the steadily expanding role of the market has constituted a second major strand of the reform program. It has three components: the relaxation of controls over prices, so that they can better reflect opportunity costs; a dismantling of the state's administrative infrastructure for allocating commodities; and greater autonomy for enterprises to operate with reference to market forces.

(a) Price Reform

4.3   Recent Developments. Under the planned system prices were fixed by the authorities using an average cost plus mark-up rule. They were altered infrequently. In 1979 came the first break with tradition. Enterprises producing four major electronics products were given a price range, instead of a single price, at which they could be sold. The use of these so-called "range" or "floating" prices was extended to other heavy industry products in June 1981. By August 1982, range pricing was being applied to virtually all products. At this stage, central or provincial bodies defined the band within which prices could fluctuate. Starting in September 1982, the prices of 160 commodities were fully liberalized, that is, they were henceforth determined by market forces. A year later, another 350 were given the same treatment, so that about 5-6 percent of retail sales nationwide became the province of the free market.a/

4.4   The next push came in January 1985 when a large number of agricultural and light manufactures were subjected to market pricing. In addition, range prices were abolished on above plan sales of commodities by enterprises. By this time, what the Chinese describe as the "dual track pricing system," was beginning to gel. It covered three modes of price setting: prices that were fixed by the state as was done in the past; prices that floated within limits prescribed by central, provincial or local agencies; and prices that were under the influence of the market.

4.5   Between 1985 and 1988 the dual track system became firmly established. Liberalization raised the ratio of market prices to nearly 50 percent (from 30 percent in 1985) and prices fixed by the state were reduced to about a quarter (from 40-50 percent two years earlier) with the balance being floating prices. As the enforcement of controls slackened, floating prices tended to approach their ceilings bringing many within close proximity of market prices. Data for December 1988 indicates that market prices for a cross-section of industrial products were 40-50 percent more than state fixed prices. The gap between state and market prices of consumer goods was far narrower.b/

---

a/ Lettered footnotes are to be found in Annex II.

4.6   By late 1988, price reform had made substantial headway in terms of the sheer number of items whose prices had been liberalized. More importantly, the majority of decisions, on the margin, were being made with reference to market prices, indicating that allocative efficiency is on the rise.c/ Planned production at fixed prices then constitutes a lump sum tax or a lump sum profit transfer--depending on relative prices between inputs and outputs--but does not affect production and investment decisions.d/ There are still many instances where enterprises obtain a percentage of their inputs or energy supplies at fixed prices, which brings average prices below those prevailing on the market. But the marginal choices are frequently made at market prices because most enterprises sell a portion of their products on the market and depend on market transactions to purchase the marginal units of energy or raw materials.

4.7   The waning of price controls was paralleled by the reduced incidence of planned direct allocation by the state. For example, as early as 1985 a major enterprise survey showed that only 20 percent of the output was determined by the state's mandatory plan and 27 percent by the guidance plan.e/ The trend since has been downwards. The share of four important industrial materials under state distribution has fallen continuously since 1979 and even in the case of steel and coal was below 50 percent in 1988 (Table 4.1). State enterprises sell most producer goods on the market including nearly three-fourths of all metal cutting tools. The distribution of some 256 of materials was a state monopoly in 1979.f/ Their numbers had been reduced to 27 in 1988. A consistent downward trend is also noticeable in the proportion of capital goods embraced by the state mandatory plan: from 80 percent to between 20 percent and 30 percent. The narrowing compass of central planning is also evidenced in the raising of project approval limits for provincial authorities (partially reversed in early 1990) (Table 4.2). The easing of clearance requirements for investment goes all the way down to the enterprise, which is now empowered to embark on small-scale, technical updating outlay without seeking a string of approvals. As indicated in Chapter 3 (iii), enterprises can meaningfully exploit their new powers because close to 30 percent of all fixed investment is financed from retained funds. Another 25 percent of funding is from local governments, profits accruing to ministries and from individual investors (Table 4.3).

4.8   Price liberalization has not yet run its course but the reforms introduced have had far-reaching effects on decision-making. On the margin, which is where it counts, resource allocation is subject to prices reflecting scarcities. In aggregate terms, the scope of mandatory planning of state monopoly and of the material supply system is much reduced. Discretion on matters pertaining to production as well as distribution has been passed down to local agencies and some of it has trickled to enterprises (but see paras. 4.48-4.50).

4.9   The exigencies of stabilization led to a postponement of attempts at price decontrol and adjustment between the last quarter of 1988 and mid 1989. In fact, during this period fixed prices were monitored with greater vigilance

Table 4.1: PROPORTION OF KEY MATERIALS ALLOCATED BY THE STATE
(In percent)

	1979	1984	1988
Steel	77.0	66.0	46.8
Timber	85.0	40.0	25.9
Coal	58.9	50.0	43.5
Cement	35.7	25.0	13.6

Source: State Planning Commission.

Table 4.2: APPROVAL LIMITS FOR INVESTMENT
(Million yuan)

Date	State Planning Commission	Provincial authorities
Before 1984	Over 10	Below 10
Beginning 1985	Over 30	Below 30
March 1987	Over 50	Below 30
March 1987 (power, transportation and raw materials)	Over 50	Below 50
January 1990	Over 30	Below 30

Note: Since January 1990, projects worth more than Y 30 million are submitted by the State Planning Commission to the State Council for approval. In a few industries, such as chemicals,
provincial authorities can approve projects valued at up to Y 50 million. Municipal
governments and local authorities can only approve projects valued at less than Y 5 million. Those in the Y 5 million to Y 30 million range need the approval of the provincial
government. This involves a significant tightening and centralization of the investment
decision process.

Source: State Planning Commission.

Table 4.3: FINANCING OF DOMESTIC FIXED INVESTMENT
(Percent of total)

	1981	1982	1983	1984	1985	1986	1987	1988
Fixed asset investment	100.0	100.0	100.0	100.0	100.0	100.0	100.0	100.0
Of which state fixed inv.	69.5	68.7	66.6	64.7	66.1	66.5	63.1	62.5
Financing of fixed inv.								
Budget	28.1	22.7	23.7	23.0	16.0	14.6	13.1	9.0
Bank loans	12.7	14.3	12.3	14.1	20.1	21.1	23.0	20.3
Foreign loans	3.7	4.9	4.7	3.9	3.6	4.4	4.8	5.7
Retained earnings and extrabudgetary funds	55.5	58.1	59.4	59.1	60.3	59.9	59.2	65.0

Source: Statistical Yearbook of China, 1988, p. 493. Total domestic fixed-asset investment
includes investment by SOEs, collectives and individuals.

as was the maintenance of floating prices between prescribed bands. However, there is no evidence as yet of prices having been reclassified from the market category to that of fixed or floating prices (See Chapter 2). Price adjustments were resumed in the second half of 1989 with an 18 percent increase in grain procurement prices followed, in October 1989, by a 120 percent adjustment in railway passenger fares along with higher charges for airline travel. On March 15, 1990, freight tariffs for rail and water transport, as well as port handling charges, were raised by between 25 and 35 percent. The government also announced plans to enlarge its control over the distribution of a few commodities, so as to lessen the incidence of profiteering associated with dual pricing schemes. Centralized allocation of caustic soda and rare metals has been increased and in the future a larger share of the coal produced will be distributed through state channels. A desire to resume more control over the allocation of investment induced the government, in early 1990, to scale down provincial approval limits to the levels prevailing prior to March 1987 (see Table 4.2).

General Guidelines

4.10   Stabilization measures that had slowed growth to a crawl by the first quarter of 1990 (industrial output grew by 1 percent in March 1990 after registering negative rates in January and February), brought the annualized rate of inflation to 0.6 percent in January-February 1990, and narrowed the gap between market and fixed prices for several items permitting price unification with the minimum of risk. Aside from these developments, a bumper harvest and significant industrial slack also decrease the likelihood that moves to adjust or liberalize prices will reignite inflationary pressures.

4.11   The design of future reform will need to take account of the following:

(a) The dual track pricing, which seems to have been an unavoidable way-station on the gradualist road to reform, is the source of much remaining distortion. Perhaps half of all prices are subject to some degree of administrative regulation by central and local agencies. The presence of such discretion keeps alive the strong strain of negotiation in economic activities. Instead of striving after efficiency, many enterprises find that the desired profitability can be more easily assured through negotiations with supervisory bodies with the power to provide inputs at lower prices or to permit sales of products to be made at more attractive rates. The negotiation of price bands, decentralized price fixing and the existence of multiple prices for many commodities undermines the parametric function of market rates. By permitting influential officials to profit from their ability to set prices and allocate resources, dual track pricing has also begun discrediting price reform.

The authorities have announced their intention to eliminate dual pricing, but the precise modus operandi and a schedule have not been revealed. Within a decentralized administrative milieu any attempt at securing uniform prices is freighted with difficulty. Under the prevailing institutional circumstances, decontrol has to be handled delicately but firmly so that it does not degenerate into endless negotiations between center and local bodies and between enterprises and their supervisors (Chapter 1). Dual track pricing comes in the way of efficiency and breeds corruption, but there is no simple way of consigning it to oblivion in a system where state ownership is to be the dominant mode and lower level provincial agencies will remain influential.

(b) In any economy a subset of prices are always subject to regulation by the authorities for political or strategic reasons or to neutralize the danger from monopolies. But in all market economies, the majority of transactions are of an arms length type, orchestrated by the Invisible Hand. In China, price reform is incomplete, as the Visible Hand of administrative directives and of negotiation continues to intervene in many transactions.g/ Meaningful price liberalization, which is required if the full efficiency gains are to be extracted from markets, is closely linked to the volume of arms-length trading. It excludes the constant negotiation of prices and taxes with administrative authorities, who represent the state's ownership rights over the goods being transacted. Efforts at creating a multiplicity of ownership forms and dispersing rights among institutions and individuals, would give more freedom to the Invisible Hand of the market.

(c) Price reforms are already well advanced in the rural sector. Product prices have been freed and in recent years liberalization has extended to factor prices as well. Rural labor markets have come into existence. Workers can sell their labor at the going wage to farmers and rural factories. They have de facto rights. Similarly, 15- and 30-year leaseholds have extended a measure of ownership rights, which could potentially be traded in land markets. These were on the verge of materializing in a few selected areas when the events of 1989 reduced the tempo of experiments with such institutions. Informal rural capital markets are flourishing, fed by the savings of rural households and managed by local financiers. Once again, makeshift institutional arrangements based on kin and village relationships extending far into the past, have helped establish individual property rights over capital, and brought the risks of transactions down to the point where market functioning is possible.

4.12   The way ahead for China might entail pursuing price reform quite rapidly in the rural sector where much progress has already been made, whereas a more measured pace and a somewhat different approach to liberalization may be warranted in the industrial sector. Because ownership rights over production factors are gradually coming into focus and putting out institutional roots, their formalization presents less of a hurdle. It is possible, therefore, in the next few years to complete the work begun over a decade ago and place the rural economy on a base of efficient markets.

4.13   Proceeding with rural price reform insofar as it affects farming and rural industry would generate additional momentum for industrial changes, as was true in the early eighties. It would, in addition, offer guidance on how ownership of assets might be diffused and the consequences of advancing beyond

the current framework, a possibility that was considered in the early
eighties. The mechanics of decontrolling some key prices are sketched below.

4.14   Specific Commodity Categories. The advantages and disadvantages of
pursuing price decontrol vary among specific commodity categories. Most
straightforward are those in which there is excess supply or an approximate
balance between supply and demand at existing fixed prices. China's policy
since 1980 has been to decontrol prices in such circumstances, and the government is now considering how this might be extended on a permanent basis to the
many additional commodities in which buyers' markets are emerging in the
course of the present macroeconomic slowdown. The prices of some of the goods
concerned may not fall much--downward flexibility of manufactured goods prices
is limited in all countries by the need to cover material and wage costs. In
the cases of some primary products subject to large fluctuations, the government may even wish to cushion the falling prices by purchasing for stock.
More generally, some of these markets may tighten in the future, and hence
prices may rise. But provided that macroeconomic control is maintained, these
price changes will be reasonably smooth and will help to maintain microeconomic balance.

4.15   Less straightforward are those categories of commodities for which
there is substantial excess demand at existing controlled prices--reflected
usually in a large gap between the official and the second-track or free
market price. In these instances price decontrol would raise the price of
those transactions currently made at official prices. Whether the unified
decontrolled price would be above or below the existing second-track price is
less certain. In some cases, especially where the second-track price is itself now held within a band, the unified decontrolled price might be higher.
In other cases, where the elimination of the low official price stimulated
production or reduced consumption, the unified decontrolled price might be
lower. But it would probably be reasonable to assume, that in most cases
unified decontrolled prices would not be far from current second-track prices.

4.16   There are three main categories of prices where there are at present
large gaps between the two tracks: the procurement prices of major agricultural products; the retail prices of some foods; and some basic industrial
intermediate goods--mainly energy, metals and chemicals. The economic and
social implications of price decontrol vary among these three categories, so
each needs to be considered separately.

4.17   Agricultural Procurement Prices. A phased adjustment of procurement
prices for major agricultural products (and of the retail price of fertilizer
and other agricultural inputs) to bring them closer to market rates is currently being debated. The first round of adjustments scheduled for 1990 will
affect prices of oilseeds, sugar and cotton. Subsequent rounds proposed
during the Eighth Five Plan (1991-96) are expected to complete the process.

4.18   The eventual goal is the abolition of direct control over most agricultural procurement prices, while retaining import barriers for some food
products, and using indirect intervention to damp short-term price fluctuations. This stage needs to be approached in steps over two or three years--
the main ones being the need for considerable additional investment in alternative marketing channels and for the authorities to learn more about indirect

regulation of agricultural markets. At first the official procurement price will have to be brought to levels somewhat below current free market prices, while maintaining a two-track system, and adjusting contracts so that almost all farmers are making some sales at free market prices. The second step will be to put in place the desired system of import restrictions and stabilization schemes (in conjunction with a realistic exchange rate). This would cause free market prices to move in directions consistent with the government's agricultural development and trade strategy. If these price changes are large, a further adjustment of official prices and agricultural taxes will probably be made prior to complete decontrol. (This could then be supported by a phased decontrol of retail food prices, as outlined in the next section.)

4.19   Retail Food Prices. The eventual target for retail food prices should be comprehensive price decontrol and abolition of rationing, with monetary compensation for ration recipients. Several successful moves in this direction have already been made, the most recent being increases in nonstaple food prices in 1988, and one option now would be to attain the eventual target in a single step. There are, however, three reasons why it might be better to continue to proceed gradually.

4.20   The first is that the economic gains from immediate decontrol are probably not large. As explained earlier, most consumers are now effectively trading at free market prices, so the waste caused by irrational official prices is limited. It is important, however, that the unofficial market in ration coupons which makes this possible should be modified in the interests of stability and consumer welfare, by assigning expiration dates to all outstanding coupons--which are effectively monetized--and by targeting eligibility to receive new coupons on the urban poor and low-income consumers. And, to the extent that compensation is provided, eliminating food subsidies would yield no immediate financial gains, though the burden might be transferred from the state budget to local sources, and the volume of subsidizaton might be made more obvious.

4.21   The second is that the necessary reform of agricultural procurement prices should probably precede decontrol of retail food prices. Otherwise, it would be difficult to determine accurately how much compensation should be given to ration recipients. For example, procurement price reforms might reduce the free retail market price of grain, in which case compensation for loss of grain coupons based on the current difference between the official and the free market price would be too generous to ration recipients, and disadvantageous to the budget.

4.22   The third reason for gradualism is that urban households are still nervous about inflation. Their fixed-price food rations (though quite small in monetary value) make them feel more secure, and for this reason should be maintained--as should indexed saving deposits--during the transitional period in which other price reforms are being implemented. Moreover, retail food price reform itself should be implemented in stages: the first step would be to complete the decontrol of nonstaple food prices (which has already occurred in most places); the second step would be to do the same for grain.

4.23   Industrial Materials Prices. The government is concerned that large increases in official materials prices, either through decontrol or through adjustment, would substantially push up the average retail price of industrial consumer goods. This concern is based on the assumption that enterprises (in some cases after seeking approval from price bureaus) would raise their output prices to cover fully any increase in their average costs. This assumption is probably not generally correct in China's present economic circumstances. In theory, profit-maximizing enterprises choose their output prices on the basis of marginal rather than average costs; and in practice marginal costs are usually governed by second-track rather than official prices. In other words, unification of input prices at the existing second-track level would not cause a profit-maximizing enterprise to raise an output price that it had previously been free to set, even though the unification would reduce its profits. Hence insofar as China's enterprises are now profit-maximizers, and insofar as second-track prices and the prices of industrial consumer goods are market-determined, decontrol of official industrial materials prices will not affect the prices that consumers pay, although it will redistribute profits (and losses) among enterprises.

4.24   The extent to which price liberalization has progressed suggests that the true impact on consumers would be much closer to this optimistic assessment than to the government's present pessimistic one. Nonetheless, the optimism must be qualified. Some second-track and industrial consumer goods prices are subject to direct control, and price bureaus, in giving permission for controlled price adjustments, pay attention to average rather than marginal costs. As a result, there would be a tendency for price increases to be passed on from enterprise to enterprise and eventually to consumers. This problem may not be serious, for two reasons. One is that as long as excess supply of many industrial consumer goods persists, enterprises would be discouraged from seeking price increases. The other is that, as explained below, some of the average cost increases inflicted on particular enterprises would be offset by reductions in their tax and profit remittance obligations.

4.25   The redistribution of profits and losses among enterprises caused by decontrol of industrial materials prices would require action by the government even where price increases were not likely to be passed on. This is because the present state enterprise tax and profit remittance system is not standardized, but tailored to each enterprise's recent profitability. The simplest and least contentious immediate response would be to adjust the terms of each enterprise's current contract in such a way as to leave its profit retention prospects approximately unaltered--increasing the remittance obligations of enterprises whose profits gained from the price adjustments, and vice versa. For most nonstate enterprises, which are subject to more standardized taxes, no such special action would be necessary.

4.26   An important objective of these immediate contractual adjustments, which should probably also cover the revenue-sharing contracts between central and local governments, would be to ensure that the state (and particularly the central government) budget was not adversely affected. This would require keeping the revenue/GNP ratio constant, while controlling the outlay on subsidies (paras. 3.34-3.40). The most important such items are key investment projects, which already account for 2-3 percent of GNP, and now obtain most of their supplies at low official prices. To ensure that these projects were unaffected it would probably be desirable to maintain mandatory allocation of supplies to them. In most other cases, price decontrol could and probably should be accompanied by the ending of mandatory output and input quotas for the goods concerned.

4.27   Plans for adjusting the prices of basic materials, transport and energy are at a fairly advanced stage. Prices of crude oil, railway freight and electricity are to be adjusted in 1990 with coal prices to be revised in 1991. Rubber will shortly be traded at a single market linked price as a part of the attempt to dismantle dual pricing regime. Cement could follow. The government expects these changes plus the ones proposed for the agricultural sector to add up to 8 percentage points to inflation in 1990. In all, taking into account the price ripples emanating from devaluation in December 1989, the anticipated rate of price increase during the year is projected by the authorities to be in the 10-12 percent range. However, as suggested in paras. 4.24-4.25, the increase in the price level may not be as high as is currently projected, allowing the authorities greater room for maneuver.

4.28   Associated Tax, Subsidy and Enterprise Adjustments. Decontrol of industrial materials prices with neutralizing adjustment of profit and tax contracts would pave the way for subsequent reforms of state enterprise taxation and management. The three next steps needed, all of which are either under experimentation or the topics of active negotiation between the center and the provinces are: to move to after-tax contracting, to introduce a standard rate of profits tax; and to make indirect taxes on enterprises more uniform (at present the rates vary partly to offset price irrationalities). Ideally these steps ought to be taken simultaneously, but under the circumstances a start is likely to be made with exclusive-of-tax contracting with the others following.

4.29   The difficult question would then arise of how to handle cases in which enterprises made losses (after paying indirect taxes), or where their post-standard-rate-of-tax profits were less than their previous expenditure out of retained profits on bonuses and other worker benefits. With the most glaring price distortions eliminated, these cases would be ones in which there was a clear economic need for basic adjustments. These might involve changes of product mix or production technology, reductions in worker remuneration or employment, mergers, and in the limit, complete enterprise closure. The government should not subsidize the continuation of loss-making activities. But it should subsidize the process of adjustment, both for enterprises with a realistic prospect of future profit, and for workers who have to leave their present jobs. Adjustment subsidies should cover nonstate as well as state enterprises and workers.

4.30   The introduction of standard taxation and after-tax contracting would in turn pave the way for other reforms of state enterprise management of the sort discussed below. These reforms should probably include alterations in the organization and exercise of the state's ownership over industrial assets and extend more generally to include property rights over factors. Until effective capital and labor markets are created, direct control of worker remuneration and investment in state enterprises will have to be maintained. But once ownership and price reforms succeed in creating stronger internal incentives for enterprises to restrain wages and invest economically, these direct controls could be relaxed or replaced by indirect controls.

(b) Sources of Inflation and its Management

4.31   Price reforms of recent years and others to be introduced in the future are altering relative prices and setting in motion an extensive realloca- tion of resources as well as substantial intergroup and intersectoral trans- fers. The economy is being required to move from a production function inhe- rited from years of centralized planning to a production surface that reflects "true scarcities" and modern technology. In spite of reforms, the price structure inherited from the past remains tilted towards capital goods and such distortions will gradually have to be smoothed over. While the nation as a whole stands to benefit, there are bound to be winners as well as losers.

4.32   Inevitably, the losers are resisting and because the earlier national consensus on objectives no longer serves, their opposition has macroeconomic repercussions.h/ As the economy moves towards the market, it is becoming clear that significant inter- and intrasectoral resource transfers are inevi- table. The intersectoral transfers will be from industry to agriculture. Intrasectoral transfers will be mainly from China's overbuilt and inefficient heavy industries, parts of which might need to be closed down, to other manu- facturing subsectors and services. In effect, the urban, heavy industry bias of past policies, that buttressed the economic position of the industrial and administrative workforce, is being succeeded by market-directed flows to other groups. As reforms proceed, the old industrial elites will only be able to maintain their position on the income scale through a determined effort at raising productivity. Relative price advantages and subsidies will continue to be shaded bit by bit.

4.33   These changes have sparked rivalrous relationships on several fronts: between urban and rural interests; between the old urban industries and the emerging upstarts in the township and village enterprise sector, that have risen from an insignificance to annex 20 percent of industrial output in 1988; and between fixed income groups in the cities and those others enriched by the recent dynamism of the urban economy. Complicating this picture are the rivalries between provinces, each of which is trying to acquire resources to further its own development. Lastly, there is the friction between the central government pursuing broad national objectives and provinces, whose concern is their own parochial interests. These rivalries are responsible for the demand and cost push pressures that have driven inflation. Rising agri- cultural prices, that improve the lot of farmers, are resisted by demands from urban workers for higher wages and a continuation of food subsidies. Higher labor costs, in conjunction with mark-up pricing rules, have led to a wage price spiral, which became an increasingly obtrusive element in the inflation picture during 1987-88. Rising production costs in heavy industries and the budgetary claims imposed by consumer subsidies squeeze the state's revenues from enterprise taxes and profit remittances. Subsidies have driven up expen- ditures. Hence the budget deficits which, though not large in comparative terms, have contributed to the increase in broad money.

4.34   Investment hunger and the excess aggregate demand it generates, is usually ascribed to sellers' markets, soft budget constraints and the general environment of tautness which pushes firms to seek all the capacity they can. This is a part of the explanation. The apparently insatiable appetite for capital is also linked to industrial and provincial claims. Aware that their future dominance is less secure, heavy industries are struggling to secure resources that will guarantee long-run income streams, and possible subsidies. Distributional concerns also underlie the opposition to the bankruptcy law and other institutional changes that would stimulate meaningful competition. Meanwhile, manufacturers of consumer goods in the collective and TVE sectors see opportunities for profit in the unfolding of demand. Both are motivated to spend on capital. In this, they are abetted by provincial and local authorities seeking higher rates of income growth, larger employment and expanding revenues. Small projects in light industry have a quicker pay-off; major heavy industry projects often bring with them resources from the central government as well as inputs at low fixed prices. Provincial authorities, therefore, have little interest in restraining expenditures. To the extent that they can, provinces with fiscal surpluses attempt to minimize transfers to Beijing and more provinces are trying to obtain net revenue flows from the center. Credit expansion is another avenue for acquiring real resources; and provincial governments have every incentive to exert all their influence to extract credit from the financial system. Which is why the local branches of the People's Bank were induced during 1984-88 to extend temporary credit in excess of the planned amounts. Not just the coastal provinces, but all provinces, have sought after bank financing to enlarge their command over real resources.

4.35   There is a correlation between the increase in broad money and prices, but that relationship is only a part of the explanation (Chart 4.1). China experienced rising prices not just because the central government's monetary policy tended to be expansionary. This undoubtedly accommodated demand pressures. But monetary controls were allowed to slip and aggregate demand became excessive because of the struggle for shares that has erupted as reforms breach old price structures, threaten inefficient industries and begin transforming the rules for allocating resources.

4.36   Each time the central authorities have arrived at a consensus on the need to stabilize demand, they have been able to empower the People's Bank to restrict credit. This was done in 1980/81 and in 1986 and a most effective credit squeeze is currently in effect. The central bank is as strong as the central government's resolve with regard to a particular variant of macroeconomic policy. It has the instruments needed to tighten credit and enforce its directives. These are canted towards the administrative but they are, nevertheless, successful in controlling liquidity. The forces unleashed by reforms gave rise to political imperatives, which at certain times militated against the application of firm credit policies. They, rather than the institutional shortcomings of the PBC, must bear much of the responsibility for the procyclical behavior of credit.

4.37   If the tempo of reforms accelerates, intergroup struggles, temporarily in abeyance, will resume and China will again be exposed to inflationary pressures. To preserve the hard-won price stability will require political action, institution building and economic reform, along with firm macroeconomic policies.

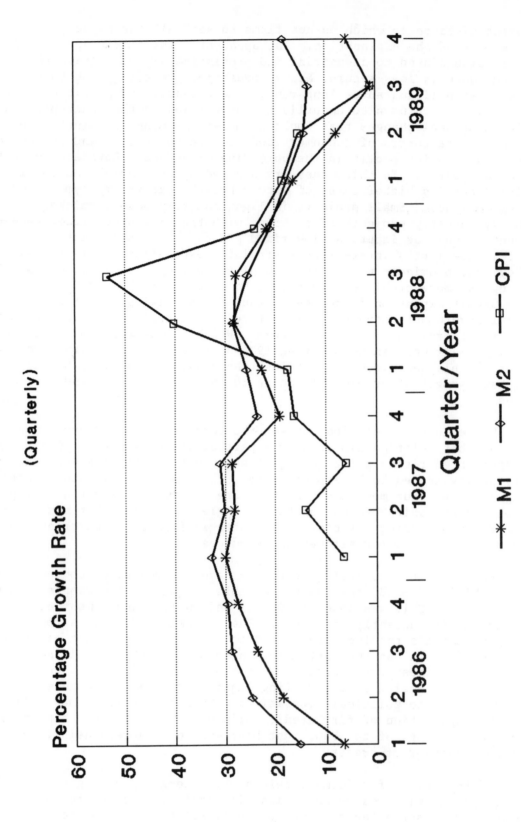

Chart 4.1:   MOVEMENTS IN MONEY & PRICES

(Quarterly)

CPI for Nation (Three month Moving Avg.)

4.38   (i) A national consensus on economic goals and the virtues of stable prices is a starting point. Countries that have at various times been conspicuously effective in holding inflation at bay, anchor macropolicy to such a consensus. Japan, Sweden, Korea (in the eighties) are examples. All of these countries depended upon an understanding between government, business and labor, on basic parameters, to coordinate macroeconomic policies, corporate pricing strategies and wage demands. The macroeconomic efficacy of political consensus has been repeatedly tested and proven in China itself. Center and provinces; urban workers and farmers; all the parties engaged in a zero sum game over income shares, must be persuaded to participate in an economic consensus entailing sacrifices, but with long-term welfare gains for all.

4.39   (ii) Expectations, behavior and demands are formed by the prevailing model of economic functioning. Enterprise managers in China can still believe that, while they might be chastised for poor decisions and losses, the state or local authorities will accommodate the deficits. In an extreme situation, a loss-making enterprise might be merged with a successful one, but for all intents, a socialist firm, especially if it is one of the larger state enterprises, is immortal. This guarantee also determines the attitudes of workers. For the vast majority, lifetime tenure is still guaranteed. Only in rare circumstances can a worker be laid off and that too for gross dereliction for which his comrades can find no mitigating factors. Having functioned for years in sellers' markets, enterprises assume that cost increases can eventually be passed on. The coming of floating and free market prices has provided further encouragement, especially because the state has been forthcoming with monetary accommodation. With administrative decentralization having stripped away some of the inhibitions on enterprise behavior and urban workers sensing that their relative income status is in jeopardy, a wage-price spiral is almost unavoidable.

4.40   Incomes policies can serve temporarily to stem the tide, but over the longer term only a change in the guiding economic model can assure stability. Enterprises and their employees are reaping some of the benefits of a market environment, without having to shoulder more of the risks--in effect, the gains are pocketed by the enterprise, losses are passed on to the government. Until reforms revise these expectations, price stability will remain an uphill battle.

4.41   Clearly the safety net, that shelters enterprises from accountability and prevents market forces from moderating wage demands, needs to be modified. Market discipline cannot be imposed administratively in a system where ownership rests with the state or a collectivity. So long as individuals do not run the risk of losing capital or losing employment, with consequences for their future livelihood, market forces are blunted. Understandably the authorities would like to avoid dramatic shifts, but on the margin, expectations must be changed. In a word, the state must begin transferring risk to enterprise owners, managers and employees. A more porous safety net, that vests ownership of some industrial assets in individuals or groups and, with it transfers full accountability, would make market discipline into a reality. Likewise, the share of tenured employment should shrink, enterprises be enabled to shed their surplus staff, and as need arises, to hire at competitive wages from a large urban labor pool. A lesson painfully learned by most industrial countries is that wage price spirals are only broken when workers are convinced that the state will not deflect market tendencies and underwrite wage demands. China may also have to bring its protected industrial workers to accept limits of state responsibility for employment and the inevitability of market guidance in wage determination.

4.42   (iii) Among the industrial countries, Japan has endured cyclical fluctuations with the smallest amplitude and has shown the most speed in adjusting to shocks. Among the factors believed to be responsible, are the so-called "flexible rigidities" in the labor market.i/ Wages are subject to political consensus attuned to the prevailing economic realities; annual syn-chronized wage negotiations take account of shocks and decide rates of increase for the bulk of the workforce; and tenurial arrangements for a core of industrial workers allow for a trade-off between job security and wage increases, helping diffuse price shocks when the need arises. As the wage contracts with the core workforce set the tone for other wage deals, market flexibility is enhanced.

4.43   Tenured employment for industrial workers already exists in China and annual wage adjustments are the norm. However, the system needs reconfiguring and fresh institutional arrangements must be sought to arrive at a political consensus on the division of the economic pie. For Chinese industrial workers, lifetime employment is a right assured by the state, whereas in Japan it is a contract involving reciprocal obligations: workers realize that their welfare is linked indissolubly to the success of the company in an intensely competitive marketplace. In addition, labor allocation in China is still largely an administrative process divorced from market pressures, which it is not in Japan. As indicated above, wage moderation and flexibility, is in part an outgrowth of consensus about the tolerable rate of price increase, which is ultimately an agreement on distribution. Equally important is the worker's realization, that his future income will in large measure be decided by his own effort and is not an administratively ordained right. This calls for a labor market wherein a worker trades his services and which sharpens his motivation, by juxtaposing rewards with the pain of search as well as jobless-ness.

4.44   Lastly, tenure is a benefit assigned to the worker. Job security is not traded off against wage adjustment because the risk of unemployment does not seriously impinge on behavior or wage demands. It could be made a factor supporting wage moderation, but the labor market backdrop against which it is viewed, will need and in fact has begun receiving the attention of reformers. Labor contracting is on the rise and serious thought is being given to the monetization of benefits received in kind so that ties of housing and welfare binding workers to enterprises can be severed and job mobility increased.

(c) Enterprise Reform

4.45   The future of enterprise reforms is closely associated with the manner in which price liberalization is tackled. After all, the functioning of markets and the efficiency of price signals depends on the nature of market participants and characteristics of their interaction. Arms-length trading, competition, freedom of entry and exit for firms, ease of contracting which lead to optimal prices, assume that the market is populated with large numbers of enterprises with substantial production and trading autonomy, the capacity to enter and exit markets and so on. Efficient markets require a particular set of rules and a certain kind of player.

4.46   Diversification of ownership and increased enterprise autonomy are central tenets of economic reform in China, though the government has consistently maintained that public ownership must remain the dominant form. The key long-term issues in the area of enterprise reform are how state enterprises should be managed, what is the appropriate balance within the public sector between state and nonstate enterprises, and how best to harness the potential of the private sector.

4.47   From its beginnings in the early eighties, enterprise reform has been steered by the cautious but widespread desire to move in stages from mandatory to guidance planning with small increments in enterprise autonomy.j/ This system assumes that enterprises will produce with reference to "suggested" targets individually assigned. While the targets can be modified depending on market conditions, the changes are "vetted" or negotiated with the relevant supervisory agency. Guidance planning enhances the choices enterprises are allowed and it displaces administrative directives with a different set of instruments for managing the economy, e.g., interest rates, taxes, exchange rates, etc. But the state retains ownership and has the potential for intervening, for instance, in the setting of prices and in personnel decisions.

4.48   Mandatory planning has not been terminated but it has come to be overshadowed by "guidance". The latter, which in the decentralized milieu is exercised by local bodies, is variously interpreted. Some planning and finance departments are less interventionist than others. This ambiguity over the operational meaning of "guidance"--and the extent to which guidance shades into compulsion--leaves the initiative to interfere with agencies of the state, who retain the right to exercise the state's prerogatives of ownership and are inclined to exercise it fully.

4.49   Guidance planning has made enterprises more autonomous, but it is a weak unstable autonomy. With independence thus circumscribed and ownership unchanged, it is inevitable that the issue of financial accountability is unsettled. The budget constraint was soft under mandatory planning; it remains soft under the guidance variety. Losses may earn bureaucratic disfavor but they do not lead to closure. As the assets of loss-making enterprises belong to the state and it is the state's responsibility to guarantee employment for the workforce, forcing enterprises to close their doors is less than meaningful. It is the state that suffers most of the pain. The absence of financial accountability in the strict market sense also means that indirect economic instruments lose some of their effectiveness. Higher interest rates, higher prices of imports or tighter credit do have an effect, but the enterprise escapes much of the pain. If its losses rise, they can be negotiated with the supervisory agencies; if credit for working capital is scarce, production is allowed to fall and the funds available used to cover overheads. No one is laid off.

4.50   The appearance of markets and the freeing of prices have begun impinging on production as well as resource allocation by enterprises. But the benefits in terms of efficiency have not been fully realized because some segments of the state sector are still sheltered from market forces. As a

- 74 -

rough rule of thumb, the township and village enterprises, accounting for 20 percent (1988) of industrial output, have the greatest independence and most responsive to market forces. By the same token, they are also the most likely to go under when the economy runs into a squall. At the other extreme are the medium and large state enterprises, some 8,000 in all, responsible for 57 percent (1988) of industrial production. Their budget constraints are soft but the guidance they receive can be heavy-handed. Collectives occupy an intermediate position. The largest ones are no different from the state enterprises. Smaller ones enjoy the fruits of autonomy to a greater measure, but must cope with the risks.

4.51   Improving the efficiency and innovativeness of state enterprises is widely agreed to be crucial. This will not be possible without changes in their external environment, including price reform and more competition, but it also requires changes in their internal motivation and management. The contract management responsibility system has made state enterprises more profit-oriented, but only in a short-term sense, with long-term success and survival still dependent mainly on good relations with administrative superiors, and with retained profits channeled mainly into workers' pockets. More generally, this system has not resolved a basic dilemma, which is that in China, relaxation of undesirable administrative control over state enterprises has usually led to an equally undesirable increase in worker control. It is of course essential that employees should be interested and involved in the management of the enterprises in which they work. On the other hand, however, a state enterprise should operate for the benefit of the whole society, not simply for the benefit of its workers as they will naturally favor high wages, restricted employment and low work effort.

4.52   Although they have one foot in the market economy, state enterprises are by and large socialist organisms and their inner workings diverge greatly from those of Western firms. A manager cannot afford to neglect supervisory agencies, whose intervention can be decisive in obtaining scarce inputs or a favorable decision with regard to prices. Bureaucratic signals are no less important than those of the market. These can reinforce each other but as frequently they pull in different directions.

4.53   The manager must pay close heed to the messages relayed by the vertical bureaucratic hierarchy. He is equally susceptible to pressures from two other sources: the Party secretary and the enterprise workforce. The former wields great influence because of his political connections beyond the firm; his role in approving appointments, links with employees, and capacity to secure materials using Party channels. The enterprise's labor force has a powerful say in what the manager decides by virtue of their monopoly power to provide or withhold work effort. Except in extreme circumstances, workers cannot be dismissed or laid off. They are inseparably associated with the firm during their active life and when in retirement. There is no labor market beyond the gates of the factory into which a discontented worker can escape and, for this reason also, the lazy and incompetent must be carried on the books. To win active cooperation, the manager must be sensitive to the workers' demands.k/

4.54   Even where decentralization has enlarged enterprise autonomy, this does not translate automatically into discretion for the manager to rationally pursue the most attractive economic goals. He can only do so to the extent that sociopolitical pressures internal to the firm allow him. His success is likely to be related to what he can provide the workers in the way of wages, bonuses, housing and benefits; his skill at negotiating with the supervisory organs; and the support he can gain from the Party hierarchy.1/

4.55   It is not surprising that for a typical state enterprise, profit or growth maximization is unlikely to be the principal aim. In fact, large profits can invite additional fees and higher guidance targets for the next period--what the Chinese refer to as "whipping the fast ox".m/ Maximizing "organizational slack" n/ so that the enterprise does not have to strain to meet its targets, and satisfactory profits, are what the manager seeks. The more fat a firm accumulates in terms of resources, the easier is the manager's job.

4.56   Freeing prices means that the market is potentially in a position to transmit signals. They will lead to efficient production if managers and workers act as maximizers. This is beginning to happen but there remain several institutional impediments to the full participation of firms in the market process. The ability of the Party to intervene in the management of a firm through its representatives in the enterprise certainly reinforces central administrative directives in a planned socialist economy, but are seriously distracting for managers, who are being called upon to respond to market signals. During 1987/88 the government was coming to accept the view that the Party should adopt a lower profile in the workplace, leaving the running of the enterprise to professional managers. Since early in 1989, Party channels have seen increased use in the center's effort to enforce its deflationary policies. If the advantages of industrial reform are not to be diluted, a return to the earlier trend is definitely called for.

4.57   Tenured employment can flourish in market economies but the institutional context is different. Both labor and management have choices. Workers have the right to leave and managers determine the employment practices to be followed. It is the boundedness of choice that is a brake on efficiency in China's enterprise sector. The worker's right to leave is narrowly constrained by institutional and practical considerations, as is the manager's ability to fire one group of workers or compete for another. Resource mobility is reduced as is the efficiency with which labor can be utilized by the enterprise. The development of an urban labor market and a redefining of the choices available to workers as well as enterprises are needed to loosen the bonds that currently bind employees to their assigned workplace. This will enhance the efficiency of labor use. But the full advantages of a system guided by market prices can only be realized by the eventual large-scale reform of public ownership and management policies.

4.58   The role of the government as owner, interested in the long-term growth of each enterprise's profits and averse to losses, has somehow to be maintained but separated from its role as an economic regulator with a range of other objectives. This point has been recognized in China, with the creation of the National Administrative Bureau of State-Owned Property (NABSOP), although its ownership rights and activities are as yet undefined. State enterprise ownership rights might also be exercised by holding companies and other public financial institutions, including investment banks, insurance companies and pension funds. If public ownership were to be organized in these ways, it might be advantageous to reconstitute state enterprises as joint stock companies with boards of directors.o/ This would permit larger enterprises to be owned jointly by several different public entities including provincial agencies, insurance companies and pension funds, thereby avoiding the problems of conflicting objectives that now arise because most enterprises are exclusively owned by a ministry or local government. Experiments with joint stock ownership have been underway for some years. They are the subject of intense debate and, since late 1989, have begun receiving renewed attention from policymakers in cities such as Shanghai. International experience makes clear, however, that there are no simple or ready-made answers in the field of state enterprise management reform and the above suggestions might only be interim solutions.p/

4.59   So long as the vast majority of enterprises in the market are state-owned, as is the financial system, meaningful competition between firms will be restrained.q/ There will be nothing resembling the entry and exit associated with functioning free-market economies. And without the hardening of budget constraints for banks, the financial system may not be able to discipline companies as it does in the industrial countries.r/

4.60   Competition between independent enterprises requires that state ownership be fragmented into parts, each of which is on its own. In effect, the state adopts the role of a passive beneficiary, who defines market rules but then also plays by these rules and, in practice, this means leaving firms severely alone. Any intermediate position which allows the enterprise partial autonomy; that transfers only a part of the usufruct, custodial and alienation rights; that blurs state ownership and prerogatives as in Yugoslavia, may fail in the above respects and may also fail to give entrepreneurship the free rein it needs. Entrepreneurial initiative assumes ownership rights, rewards from the success of a venture and the acceptance of risks.s/ The experience of China and other East European economies in the agriculture sector shows that entrepreneurship is sparked by long-term contracts or private leasehold over land, backed by dependable legal guarantees. This is still a halfway house because these rights are not necessarily portable. Leasehold rights cannot yet be sold in China and the capital used for some other industrial activity.

4.61   State ownership provides a direct command over resources, which definitely facilitates planning, the raising of revenues and the management of income distribution. But production, fiscal and distributional goals can be achieved without undue difficulty, even if state ownership, while remaining dominant, is reduced in scale. In fact, such a division of shares promises additional advantages: higher efficiency and growth for the whole economy.

4.62   Ownership questions might first be tackled on the fringes of the formal industrial sector: in agriculture; township and village enterprises; and service industries. In all these cases, the ground has been prepared with a multitude of private or quasi-private enterprises in existence. These firms must be encouraged to compete with state enterprises. Progressively, as the infrastructure of legal rules and regulatory institutions is introduced, the latter could shift increasingly to joint stock forms of ownership except the ones in core sectors which, for reasons of natural monopoly or strategic interest, must remain directly under state control.

4.63   Township and village enterprises, clustered mainly in the Eastern provinces, have rapidly increased their share of industrial output. (see Table A9.1). They have broadened the spectrum of ownership forms. Their absorption of surplus agricultural labor and contribution to raising rural living standards is much appreciated, but they are also seen as technologically backward, and as inefficient users of agricultural land and valuable raw materials.t/ This has led to periodic attempts by the central authorities to curb their expansion, the latest of which occurred in 1989. It is true that some of these enterprises are of little or no economic value to society, being profitable only because of price distortions or market imperfections. Administrative weeding, however, is a crude and ineffectual approach to this problem, for which the only efficient and lasting solution is price reform and other actions to make markets work better. Administrative improvements are also needed, but mainly to ensure that nonstate enterprises pay their due taxes and comply with the safety and environmental regulations to which state enterprises are subject.u/

4.64   More generally, it is not possible as yet to judge reliably whether township and village enterprises are more or less efficient and technologically progressive than state enterprises.v/ Not only has there been little scientific study of this issue, but also the comparison is inherently difficult. This is partly because of the manifest diversity of performance within both enterprise categories, and partly because township and village enterprises do not have equal access to skilled manpower and advanced equipment-- though this has improved in recent years. In certain respects, township enterprises are similar to small state enterprises. But they are free of some of the causes of state enterprise inefficiency: they have much less access to subsidies and soft loans; their owners cannot protect them as easily from outside competition; and their employment and wage decisions generally involve a better balance between the interests of their workers and those of the whole local community. In some sectors, they are also a valuable source of competition which has improved the performance by state enterprises. So although the issue merits further study, it seems likely that continued expansion of rural and other nonstate public enterprises, albeit at a more moderate pace, would be to China's long-term economic advantage.

4.65   Private enterprises and individual self-employment are permitted and protected by China's constitution, and have been governed since 1988 by well-defined State Council regulations.w/ The number of privately owned businesses at the end of 1989 was 12.4 million down from 14.5 million a year earlier, and they provided employment to over 19 million people. Private businesses are most heavily represented in repair activities, small scale construction, retailing, food and beverages production, agricultural sideline production, light manufacturing and in services. But there remains disagreement about their future role, scale and scope in China's socialist economy. Moreover, criticisms of the private sector have recently been intensified as part of the rectification campaign. This has arisen, because some private enterprises did engage in illegal activities and tax evasion, and it is essential that private enterprises should comply with laws and regulations. However, these justified criticisms should not be exaggerated, and ought not to obscure an objective assessment of the advantages and disadvantages of legitimate private enterprise in China's economic development.

4.66   On the basis of recent Chinese as well as all foreign experience, there can be no doubting the power of private enterprise to harness the effort and initiative of individuals and families. In most countries family businesses account for the overwhelming majority of small and medium-sized nonagricultural enterprises. For this reason, it may be advantageous to promote such businesses in China, while retaining public ownership of all large enterprises. Such extension of private ownership, starting in the rural sector, would not make it any harder to plan and manage the economy than if it consisted entirely of autonomous public enterprises, because either way, regulation would have to be indirect. The real problem with an extension of private ownership in China instead appears to be its effect on income inequality. The very high incomes that a few successful entrepreneurs earn, even after paying progressive personal income tax, provide a valuable incentive for all the others to work and to take the large risk of financial failure. But the social justification for very high incomes is only gradually becoming accepted in China.

V. TRADE, FOREIGN EXCHANGE AND CREDITWORTHINESS

5.1   "Open door" policies have transformed China's trade relations with the rest of the world. In a little over ten years, the ratio of trade to GDP tripled, approaching nearly 28 percent in 1989 and trade now exercises a strong direct influence on growth and a profound indirect effect on the modernization of the economy through the impact of technology, marketing skills, as well as the contacts with other nations. The rising importance of trade in economic calculations has spurred efforts to change the composition of exports along with those of imports, so that China can maximize the growth impulse imparted to the economy. Manufactured exports have displaced raw materials and accounted for 70 percent of the total in 1988. Among them, garments, consumer electronics, office and telecommunications equipment, toys and machinery have risen to prominence, while the share of foodstuffs has diminished. Raw materials and intermediates still comprise a somewhat incompressible third of China's imports, but the proportion of capital goods rose to 34 percent in 1988 from 19 percent ten years ago. Since the mid-eighties, merchandise exports have increased at an average rate of 15.2 percent per annum, reaching $52.5 billion in 1989 (Table A3.3). With respect to the growth of world trade, this represents an elasticity of 1.3 (Table A3.7). Imports, which grew explosively in 1985 coinciding with the second round of reforms, were restrained in 1986/87. As a part of the government's stabilization policy, the flow of imports expanded rapidly in 1988 and the first half of 1989, but slowed down in the second half. Imports for 1989 reached $59 billion, a 18.2 percent per annum increase since the middle of the decade (see Table A4.3).

5.2   After agriculture, trade is the area where reforms have been most successfully introduced. They have contributed significantly to industrial progress and bolstered creditworthiness. The role of trade during the nineties promises to be even larger, as a source of growth and technology. It will also remain the principal bulwark of China's credit standing. The momentum certainly is there. By building on past reforms, it can be sustained, assuming that world trade expands at 4-6 percent per annum as it has done in 1985-89.1/ This section reviews trade prospects and the policies required; the following one examines trends in external borrowing and creditworthiness.

Trade Prospects and Policies Required

5.3   In the pre-reform era, China, much like other socialist countries, relied on imports to make good domestic shortages of materials and the unavailability of various kinds of capital goods. These were financed by exporting items for which surpluses could be generated such as rice, petroleum, processed food and other minerals. After decentralization transferred some of the initiatives to provincial bodies, market opportunities, the chances to earn profits, have introduced new dimensions into trade strategy. Where once a handful of centrally controlled, foreign trade corporations (FTCs) were responsible for all transactions, the numbers had risen to over 6,000 in 1989. Furthermore, the trade responsibility system, allied with guidance planning,

---

1/ The volume of international trade grew by 7 percent per annum during 1987-89. World Economic Outlook, IMF, April 1989, p.11.

vastly improved the attractions of exporting for enterprises and local governments. Exporters can retain 25 percent of the foreign exchange earned for
quota sales assigned by the center and 75 percent of above-target business,
the balance being transferred to the central government. Of the retained
amount, they share half with the provincial government. All parties have a
stake in the growth of trade.

5.4   Aside from the reforms that led to trade contracting on a decentralized basis, the other important step was the creation of Special Economic
Zones, which have attracted direct foreign investment in processing and assembly industries. In 1989 these Zones, led by Shenzhen, accounted for $3.8 bil-
lion (7.2 percent) of China's merchandise exports.a/

5.5   The future of trade will be decided by industrial strategy alluded to
in Chapter 3 as well as by trade and exchange rate policies. Some of the more
important ones are discussed below.

5.6   <u>Export Composition</u>. It is quite probable that the share of raw
materials in exports will shrink even more. Petroleum production is stagnat-
ing in the face of rising domestic consumption, and the need to satisfy grain
targets holds down the output of cotton. Petroleum accounted for 26 percent
of China's exports in 1985 and 6 percent in 1988. Manufactures, initially
labor-intensive ones, but increasingly producer goods, that capitalize on
China's substantial experience in this field, will emerge as leading exports,
as they have done in the case of South Korea.

5.7   There are several commodities which have shown growth rates consistently above the average rate for the last few years: silk piece goods;
embroidered articles; other garments, especially of cotton; carpets; and "products exported after inward processing of imported materials," which are, in
particular, soft toys, electronic items, such as radios and cassette players,
and garments. Typically, these are being exported out of Guangdong and
Fujian, as described above. All of these products have one thing in common:
they rely on a large supply of cheap, but semiskilled labor.

5.8   Many countries can claim such a resource, but China has been able to
put it to better use for two reasons. First, China is benefiting enormously
from its relationship with overseas Chinese in Hong Kong, Taiwan, China, and
Singapore. Contacts between overseas Chinese and their relatives or simply
their villages of origin are very important, and seem to be the reason--along
with the sound underlying business rationale--why there has been so much small
scale, export-oriented foreign investment in these two provinces. Moreover,
this development is in the interest of the other East Asian countries who are
faced with rising labor costs.

5.9   Second, China's producers have encountered few difficulties in adapt-
ing to the quality standards demanded of exports. Certainly, labor needs
vigilant supervision in Chinese factories, but, in the case of the Guangdong
enterprises for example, the rates of productivity have been close to those of
the Hong Kong enterprises, with any shortfalls fully compensated by the very
large wage differential. Part of this is explained by the common language and
culture of most of the quality and production supervisors sent to the Chinese
enterprises; part of it may also be that there are real incentives for the

---

a/   Lettered footnotes are to be found in Annex II.

Chinese entrepreneurs and enterprise managers to achieve the standards required; and part, it must be said, may be the apparent natural tendency to high productivity of the people and cultures of East Asia, when offered appropriate rewards.

5.10   What this suggests is that garments, toys and footwear, that are already among China's major exports, will continue to perform strongly for years as they have done in the case of South Korea and Taiwan, China. What China lacks is design, production and marketing technology. This will develop with time as a natural process, as it has in Hong Kong, and, indeed, is already doing in China's silk goods. At present, China is facing growing protectionism, and already has limits to growth with the US and EEC markets. Following the pattern of Hong Kong, it will need to diversify its markets and establish niches in the dynamic economies of East Asia.

5.11   Among the emerging export industries, electronics assembly is one which is the most promising. It is entrenched in the Special Economic Zones and the Economic Development Areas. The OEM (original equipment manufacture) route is the one China is now following by assembling or producing items for large foreign companies. But it has the option of developing and marketing its own brand names as both South Korea and Taiwan, China have begun doing. There appears to be scope for both strategies in China, but whichever is followed, it appears certain that there will be strong comparative advantage in China in the coming years for consumer electronics, including TVs, radios (which are already quite strong), microwave ovens and computers. Just as these exports have moved from the USA to Japan and then to South Korea and Taiwan, China, so they will also move to the mainland. It is quite likely that this sector would be a particularly relevant one to target for greater foreign investment--to follow the first strategy--which could be attracted by access to the Chinese domestic market. As the internal market is now adequately supplied with many basic consumer durables, the export market should become increasingly interesting for producers of commodities such as refrigerators and bicycles.2/

5.12   There also appear to be two other industries that can be groomed for a larger export role in the near term. The pharmaceutical sector has performed creditably in the last few years, as a result of a growing interest in Chinese traditional medicine, but also because of the increasing availability of fine chemicals. This beachhead can be expanded by drawing on the strength of the domestic market. Similarly, China has seen growth in its exports of hand tools and small machine tools, which its vast engineering sector is equipped to produce in quantity. China is by far the world's largest producer of machine tools and can mount a strong push in the export market if problems of quality and technology can be overcome.

2/   It is estimated that 2 million bicycles, half a million more than in 1988, were exported in 1989, from a total output of 38 million. Production capacity, spread across 78 factories, is 50 million. There are eight bicycle exporting "bases" in Shanghai, Tianjin, Jiangsu and Guangdong. "Nearly 2 Million Bicycles Exported," China Daily, December 23, 1989.

5.13   Much of the recent growth in exports of light manufactures has come from small producers in the south of the country, working to orders provided by buyers in Hong Kong. This suggests that two elements of general policy are critical: a moderately supportive policy towards township and village enter-prises, which already account for $10 billion in exports, or about one-third of all manufactured exports, so that they can fulfill export orders; and a maintenance of the Hong Kong/Taiwan, China special relationships, which will continue to be the main real source of export growth.

5.14   Trade Reforms. The last two years have seen two phases of trade reform, followed by the present phase of rectification. The first phase, in September 1987, selected three sectors where price distortions were relatively absent: garments, light industrial products (including electrical and electronic goods) and arts and handicrafts. The reform offered a carrot and a stick: (a) for these sectors, rates of foreign exchange retention were raised to between 60 percent (garments) and 100 percent (electronic components). If the enterprises/localities did not wish to use this foreign exchange for imports, they were permitted to sell excess foreign exchange in the newly created foreign exchange adjustment centers, where rates have on average been 75 percent above the official rate (see Section D for more details on these centers); and (b) the stick was the complete removal of subsidies and of official allocation of foreign exchange, so that the industries were by and large fully independent.

5.15   The second phase came at the beginning of 1988 with the introduction of the trade responsibility system. MOFERT devised and signed contracts with all the provinces, municipalities and major cities (i.e. those with separate planning), each for a three year period. These contracts are actually rather simple documents, and they have three essential components: (a) they define an annual export earnings target for the contracted period; (b) they define the rates for the sharing of foreign exchange between the center and the con-tractor, with one rate (usually 75-80 percent) for above target earnings; and (c) the contracts specify the "economic results" of the export activity. This means that the contracts fix the level of subsidy (if any) that the central government will provide over the life of the contract. In general, targets and subsidies were based simply on their 1987 levels. As far as is known, there was no nominal increase in subsidies provided over the three-year period.

5.16   These reforms were accompanied by administrative decentralization. This was in two respects. First, the authority to approve the creation of new foreign trade corporations and to grant direct trading rights to enterprises was decentralized to the local bureaus of foreign economic relations and trade. It fostered a major growth in the number of the FTCs operating at the local level. Excluding Guangdong province, the number of FTCs rose in 1988 alone to well over 5,000 from about 4,000, and in Guangdong the number of companies increased by almost one third to over 1,000 from under 800. In all, about 2,000 new foreign trade enterprises emerged in 1988. The trend was halted in July 1988, when the approval of new FTCs was suspended.

5.17   A second related reform was the delegation by MOFERT of some aspects of trade administration to the newly created Special Commissioners' Offices, and the creation of quasi-governmental Chambers of Commerce for Import and

Export, to act as information exchanges, provide consultancy, and market advice. In short, this involved a division of responsibility for business and administration in the large FTCs, and for policy formulation and administration in MOFERT.

5.18   More recently, MOFERT has launched a third phase of reform, in line with the macropolicy of improvement and rectification. The Government's view is that too many new FTCs were created, and that they have contributed to inflation by bidding up procurement prices, and through their own administrative costs.3/ All FTCs are to be screened, and "illegal and unqualified ones will be dissolved, merged or deprived of import and export rights." Over 80 percent of the trading enterprises created in 1988 were pure trading companies, with under 20 percent being producing enterprises granted trading rights. It has been stated that rectification will concentrate on these pure trading companies, and that there will continue to be progress in granting direct trading rights to producing enterprises.

5.19   A prelude to this effort was the government's response to the so-called "silk war" in the summer of 1988. Silk is (or was) among the most profitable of all China's exports, being a high-value export with relatively low production costs. The freedom to create new FTCs led to a situation where many new FTCs signed silk export contracts prior to securing a source of supply and then competed for the limited supply of silk cocoons.4/ Fierce interprovincial competition to secure raw material supplies erupted. Two consequences alarmed MOFERT: first, cocoon prices were bid up sharply and export profit margins cut (which was a good thing, but affected seriously the profitability of the National Silk Import and Export Corporation); and the second was the breaking of large numbers of export contracts, which was rightly perceived by MOFERT as damaging to China's market reputation. MOFERT responded by unifying control of the silk trade under the National Silk Import and Export Corporation.

5.20   In its attempts to correct the mistakes made earlier, MOFERT has no intention of reneging on or renegotiating the three-year trade contracts. Thus, the reforms of the trade planning system will remain intact. Furthermore, the September 1987 reforms, which liberalized trade in selected sectors, will also be preserved, although not necessarily extended to other sectors. Within the three components of the recent reforms--the foreign trade contract system, higher retention ratios coupled with the abolition of subsidies and

---

3/   Since pricing for many commodities in China is based on a simple cost-plus pricing rule, there is a generalized belief among Chinese policymakers that additional agents in the distribution field must automatically increase total production costs and thus raise prices. There is no concept of competition spreading rents wider, or of the generation of efficiency gains in distribution via increased competition.

4/   This also reflects remaining price distortions, in that large profits were generated in exporting, but under the prior system, this profitability had not been adequately transmitted to the silk cocoon production level. Thus, while export demand was growing rapidly in 1988, cocoon output actually fell.

decentralization of administration--it is only the right to approve new FTCs that has been reversed.

5.21   There are two comments to be made with respect to the current reassessment of foreign trade policies. It is indeed important to ensure that trading companies (FTCs) abide by laws and regulations and that they do not damage China's market reputation, either by reneging on contracts or by exporting substandard products. It is, therefore, appropriate to strengthen export certification capacity and to clarify rules and regulations for the qualification of trading companies. To the extent that this is the motivation and rationale behind the recent changes it is to be supported. However, there is also an element of judgment by government that there are simply "too many" FTCs, although it is by no means clear that the central administration--as opposed to the market--can determine the appropriate number of trading companies. The creation of more FTCs, and especially of more enterprises with direct trading rights can ultimately only be good for the efficiency of exporting, provided, of course, it is done within an appropriate regulatory framework. Overall, therefore, consolidation should be pursued with caution, and some of the energy and effort being expended upon it could be better allocated to improving the regulatory framework.

5.22   With respect to the two continuing elements of reform, they both clearly represent progress in the bringing to bear market forces in the area of trade and the reduction of micro planning. However: (a) the trade responsibility system leaves major power in the hands of local governments, rather than enterprises. Local governments tend to take the broad export targets of the contract system and convert them into mandatory targets for their FTCs, just as they used to do with central guidance plans; and (b) the use of high retention ratios and parallel exchange rates are of course powerful export incentives, but also a major distortion in the trading environment. Therefore, these two measures should be regarded as transitional mechanisms, rather than as final goals.

5.23   While macroeconomic restraint is being observed over the next two years, there are several issues that could be taken up. They fall into five areas: trade organizations; reform of the present foreign trade responsibility system; treatment of credit allocation; licensing and tariffs; and export promotion policies.

5.24   <u>Trade Organizations</u>. The most notable feature of trade reform in China has been the explosive growth of foreign trade corporations since 1984. This has injected vigor into exporting, creating competition for export supply, and generally "raising the enthusiasm" for exporting. Over the years, a number of deficiencies have been noted in this approach, but the authorities have usually reacted by tightening administrative controls, as is occurring at the present time. Three problems require attention:

    (a) While many new foreign trade corporations have been created, relatively few direct trading rights have been granted to producing enterprises. These would raise the efficiency of the export drive and enlarge benefits in the realm of technology transfer and product upgrading.

(b)   The new trade corporations have suffered from the same drawbacks as the ones in the prereform era, in that they purchase goods and export on their own account. As a consequence, they fail to pass on fully to exporters changes in world market prices. This has been compounded by the fact that the new FTCs are frequently the product of provincial government initiative, committed more to quantitative export targets than the economic efficiency of such exports.

(c)   The creation of new FTCs has occurred in spurts during periods of decentralization. This has had two consequences: some of them lack experience and qualifications, making it difficult for them to satisfactorily deliver on export contracts.b/ The usual reaction has been to place artificial limits on growth of FTCs, recentralization of trade rights granting authority, and, as now, administrative closures of new FTCs.

5.25   Clearly, there is a need for policy action with respect to trading organizations. They should be directed towards three main areas:

(a)   A vigorous program of granting direct trading rights to qualified producing enterprises, together with the development of assistance to these enterprises so they can enter world markets.

(b)   The strict application of hard budget constraints on foreign trade enterprises, and the replacement of trading for their own account with the export agency system, as has been done successfully in the area of imports.

(c)   The development of clear rules, regulations (including audit provisions) and qualification requirements for foreign trade corporations.

5.26   Chinese trading corporations, like their counterparts in South Korea and Japan, have a vital role to play for many years.c/ There are many production enterprises that will not wish to export directly, nor would they find it economic to do so. Many importers from China also find the FTCs essential in their role of identifying export producers, supervising production, and guiding the importer through the bureaucratic maze. The same goes for the exporter to China. Moreover, many of the FTCs such as ChinaTex have now developed expert knowledge of overseas markets, as well as a network of contacts, and this expertise should not be lost. What the above proposals would do is heighten their efficiency and enable them to contribute more fully to the diversification of China's trade.

5.27   <u>Reforming the Foreign Trade Contract Responsibility System</u>. The existing set of foreign trade contracts will need to be renewed at the end of 1990. The system is to be retained, but three options are under active consideration:

(a)   A widening of the current system of provincial contracts;

(b)   A replacement of the provincial contracts with "commodity contracts" negotiated between MOFERT and the FTCs;

(c)   An extension of the September 1987 reforms, which generated higher retention ratios to certain sectors (as described in para. 5.14).

While the power of the September 1987 reforms is recognized by the government, there are concerns that its broader application could cause shortages of foreign exchange at the central level.

5.28   There should be scope for each of these three elements to be incorporated into a revised trade contract system. The present system has encouraged provincial initiative, and reduced the subsidy burden on the center, and thus elements of this framework need to be retained. However, there remain some features of the old mandatory trade plan for certain raw materials, which could be superceded by some form of commodity contract system. For the provincial contracts to be replaced by commodity contracts would seem, however, to be a regressive step, as it would involve a greater level of central planning.

5.29   Finally, the third option would have considerable benefits, as it would both enhance export incentives and foster the further development of the foreign exchange market. With regard to the question of whether it would cause shortfalls in central access to foreign exchange, the answer would be that the government could always purchase foreign exchange in the adjustment centers through the People's Bank to meet any such needs. It would have to pay the market price, but this would be a further encouragement to continue to move towards the unification of the official and parallel rates.

5.30   Credit for Exporters. In a time of credit restraint it is very important to ensure that export enterprises have the ability to finance their export production. As long as there continues to be a very significant element of administrative allocation of credit in China, provisions will need to be made to ensure that exporters have access to pre- and post-shipment financing.

5.31   Without such provisions, there is a danger that either the banks may be unable to provide adequate levels of credit, given competing demands in the face of an overall shortage, or they may be able to force the People's Bank to create excessive levels of credit in order to fulfill the policy, as has occurred in the past--for example in 1988--in the area of credit for agricultural procurement. In such circumstances, the correct approach is for the PBC to set aside part of the annual credit plan, and of PBC credit creation in particular, to meet the pre- and post-shipment needs of exporters. In this way, credit for exporters can be accommodated within the overall credit plan, but banks would not feel restrained in granting credit for export production.

5.32   What must be stressed is that credit allocation for exporters should be at regular interest rates. The issue is access to credit, not the cost of credit. Indeed, to subsidize credit would be exactly the same as directly subsidizing exports. But ensuring access to credit in the current framework of credit restraint through the suggested mechanism would be a powerful instrument that the government could institute to accompany the foreign exchange rate policy in encouraging the rapid growth of exports.

5.33   Licensing and Tariffs. In the last ten years, China has moved a long way from its old, highly centralized system. Now, the exchange rate and the tariff system do play a major role in the level and composition of exports and imports. But China continues to direct both its imports and exports to a considerable degree through an extensive system of licensing, and further progress towards an indirect system of trade control seems warranted. A tightening of import licensing contributed to the reduced growth of imports in mid-1989 and it is the export licensing of raw materials which has been a critical determinant in domestic availability.

5.34   On the import side, there is great reluctance to move from this quantitative system to one which relies more on the price mechanism via tariffs. There are two reasons for this reluctance: the government believes that so long as enterprise budget constraints remain soft, the demand for imports in the absence of such controls will be excessive; and, second, that tariffs would be very hard to collect and could be a further source of corruption in the system. (In many other countries, it is the fear of corruption or its existence that moves governments to replace quotas with tariffs.) Indeed, the current degree of domestic price distortion means that tariffs would have to rise to very high levels for some commodities--if they were to replace import quotas at an equivalent level of protection--that collection would pose serious administrative difficulties. Nevertheless, the medium-term goal should remain the replacement of import quotas by tariffs, holding the level of protection constant. Over the longer run, the degree of protection should be reduced.

5.35   In the meantime, the ground can be prepared by the gradual elimination of exemptions on tariffs. The effective rate of tariff collection is only 4.6 percent of imports, whereas the tariff rates would imply a taxable level at least ten times higher. This can only be attributed to widespread exemption of tariffs and duties. It is a practice that should be ended, both in order to boost revenues--for these taxes are a way for the government to capture the rents associated with actual imports in the face of excess demand for imports--and to develop the administrative mechanisms, together with the trained personnel needed to administer a system, that will eventually rely on tariffs rather than on licenses.

5.36   But these same considerations do not apply to the export side. The reasons for quantitative controls at the present time fall into three types:

    (a) On commodities in which China has a dominant supplier and in a position to extract monopoly rents. The frequently quoted example is China's food exports to Hong Kong, which are administered very strictly.

    (b) On commodities where China is facing quota restrictions in the market, as in the case of garment exports to the United States and the European Economic Community.

    (c) Where the domestic price for the commodity is very low, but the commodity is in short supply at home. Here, China is applying export controls in order to prevent the emergence of domestic scarcity.

For the first two situations, there are theoretical economic solutions (notably export taxes and auctioning of quotas) that would have the same result in terms of the volume of exports, but it must be recognized that such solutions may be difficult to design and implement. Moreover, it appears that the current arrangements are operated rather well. While there is little immediate need for reforms in these areas, experiments with the auctioning of garment export quotas could be broadened if they prove workable.

5.37   It is in the third area that more immediate actions seem to be warranted. The purpose of the quota is to compensate for the differential between fixed domestic and world market prices. This is a classic case where the application of appropriate export taxes would be more efficient than the current approach. China may be missing out on useful export opportunities because of the imperfections of planning, and because of the difficulties of accurately forecasting domestic demand and supply of these commodities. For example, it could easily prove to be the case that as demand patterns change, domestic supply of certain types of steel move into surplus, while there remains a shortage of other types. In such cases, it is more efficient to export the surplus type and import the shortage type, than to attempt to force the domestic market to accept what is available. A policy of replacing many or most of the 173 export quotas, now in place, with export taxes at a level that covers the difference between the domestic price and the world market price would be highly appropriate. As price reform progresses, these taxes can be gradually removed, in line with the application of world market prices in the domestic economy.

5.38   Export Incentives and Export Promotion. China has made progress in the last few years with the application of a system of tax drawbacks and exemptions, so that export producers can obtain their imported inputs at world market prices. This system should be maintained and perfected. Less progress, if any, has been achieved in the drawback of domestic indirect taxes on inputs to exports. This applies in particular to the industrial and commercial taxes levied on domestically produced inputs for exports. The principles are exactly the same as for the drawback of import duties, except inasmuch as many of these exemptions take place at the time that imports actually occur, and duties have to be paid if the imported inputs are not used in export production. However, action on this front is constrained by the inclusion of such taxes within the enterprise contract responsibility system. Therefore, this factor should be incorporated into the current tax reform efforts and experiments, so that an eventual indirect tax drawback scheme could be built into a reformed tax system.

5.39   The government already makes fairly strong efforts in the area of general export promotion, by mounting trade fairs, and arranging for participation of producers and FTCs in overseas trade fairs. This effort should not be minimized, and has certainly assisted in export growth. In addition, some of the FTCs, such as Chinatex, have proved to be very adept in identifying overseas markets, and in searching out potential buyers and contractors. Both of these activities should be maintained. However, the relationship between the FTCs and the export producers is essentially a contractual one, and while the exporters may learn quite a lot about export standards, they learn little about the actual marketing of exports.

5.40   Steps are being taken to change this situation, with the gradual separation of market information and consulting services from the FTCs into the newly created Chambers of Commerce for Import and Export. This is a process that should be accelerated and supported financially. The FTCs will always regard themselves as competitors with the export producers for the available supply of exports, and so long as they retain the dual roles of being trading companies as well as being responsible for technical assistance to exporters, the latter function will be short-changed. Thus the creation of specialized institutions to assist the exporters is a useful step that should be pursued with vigor.

Exchange Rate Developments

5.41   The last two years have seen major developments in the exchange rate system in China. First, the introduction of the foreign exchange adjustment centers (FEACs), which led initially to the development of a wide differential between the official and parallel exchange rates; second, the tightening of domestic credit and import licensing, which led to a narrowing of the two rates; and third, of course, the devaluation of the official rate of exchange by 21 percent on December 15, 1989, from Y 3.72 = $1 to Y 4.72 = $1, which substantially closed the gap between the official and parallel rates.

5.42   The official exchange rate in China is theoretically linked to a basket of currencies, with the US dollar as the currency of intervention. In practice, this has tied the rate for the renminbi yuan to the US dollar, and the effective rate of exchange has moved in line with the US dollar against other currencies. As most of China's exports are traded in US dollars, this policy has merits, provided that periodic adjustments are made to the intervention rate. Since the beginning of 1988, the US dollar has been appreciating against other currencies--notably the Japanese Yen--and causing the nominal rate of exchange for the Yuan to appreciate also. Taking 1980 as 100, the nominal effective exchange rate index fell to a low of 51 in December 1987--following several official devaluations, notably that of July 1986--but with the appreciation of the US dollar, the nominal effective rate had risen to about 6 percent by December 1989.5/ The devaluation of December 1989 restores the nominal rate to its most competitive level. The real effective exchange rate index had, of course, moved even faster, and from a low of 38.5 in December 1987, it had appreciated by 26.8 percent by December 1989. The devaluation helped to correct the recent appreciation, but did not compensate for it entirely. Very low rates of inflation in the first half of 1990 has, however, narrowed the gap still further.

5.43   Until the beginning of 1988, the FEACs had only been available to joint ventures, for whom it was a major development, as it virtually eliminated the difficulties previously imposed by the "foreign exchange balance" policy that had been in effect up to that time. The recent trade reforms

---

5/ The nominal effective exchange rate measures the exchange rate by weighting the actual rate against other currencies according to the shares of those currencies in China's trade. Thus, in the case of China, major weights are assigned to the US dollar (which includes the Hong Kong dollar, as this is also tied to the US dollar) the Yen and the Deutschmark. The real effective exchange rate adds the impact of differential rates of inflation to the calculation.

raised retention rates for a range of commodities, and opened the FEACs to domestic enterprises, both those which now had a surplus of foreign exchange to sell given their higher retention rights, and those which had been unable to obtain foreign exchange at the official rate to meet their import purchase requirements. From only a few hundred millions in transactions among joint ventures in 1987 6/ the level of transactions rose to $6.5 billions in 1988, and to about $7.5 billions in 1989, or about 15 percent of total export earnings. The average rate moved from about Y 6 = $1 at the beginning of 1988, to a peak of Y 7 = $1 in September 1988, and again in February 1989. It then began a steady decline because of tighter credit and control over import licensing, falling sharply to a level of only Y 5 = $1 in November.

5.44   The conduct of foreign exchange policy can be judged to be an area of some success in the overall reform effort of the last few years. It is no coincidence that garments and light manufactures, which have the highest rates of retention, have continued to show strong growth even when the official rate has been appreciating. Moreover, the government is to be applauded for taking the opportunity of the narrowing of the differential to devalue the official rate. It can be assumed that it was the pressure from the existence of a parallel rate, that caused the authorities to pay attention to the competi- tiveness of the official rate, and to move at an ideal time to adjust the official rate. With the gap between the two rates at its lowest ever level, and with domestic demand sluggish and inflation falling, this was indeed an opportune moment at which to adjust the official rate. It is very clear that the real appreciation of the official rate of exchange during 1989 caused a strong reduction in the interest of producers to export, and in the ability of the FTCs to offer competitive procurement prices. Furthermore, the trade responsibility system, offering as it did only limited subsidies to exporting, made the exchange rate much more relevant to the level of exports achieved, as it constrained to a much greater degree than before the ability of the FTCs to export at unprofitable prices. Thus, to a very significant degree, it was the developments in trade policy in the last two years that forced the government to move on the exchange rate.7/

6/   At this time, transactions were also permitted between joint ventures outside the confines of the FEACs, which were seen as a facilitating institution at the time, and thus the total volume of transactions was undoubtedly higher. It was also possible for Chinese enterprises to sell foreign exchange between each other, but the lower rates of retention made this a relatively rare occurrence.

7/   It should be recalled that an exchange rate change in China is not neutral for the budget. The devaluation will have major expenditure implications in three respects: first, it raises the cost of import subsidies on essential raw materials (and hopefully exerts more pressure for domestic price adjustments, but this remains to be seen), and these are not covered by the provisions of the trade contracts; second, it raises the cost of external debt servicing; and third, it has no impact on the costs of export subsidies, as these were fixed by the trade contracts. It should therefore be obvious that while MOFERT and the provincial authorities were pushing strongly for a devaluation, the Ministry of Finance was reluctant. This devaluation may well have been part of the price for extracting the agreement of the provincial authorities at the Fifth Plenum for the continuation of the austerity policies.

5.45   The devaluation in no way reduces the usefulness of the role of the FEACs, and it is strongly recommended that they be maintained for the present. There are three main reasons for saying this:

(a)   The FEACs have indicated to the authorities, the direction in which the official rate should be moving, and in a much more powerful way than, for example, real exchange rate calculations.

(b)   The FEACs are a true market, being a forum where willing buyers and sellers meet to negotiate freely. The allocation system for official foreign exchange remains an administrative system, where officials decide between competing applications on the basis of the government's industrial policy. Therefore, without the FEACs, many importers with the ability to pay would be unable to obtain foreign exchange, and as the official allocation system has a natural tendency to favor the state-owned enterprises, the FEACs have served to allocate significant amounts of foreign exchange to the more efficient and dynamic sectors of the economy.

(c)   The parallel rate has helped to provide a significant export incentive, and has undoubtedly helped to generate export growth, especially in 1988, and has averted a further decline in the rate of growth of exports in 1989. Given the need, and the stated policy aim of maintaining a rate of growth of exports above that of GDP, removal of this incentive would seem to be premature at the present time.

5.46   But there are certain drawbacks in the FEAC system at the present time, and the government should use the opportunity created by the official devaluation to address these:

(a)   It is only selected sectors that have higher rates of retention, and this arbitrary discrimination leads to the thinness--and volatility --of the market at the present time. It would thus be appropriate to consider widening the number of sectors with the higher retention rights, and raising the general level of retention. This could be accompanied, as it was in the reform experiment of September 1987, by an elimination of export subsidies. At the same time, restrictions on eligible import transactions for which foreign exchange can be purchased at the FEACs could be broadened.

(b)   The market is not a national one, and provincial authorities have been permitted to exercise provincial protectionism over "their" foreign exchange. The efficiency of the market would be enhanced if the SAEC could devise rules and exert supervision to ensure that foreign exchange could flow between different FEACs to reflect the pattern of regional demand.

5.47   While the role of the parallel market is useful in the short term, it should be noted that all such markets--as with the two-tier price system in general--create distortions and incentives for corruption. Therefore, in moving to refine and improve the functions of the parallel market in the short term, this should always be in the context of a goal of moving to a unified, market-based exchange rate determination system. Further, recent experience in China demonstrates clearly that the economic system is responsive to exchange rate movements, and it is the effective exchange rate which is the most important of all export incentives, even in China. The maintenance of a competitive exchange rate is an issue of critical importance to the achievement of China's export targets, and, as the Minister of MOFERT put it, "to the scale and program for (China's) domestic economic construction".

External Borrowing and Creditworthiness

5.48   Future Trends in Debt Indicators. China's trade performance has contributed significantly to the country's creditworthiness. Other factors that have helped maintain access to international capital markets are the country's impressive growth rate that has kept the ratio of debt outstanding and disbursed to GDP to a modest 10.6 percent ($43.9 billion or 10 percent if the DOD is assumed to be $41.3 billion) in 1989;8/ and the high rate of national savings that holds down the current account deficit, insulates the economy from external shocks and supports the expansion of exports. In the medium term, the economy is projected to grow by between 3 and 6 percent with

---

8/   A major discrepancy exists between the amount of China's external debt reported in the World Debt Tables (WDT) and the OECD. The amount of total debt reported by OECD is $49.6 billion for 1988 as against $42.0 million in the WDT. The bulk of the discrepancy lies in the estimation of short-term debt. OECD supplements the short-term debt figures from the creditor reporting system with aggregate figures from Bank of International Settlements (BIS) surveys. As a result, the short-term debt items included in OECD's estimate differ from the calculation by China's government, specifically SAEC. OECD's estimate may overstate China's short-term debt because it includes debt with a maturity of less than 90 days and debt for which an agreement has been signed but has not been disbursed, while SAEC does not include these items. SAEC's exclusion of undisbursed loans rests on the opinion that a loan agreement does not become debt until is is disbursed. Other differences are: OECD includes debt incurred by branches of Chinese companies not resident in China; OECD includes all guaranteed debt while SAEC only includes such debt when obligations are assumed; SAEC values debt at the exchange rate at a particular time and OECD uses the exchange rate at the time the transaction takes place. Data are not available for calculating the specific influence of each difference between OECD's and SAEC's definitions of short-term debt but these differences can easily account for the discrepancy in short-term debt figures from OECD and SAEC. For example, substantial financing of trade with credit of less than 90 days could account for a large part of the discrepancy. In Shanghai it was reported that over 90 percent of short-term debt is less than 90 days. Also, the source of funds is important in the calculation of external debt by Chinese officials. For example, if the funds borrowed from the branch of Citibank in Shanghai emanate from local enterprises' foreign exchange deposits, they are not considered external borrowing. Consequently, the discrepancy raises questions about the definition and coverage of short-term debt. They do not relate to the actual level or accuracy of reporting.

longer-term growth falling in the 6.0-7.0 percent range. The increasing share of manufactures in exports will also help to sustain export trends. Exports are projected to rise by about 7 percent in the first half of the 1990s, with manufactures growing by 8-9.0 percent per annum. As savings propensities are likely to remain strong and the share of investment in GDP should decline somewhat (counterbalanced by increased efficiency as reforms unfold), the resource gap should remain fairly small, moderating China's net borrowing needs. The continuation of relatively contractionary policies during the first half of 1990 and modest reflation in the second half of the year will limit the growth rate to 2.5-3.5 percent (paras. 2.53 and 6.3). The current account deficit is projected to remain at well below 1 percent of GDP through 1995.

5.49   This pattern of growth and external borrowing will keep the debt servicing burden down to manageable levels and sustain China's creditworthiness. Table 5.1 present the external accounts and the various indicators which measure the burden of indebtedness under the base scenario which is predicated on continuing reforms and openness. The principal assumptions underlying these projections are given in Table 5.3. The ratio of debt outstanding and disbursed to GDP in 1990 will be under 8.5 percent and the total debt service ratio 9.2 percent (see para. 2.30).d/ Total repayments of public and publicly guaranteed medium- and long-term debt (including interest) will rise through 1992 and then decline somewhat by 1994, followed by another upturn in 1995. The debt service ratio, however, should fall steadily to 5.7 percent in 1995 with total debt outstanding and disbursed to GDP reaching 6.3 percent.

5.50   To realize the export growth rates and finance even the relatively modest external borrowing requirements projected in the base scenario, China will need a hospitable international environment. Furthermore, an unwillingness on the part of the international banking system to meet China's needs for term financing, on terms commensurate with its credit standing, could curtail China's growth prospects and may necessitate protective policies inimical to further reform.

5.51   A possible outcome of an unfavorable external environment is spelled out in the low case scenario. There would be less growth, resources would be utilized inefficiently (because measures to secure economic self-sufficiency and central control would take precedence over market oriented reforms) exports would grow at a lower rate and there would be a marked tendency to control imports for the sake of balancing the current account, thereby minimizing reliance on the international capital market. In the low case scenario, China's creditworthiness, on the basis of modest external borrowing, is not impaired. Indeed, by some indications, it improved in the medium term, but it must be recognized that insular policies and an increased reliance on planning and control would undoubtedly hurt the country's long-term development prospects and lead to stagnation.

Table 5.1: CHINA: Creditworthiness Ratios: BASE CASE

	1988	1989	1990	1991	1992	1993	1994	1995
Interest Payments/XGS	3.0	3.9	3.8	3.3	3.0	2.6	2.3	2.1
Total debt service/XGS	6.9	7.6	9.2	8.6	8.4	7.1	5.8	5.7
DOD/XGS	60.3	59.1	53.9	50.0	45.1	41.4	39.3	38.6
DOD/GDP	8.6	8.1	8.5	7.9	7.3	6.9	6.5	6.3

Table 5.2: CHINA: Creditworthiness Ratios: LOW CASE

	1988	1989	1990	1991	1992	1993	1994	1995
Interest Payments/XGS	3.0	3.9	3.7	3.1	2.7	2.2	1.9	1.6
Total debt service/XGS	6.9	7.6	8.9	8.1	7.9	6.6	5.3	5.0
DOD/XGS	60.3	59.1	51.1	44.7	39.2	34.8	31.1	27.5
DOD/GDP	8.6	8.1	8.3	7.4	6.6	6.1	5.5	4.9

NOTE: XGS: Exports of goods and services.
DOD: MLT Debt outstanding and disbursed.

Table 5.3: CHINA: Model ASSUMPTIONS

	1988	1989	Base Case AVERAGE 1990-5	Low Case AVERAGE 1990-5
EXOGENOUS				
Export Growth Rates (%)				
XGNFS_GR Total GNFS (endogenous)	17.46	8.95	8.71	6.87
of which XMANUF_GR Manufacture	17.79	13.53	8.50	8.60
Import Growth Rates (%)				
Total cif Imports growth rate (MGNFS) (endogenous)	18.98	8.19	5.77	3.96
Other Ratios & Growth Rates (%)				
A10 Investment/GDP	37.59	36.50	33.92	33.92
ENDOGENOUS				
GDPGR GDP growth rate (%)	11.20	3.89	5.84	4.66
Current account balance/GDPCUR (%)	-1.02	-1.08	-0.46	0.82

5.52   <u>External Debt Management</u>. As the opening of the economy multiplied the range and complexity of foreign contacts, earlier regulatory procedures were found to be inadequate. Since the mid-eighties, the government has moved to centralize and systematize external borrowing in order to contain the risks inherent in economic liberalization. The State Planning Commission formulates the overall borrowing plan, in consultation with the People's Bank and the Ministry of Finance, but ratification is still required by the State Council. Bilateral lending is managed by MOFERT and the MOF is responsible for borrowing from the World Bank. However, the activity of data gathering, and the supervision of commercial borrowing is the task of the State Administration for Exchange Control (SAEC). Created in 1985 as an entity within the People's Bank with branches throughout the country, the SAEC has, after an uncertain start, improved its administrative capacity and technical skills. These qualities, which seemed somewhat tentative in 1988, were put to the test in late 1988 and 1989, when the authorities acted first to increase the scale of imports to dampen domestic demand pressures, and followed this up with a policy of tight restraint on all commercial foreign transactions, starting in the third quarter of 1989. By and large, the framework for assigning quotas, reporting, cross-checking and enforcing that has been put in place, appears serviceable although more experience and the accumulation of trained manpower, will certainly improve matters. The situation that prevailed during 1984-88, when not just the ten officially designated borrowing windows 9/ but also a few hundred provincial financial entities, were raising funds overseas has been checked for the most part, through the rigorous use of administrative pressure. No doubt the lack of receptivity in international capital markets, during the latter part of 1989, has eased the SAEC's task, but as an organization it has apparently gained in strength and credibility.

5.53   Administrative capability to manage external borrowing is one facet of creditworthiness and the changes introduced, seem to be bearing fruits. The reporting net is still far from watertight--some borrowing by Chinese entities with operations in Hong Kong is probably not captured by the statistics--but the leaks are few. Another equally important facet is the composition and management of the existing debt portfolio.

5.54   China has shown considerable bargaining skill in overseas markets, fully exploiting the attractions of its market, its low exposure and the strength of its economic performance, to extract the most favorable possible terms from lenders--especially Japanese banks. Borrowing from Japanese institutions has been at 15 points below LIBOR and from others, the rates have averaged 25 points over LIBOR. Concessional funds have been sought where possible. From 1.1 percent of the total in 1981, concessional borrowing rose to a peak of 22.7 percent in 1985 before settling at just under 20 percent in 1988. Average interest paid on such borrowing has declined from 5.9 percent in 1984 to 4.3 percent in 1988. For the entire portfolio, average interest charges were 7.1 percent in 1988, close to par for the eighties although maturity on both concessional and overall borrowing is down to 22.7 years and 12.7 years, respectively. About 40 percent of the borrowing is at variable

---

9/   These are: The Bank of China, the Communication Bank of China, the China Investment Bank, the China International Trust and Investment Company, and the Guangdong, Fujian, Hainan, Shanghai, Tianjin, Dalian international trust and investment companies.

rates which is close to the norm under current market conditions and does not expose China to unusual risks (Table A5.3).

5.55   The ratio of short-term to total debt is another index of portfolio quality. When China was a newcomer to the international capital market, much of its borrowing was for purposes of trade and tended to be of short maturities--41 percent in 1983. Such lopsidedness, that would be highly unwelcome in the event of a crisis, has been quickly corrected. The share of short-term borrowing was under 26 percent in 1986 and down to 21 percent in 1988--about normal for an economy with a trade to GNP ratio of nearly 28 percent.

5.56   As Japan has been the principal net supplier of capital in the international market and Japanese banks have sought close relations with China, much of the borrowing in the mid-eighties was Yen-denominated and at quite low rates. The appreciation of the Yen in 1986/87 triggered a change in portfolio composition, the percentage of dollars being increased to 40 percent by 1989 and the Yen share brought down to 34.3 percent. In hindsight, the shift may not have been wisely timed given the strength of the dollar during 1987-89, but future trends for the dollar and the proportion of China's trade denominated in that currency favor the maintenance of the current ratios.

5.57   A third determinant of credit standing is the size of a country's liquid reserves that can enable it to ride out an emergency. Reserves equivalent to three months of imports are generally considered adequate. China has allowed itself a more comfortable margin: reserves amounted to $12 billion in 1986 (4 months of imports), rising to $19.1 billion (5.3 months) in 1988 (Table 1.1).10/ The need to finance debt servicing obligations and other claims in 1989, when MLT credit became unavailable, forced China to dip into its reserves which fell to a low of $15.0 billion at the end of August. However, the recovery of trade brought about some relief and at the end of 1989, total reserves were estimated at $18.5 billion--about a third with PBC and the balance held by the Bank of China. These were equivalent to 3.5 months of imports. Trade surpluses and capital flows pushed reserves close to $25 billion (nearly six months of imports) at the end of April 1990. In actual fact, China's reserve position may be stronger than the published statistics indicate. The country may now be the sixth largest producer of gold. In 1988 output was estimated to be over 90 tons, rising close to 100 tons in 1989.e/ This could be used to augment gold reserves that have remained constant at 12.67 million ounces for several years. It is believed that substantial sales and forward transactions in gold during June-August 1989 were a source of additional liquidity at a time when overseas branches of the Bank of China were faced with mounting withdrawals.

5.58   By economic indices, China's credit standing looks firm and the country compares very favorably with other developing countries in South and

---

10/ Includes gold, SDRs and reserve position at the IMF.

Southeast Asia, not to mention the Latin American region.11/ However, the problems that arose in mid-1989 have aroused fears regarding future political stability. These concerns, that have been stilled somewhat with the return of normality, have led credit rating agencies such as Moody's to mark China's creditworthiness from A3 to BAA. They have also induced lenders to reexamine their exposure in China and future plans for acquiring Chinese paper.

5.59 Future Actions. Some improvements in debt management merit attention in the coming years. External borrowing decisions still remain dispersed over several agencies. The SAEC has begun filling its role in a fairly short space of time, but there are gaps in its coverage and lingering uncertainties about the volume of debt contracted in the 1984-86 period, before reporting rules were tightened. The amounts involved are probably a few hundred million dollars. Nevertheless, these must be made precise and the obligations of the state specified. Essentially, this is a matter of perfecting the information feedback system and verifying what is received. The regulatory powers of the SAEC might also be put on a more formal basis so that it is able to police borrowing and impose order among borrowers, when rectification imperatives are succeeded by normal times.

5.60 There remains some confusion over what is China's sovereign debt, and what rests on the creditworthiness of the borrower alone. Sovereign liabilities include, potentially, all borrowing and guarantees by Chinese borrowers and obligations of joint ventures and borrowing by overseas Chinese enterprises. Creditors' behavior suggests that they consider the bulk of China's

---

11/ China's record in servicing its debt has been good but certainly not flawless and in recent months problems have been reported, particularly in connection with lending in the mid-1980s. At that time, foreign banks were aggressive in seeking business, skimped on documentation and did not look too closely at the guarantees mobilized by the many provincial agencies that trawled East Asian financial markets for funds. Now some of these guarantees are being called, there is a concern that a few of these might have been "improper" and may not be eligible for repayment. In the past twelve months, cases have been brought against Chinese entities by First Chicago Bank, Lloyds Bank, the Hong Kong and Shanghai Banking Corporation, and Security Pacific. The latter concerns bankers acceptances guaranteed by the PCBC branch in Shenzhen (this appears to be nearing resolution). Lloyds Bank sued the CITIC Industrial Bank branch of Shenzhen for nonpayment of $1 million in letters of credit, but this case was settled in March 1990. The Hong Kong and Shanghai bank is involved in lawsuits with three Chinese guarantors for a total sum of $81.3 million. Finally, the First National Bank of Chicago has brought a suit against the China National Machinery and Equipment Corporation to claim $14.65 million that were guaranteed by its Guangdong branch on behalf of Carroway Enterprises, Ltd., registered in Hong Kong. The decline of tourism in 1989 has clouded the future of hotel projects in Shanghai, Beijing, Xian and Guilin, and many of these are being rescheduled or restructured. Other complaints refer to small delays in the repayment of loans and trade credit, which in the current atmosphere are causing irritation. But Hong Kong bankers, who are among the most sensitive, admit that, by and large, Chinese borrowers have been quite scrupulous in servicing their loans at least thus far and that delays may affect 3-5 percent of loans.

external debt to be sovereign. The Chinese authorities argue that this is not so, and that even the BOC borrowing on behalf of the government is only an organ of the state, not the state itself. As a practical matter, however, it appears that most debt in the event of difficulties, would come to be sovereign if China places a high premium on its future credit standing. Thus, BOC's borrowing must be considered sovereign debt; in addition, any borrowing by the nine other institutions is also fairly clearly sovereign borrowing.

5.61   The distinction between sovereign and nonsovereign debt, and between sovereign and debt and guarantees and nonsovereign debt and guarantees, could be accomplished by the dissemination of a State Council pronouncement expressly, forcefully, and publicly disclaiming responsibility, legally and in fact, for the debt of all but a narrowly defined (preferably expressly named) group of borrowers. This disclaimer could be made by a carefully drafted letter, delivered to, say, the 500 largest foreign commercial and investment banks. In addition to the general disclaimer, the letter should specifically state that any "comfort letters" or other representations made by any ministry or other organ of government are without effect.

5.62   This approach is consistent with the effort to decentralize enterprise accountability and management, since it would make clear that enterprises must be financed on their own merits. It will make it difficult or impossible for foreign banks to justify credits to these enterprises on the basis of implicit sovereign guarantee and can be expected to dramatically reduce the availability, and raise the cost, of foreign credit to these enterprises. Meanwhile, with expressly guaranteed borrowers enjoying substantially cheaper access to foreign borrowing, they will become the most attractive source of foreign exchange for enterprises, thus providing an incentive for the development of a viable internal intermediation system.

5.63   It is quite likely that, for borrowing activities in 1990, terms may be harder and lenders less inclined to shave margins for the sake of future business with China.f/ In these circumstances, the borrowing strategy might have to be better orchestrated so as to keep costs down. This will require using China's most creditworthy institutions in the proper sequence; avoiding market saturation through appropriate spacing and dispersion of markets; and choosing the borrowing instrument, e.g., syndicated loans or bonds, with an eye to receptivity.12/ There is, at the moment, no problems of excess but neither is there much of a secondary market for Chinese paper that would serve to enhance absorptivity.

5.64   It would be useful for China to consider advice given to Korea a few years ago, which is to develop correlations between China's terms of trade and various exchange rates and use these expected exchange rates to guide the choice of currency in future borrowing.h/ China's pattern of external trade is an important determinant of the currency composition of its foreign exchange. External liabilities and assets should be managed in an integrated fashion because what really needs to be managed are net liabilities, that is, external liabilities minus external assets such as foreign exchange reserves.

12/ The increase in bond issuance is one of the most prominent current trends in international capital markets. Gross issues of international bonds have increased from $75.5 billion in 1982 to almost $252.1 billion in 1989. Although OECD countries and international organizations dominate the market, China has increased its activity in this market. A recent World Bank report describes a number of trends in this market having implications for future external financing in Korea--implications that apply to China as well. These trends are: (a) the resurgence of fixed-interest bonds after a substantial decline in their popularity following the high inflation and high interest rates in the late 1970s and early 1980s. With low inflation in key industrial countries in the foreseeable future, investors have been drawn back to fixed-interest bonds. Longer maturities, together with the option to issue callable debt, which prevents issuers being locked into high interest rates, are attractive to borrowers who need to reduce their exposure to future high interest rates while at the same time reducing their use of short-term debt; (b) the easing of regulations in a number of countries, including Japan and Germany, which should improve the prospects of currency diversification in this market; (c) the increasing popularity of equity-related bond instruments such as convertible debentures and warrant issues. Issuing equity-related debt can be an attractive option for certain types of enterprises, such as joint ventures. It can be a cheap form of finance for an enterprise with high earnings potential.

VI. THE NINETIES: AGENDA AND PROSPECTS

6.1   The Chinese economy emerged from the first quarter of 1990 with growth at a virtual standstill, unemployment approaching 3.5 percent, inflation running at 3.9 percent over the same quarter of 1989 and a trade surplus amounting to $0.82 billion, as a result of an 11.6 percent increase in exports while imports fell by 13.7 percent (Table 2.6). Aside from the trade sector, there were, at that stage, no other sources of growth pulling the economy with investment stagnating, household saving inching upwards and the government's own spending decisions constrained by a tight revenue situation as well as the intention voiced during the Fifth Plenum of eliminating the budget deficit within the coming 2-3 years. A large overhang of inventories accumulated over the course of 1989, and during the first five months of 1990, means that the responsiveness of production to reflationary stimuli will be subject to a lag and excess capacity in many manufacturing subsectors will dampen investment for a few quarters.[1]

6.2   Concerned over the economy's sharp slide into recession in the final quarter of 1989, the authorities injected an additional Y 25 billion of credit. This was counterbalanced to a degree by reducing currency in circulation by Y 20 billion in January-February 1990 to about the level prevailing at the end of 1988. In the first half of 1990, credit expansion has been eased somewhat and more funds made available to priority industries, the export sectors and for the purposes of institutional consumption. To stimulate labor absorption and promote China's trade in manufactures (paras. 2.12, 2.53, 4.63 and 5.13), the credit supply to TVEs was eased in early 1990, a move the Bank has recommended. In provinces such as Jiangsu, the TVEs are being actively encouraged to step up exports by establishing direct links with foreign buyers and entering into new joint venture arrangements. The government has also marginally reduced lending rates and is considering the possibility of stimulating consumption a notch or two by shaving deposit rates. In the first quarter, M2 rose by 22.5 percent and total credit supply grew by Y 55 billion.

6.3   The government's guarded efforts at reflation began producing results in the second quarter, helped along by a bumper summer grain harvest of 98 million tons. By the end of June, industrial production was growing by 5.9 percent and the rate for the first six months averaged out to 2.2 percent. Meanwhile, GNP rose by 1.6 percent, well short of the annual target but a distinct improvement over the first quarter. Prices remained stable with inflation through June amounting to 3.2 percent (over 1989) as against 4.1 percent at the end of January. The trend in external balances persisted, in fact steepened in the second quarter of 1990. In the first half of the year, China's merchandise exports rose 15.4 percent to $25.65 billion, while imports declined 17.7 percent to $23.09 billion. The overall trade surplus was $4.54 billion, with the current account showing a surplus as well.

---

[1] Devaluation and price adjustments are additional sources of deflationary pressure.

6.4   The actions thus far are cautious ones and very much in the spirit of the austerity program, that has mandated single digit inflation but also calls for 4-5 percent growth per annum. A second year of very low growth would be politically unpalatable and painful in economic terms even under conditions of zero inflation. If the government tailors reflationary policy with reference to program announced by the Fifth Plenum--and this was reaffirmed in speeches by senior leaders at the National People's Congress in March--credit expansion should remain within planned limits (15 percent over 1989, see para. 2.54). GDP growth, for the year as whole, is likely to be in the region of 3-4 percent (as against the government's target of 5 percent) and core inflation--with the benefit of a good harvest--might be held to the low single digit range. However, when the effects of price adjustments proposed later in 1990 and the ripples from the devaluation in December 1989 are factored in, inflation might edge close to the double digit range. At the projected rates of growth, with household savings behavior largely unchanged and import controls on consumer goods sustained, a sizable trade surplus and a smaller one on the current account appear likely.2/

6.5   The outlook for 1991 depends on how the austerity program evolves; on international relations; and on access to capital markets. If core inflation shows no signs of reviving and the external environment is favorable, growth could be faster and there may be less need to strive for balance (or a surplus) on external account. On the other hand a deterioration in either of these areas might necessitate a continuation of the current policy stance favoring retrenchment.

6.6   So much for the short-term macroeconomic picture. Of possibly greater importance is the manner in which reforms are introduced to enable China to meet its medium and longer run goals of modernization. Some of the critical issues were identified by the Fifth Plenum, including centralizing macromanagement, the abolishing of dual prices, and enterprise reform. However, the explicit content, phasing and direction of these reforms as well as reforms in other important areas still remain to be explicated. Preparing such an agenda so that it can guide development in the Eighth Five Year Plan, should have the highest priority.

Medium-Run Macroeconomic Reforms

6.7   A particular issue raised by the Plenum's economic policies is the analysis underlying them. The implication of the decision is that the problems that emerged in 1988 were the result of haste in pushing forward reforms in the past and the fact that this haste was accompanied by a pursuit of an excessively high growth rate. Thus, the program would, essentially, do two things: strengthen macroeconomic management controls to prevent excessive growth rates from reemerging; and utilize the planning system to overcome the difficulties that have arisen in the course of reform.

2/   A normalization of China's external relations which permitted a more liberal trade policy could lead to the contrary results reflected in the Base Scenario (para. 5.49).

6.8   It is at this point that a serious dilemma emerges. The reform program is, at heart, an attempt to correct the mistakes of the old central planning system, and to introduce mechanisms in the economy that permit economic agents to take rational resource allocation decisions, instead of leaving such decisions to the planners. The program adopted at the Fifth Plenum suggests that the problems that have emerged during the course of the reform can now be solved by the very same mechanisms--price control, unified materials distribution, central investment approvals--responsible for the distortions that the reform was designed to correct. The emphasis on planning does not reflect a change in the predispositions of policymakers towards reforms, but a recognition of weaknesses in the instruments for macroeconomic control.

6.9   The strengthening of China's institutions responsible for macromanagement will require improvements in its budgetary, monetary and trade policies. The central budget, for example, should be a programming framework for all government current and capital expenditures, matched by tax revenues and other clearly defined sources of funds. Control of base money supply, through the lending and reserve ratio policies of the central bank, should gradually substitute for the use of credit controls. Interest rates should be employed more flexibly to manage savings and investment, within the framework of meaningful budget constraints on enterprises. Finally, ways should be sought to make the allocation of foreign exchange more market-determined.

6.10   Regarding pricing and marketing, it is important that the government reaffirm its commitment to moving towards market-determined prices. Recently imposed price controls should be removed as soon as possible and a plan of action specifying priorities for future price reform developed. The prices of key agricultural commodities and of several basic inputs for industry are candidates for early action. Parallel to price reforms, it is equally important that impediments to the free interprovincial flow of commodities be removed and that the list of goods still subject to quantitative allocation be reduced further.

6.11   During the period when macroeconomic and price reforms are being conducted any significant easing of the monetary policy could jeopardize the stability that has been so painfully achieved. The time to relax austerity measures should be after fundamental macromanagement problems and price distortions have been removed. As indicated in earlier chapters, the current downturn in the economy and the consensus regarding the macro framework present an excellent opportunity for proceeding with price adjustments.

The Longer-Term Agenda

6.12   China has brought plan and market together under one roof but the relationship is proving more stressful than was anticipated. Simulating markets within a framework of planning and collective ownership has yielded mixed results;a/ and seeking enterprise autonomy through administrative decentralization has proven to be problematic. In this respect, China's experience replicates that of countries like Hungary, with an even longer history of reform. One fact is emblematic. Between 1968 and 1980, bankruptcy was practically unknown in Hungary. Instead of being liquidated, virtually all the lossmakers were rescued by the state.b/ Much the same can be said for China.

---

a/ Lettered footnotes are to be found in Annex II.

Competitive forces have not been allowed to weed out the weak, only two enterprises having been consigned to bankruptcy. Market and plan pull in different
directions and when efficiency collides with employment security, and the
imperatives of annual production targets, the market is the one made to
yield.c/

6.13   In the early stages of reform, the difficulties of coordinating plan
with the market tends to be obscured. When controls are slipped and material
incentives enhanced, resource utilization long held at suboptimal levels,
improves markedly, resulting in high rates of growth. Once the economy
approaches the production frontier and its expansion slows, the contradictions
are more apparent. If a transition from a planned to a more market-centered
system is intended, the time to do this is when the economy is still in the
catching-up phase and growth momentum is high. Many of the costs in terms of
dislocation and unemployment can be minimized when the economy is at full
stretch. China's development prospects in the nineties will depend on specific economic policies and the continuation of institutional reforms, some of
which were outlined in Chapters 3-5. After a series of reform cycles, the
sources of systemic instability can be identified. It is also possible to
make some educated guesses as to the path China must tread in its pursuit of
efficiency and technological dynamism, the wellsprings of growth in a modern
economy.

Decentralization and Enterprise Reform

6.14   Administrative decentralization, as currently practiced, may not be
the recipe for the longer term. From the very outset, the People's Republic
has been ambivalent about bureaucratic formalization. In the late fifties and
again ten years later, the center transferred power to provincial authorities
and sought to minimize the role of the government bureaucracy (Chapter 1).
Instead of managing the economy using mainly bureaucratic machinery, the state
drew heavily on its capacity for political mobilization to achieve its ends.d/
This approach gave added impetus to historical tendencies towards localism.
It also detracted from the institutionalization of the center's administrative
powers and the creation of a system geared for routine management of economic
activities. While local administration became increasingly better articula-
ted, the central government's ability to intervene at the microlevel was
modest, except when the full political energies were brought to bear through
periodic rectification campaigns. To compensate for its administrative weakness and assure at least the fiscal responsiveness of the coastal provinces

with surplus revenues, the center relied upon the nomenklatura system.3/
Provincial governors and city mayors were usually not from the provinces to
which they were appointed and the senior leaders of the key provinces were
often drawn from central economic ministries.e/

6.15   When the push to decentralize commenced in the late seventies, it was
difficult for the reformers to do what was needed, which was to greatly
enhance the central government's capacity for routine macroeconomic management, while freeing enterprises from the coils of local agencies and giving
them a meaningful degree of autonomy (Chapter 1). Decentralization made local
authorities more independent and brought about a decline in the center's ability to direct the evolution of a market system, to stimulate competition and
to introduce rules that would promote orderliness and check abuses. The rise
to mayoral positions of men, many of whom are from the cities they now manage,
has increased the pull of local interests.f/ It has also complicated the center's efforts at preserving macroeconomic stability and introducing further
reforms.

6.16   Attempting to reverse decentralization would most likely incur very
high economic costs and might not restore the central government's control.
By the same token, a loss of local initiative at this stage could lead to
stagnation without stemming the steady erosion of central discretionary power.
It is vital that the central government use the breathing space afforded by
the political consensus underlying the current rectification program to make
decentralization work on an economic plane as it was originally intended to
do. Instead of strong local governments and dependent enterprises, each
linked to its supervisory agency by the umbilical cord of a soft budget constraint, there is a need for autonomous enterprises, disciplined by the market
and subject to general rules defined by central regulatory agencies. It is
only by freeing enterprises from the grasp of local governments that the center can circumscribe local political influence and continue with the work of
developing an integrated as well as an efficient national economy. This is an
essential part of enterprise reform (Chapter 4).

6.17   A more durable political consensus on future goals and how they are
to be reached must reverse the trend towards localism, protectionism and zero-
sum gamesmanship (Chapter 4). As worries regarding the distribution of income
and wealth are at the core of the problem, both political and market processes

---

3/ The zhiwu mingcheng hiao (nomenklatura) system comprises lists of leading
    positions over which Party committees have powers of appointment. These
    extend from the central government all the way down to the 2,000 county-
    level units, and are the main vehicle through which Party control is
    exercised. In November 1987, the Thirteenth Party Congress endorsed further
    decentralization of appointments and the gradual dissolution of the Party
    core groups found in all central and local organizations. While some
    attempts were made to implement this in 1988 and work was begun on the
    creation of a professional civil service, the status of reforms in this area
    is uncertain. "China's Nomenklatura System," John P. Burns, Problems of
    Communism, September/October 1987, pp. 36-38, 50-51; and "China's Civil
    Service Reforms: The 13th Party Congress Proposals," by John P. Burns,
    China Quarterly, No. 120, December 1989.

will have to be employed: market avenues to promote factor mobility, which will multiply employment opportunities and the prospects for earnings higher returns on labor and capital; and, political understandings that accommodate some fluidity in income distribution, so that market signals can produce actual results. The two mechanisms must work side by side. Arms-length market arrangements to loosen the hold of local networks, to lessen the incidence of negotiation, and to render decisions regarding prices, wages and resource use as impersonal transactions. Thus, the market can erode parochialism and diffuse interprovincial rivalry, making room for the national political consciousness that will underwrite a dynamic economic strategy. For people to frame their decisions with reference to the national interest, impersonal market forces that are viewed as basically fair should dislodge localism. Furthermore, the center must subsume local into national interests by redefining the fundamentals of its long-term reform strategy and show that it has both the resolve and the institutional ability to see it through.

6.18   In this context, a continuing support for a wider spectrum of ownership which provides a secure legal basis for TVEs, and private business would greatly enhance the robustness of the market system and introduce a pattern of financial accountability, that enterprises in the dominant state sector could be induced to emulate.g/

Labor Market

6.19   Employment and wage-setting practices will have a profound influence on cost-push and on productivity growth. Tenurial arrangements can moderate wage demands but only in the context of a functioning labor market that permits mobility and the right of firms to employ and dismiss workers. Present rigidities, by binding workers and enterprises, breed inefficiency and make it difficult to resist the demands of employees. Progress with labor contracting and experimental social security reforms that transfer pension and health obligations from enterprises to the government, and that privatize housing could remove major barriers to market functioning.h/ In many countries, profit-sharing within enterprises has a measurable effect on productivity, especially when it partially substitutes for wages. Bonus payments to Chinese workers might be restructured so that the link with profits and productivity is made tighter and bonuses are not simply add-ons to wages.i/ Again, this is something that may require price and ownership reforms before it can be introduced in an efficient fashion.

Social Security

6.20   A social security system that is enterprise based not only impairs labor mobility, but also limits enterprise autonomy and efficiency. Social security reforms that transfer the financial responsibility for pensions from enterprises to provincial or central authorities would facilitate reforms of prices and taxes which are, at times, manipulated to subsidize firms burdened with heavy pension payments. This would also allow the government to tackle, in a comprehensive manner, the financial implications arising from a growing number of retirees and lengthening life spans.

Industry

6.21   A major goal should be institutional developments that facilitate entry and exit of industrial firms, not just those in the township and village sector, but state and collective enterprises as well. These should be combined with policies that help modify the composition of the manufacturing system. As China moves towards production and demand patterns observed in other industrial economies, subsectors producing consumer durables, electronics and transport equipment might be best positioned to play the leading role. The claims of heavy industry on resources will have to be moderated and increased volume of investment allowed to flow to industries favored by income elasticities as well as technology.

6.22   Investment allocation and the absorption of technology made available through R&D, direct foreign investment and licensing will strongly influence trends in productivity and China's success as an exporter. Industrial productivity, by defining the scope for a transfer of resources to agriculture, will also affect supplies of foodstuffs along with the degree of self-sufficiency.

Resource Mobilization

6.23   Savings is the remaining key element in the long-run growth equation. High savings yields inestimable benefits: without it, China could not afford the levels of investment that have underwritten growth. It permits the country to absorb external shocks without undue hardship and reduces reliance on foreign capital. And it gives the government flexibility with respect to expenditure policies, because modest deficits can be financed in a noninflationary manner without excessive crowding out. Growth and savings follow each other in a virtuous circle.j/ Private financial savings can also, to an extent, be buoyed by interest rate policy.k/ Demographic and other factors are likely to sustain China's saving performance with some help from financial policy.l/ If resource mobilization of a high order can be combined with flexible, market-directed allocation, China would be well placed to realize its growth potential.

6.24   How China's economy fares during the nineties depends, substantially, on the institutional changes that are put in train and on the steady implementation of reforms already identified. But the willingness as well as the ability to institute these changes is likely to be significantly influenced by the nature of the international environment. Limitations on access to capital markets; emergence of trade barriers; and a declining flow of foreign direct investment may inhibit a further opening of the Chinese economy and slow the process of integration with the world economy which the authorities have pursued over the last decade. These developments could lead the government to reverse some of the reform measures being adopted or planned and to seek economic security through greater planning. The longer term costs of such unfavorable developments could be high.

ANNEX   I

STATISTICAL   ANNEX

Table 1.1 : CHINA: National Accounts
(in billions of yuan in Current prices)

ORIGIN AND USE OF RESOURCES	1978	1979	1980	1981	1982	1983	1984	1985	1986	1987	1988	1989
A.1. GDP at market prices	358.81	399.87	447.15	477.51	518.58	578.46	692.44	854.06	971.99	1135.71	1385.77	1573.11
2. Net indirect taxes	..	..	..	..	..	..	..	..	..	..	..	..
3. GDP at factor cost	117.55	146.35	160.75	182.89	209.72	234.91	275.94	302.68	335.24	384.32	449.54	..
4. Agriculture	177.25	194.34	218.66	223.00	237.10	261.23	308.34	384.16	440.31	519.36	639.53	..
5. Industry	64.01	59.18	67.74	71.63	71.77	82.32	108.16	167.23	196.44	232.03	296.69	..
6. Services, etc.												
B.1. Resource balance	-0.63	-1.29	-0.12	3.88	10.04	6.25	2.66	-36.11	-30.99	-1.06	-12.45	-11.28
2. Exports of GNFS	17.70	23.07	29.77	41.41	46.54	48.52	66.25	87.98	117.15	159.79	193.20	213.80
3. Imports of GNFS	18.34	24.37	29.89	37.53	36.50	42.27	63.59	124.09	148.15	160.85	205.64	225.06
C.1. Domestic absorption	359.45	401.16	447.27	473.63	508.54	572.21	689.78	890.17	1002.99	1136.77	1398.22	1584.37
D.1. Total consumption, etc	239.65	261.61	303.29	334.19	354.52	396.20	465.61	559.45	620.75	691.81	859.34	1012.16
2. Private, etc	188.84	215.41	251.17	279.33	304.08	332.93	383.11	478.50	544.05	621.85	781.67	..
3. General government	50.81	46.20	52.12	54.87	50.45	63.27	82.50	80.95	76.70	69.96	77.67	..
E.1. Gross domestic investment	119.80	139.55	143.98	139.43	154.02	176.01	224.18	330.72	382.23	444.96	538.88	572.21
2. Fixed investment	96.28	100.69	107.39	96.10	123.04	143.01	183.29	254.32	301.96	364.09	449.65	400.00
3. Increase in stocks	23.52	38.87	36.60	43.33	30.98	33.01	40.89	76.41	80.27	80.87	89.23	172.21
Memorandum Items:												
G.1. Net factor income	-0.01	-0.07	-0.15	-0.21	0.72	2.44	3.76	2.74	0.61	-0.61	-0.47	-5.41
2. Net current transfers	1.01	1.02	0.98	0.79	1.00	0.86	0.71	0.50	0.88	0.93	-1.23	-0.80
3. Gross national product	358.80	399.80	447.00	477.30	519.30	580.90	696.20	856.80	972.60	1135.10	1385.30	1567.70
H.1. Gross domestic saving	119.17	138.26	143.86	143.32	164.06	182.26	226.84	294.61	351.24	443.90	526.43	580.95
2. Gross national saving	120.16	139.21	144.67	143.90	165.78	185.56	231.30	297.85	352.73	444.21	524.73	554.74
J.1. IFS conversion factor	1.684	1.555	1.498	1.705	1.893	1.976	2.320	2.937	3.453	3.722	3.722	3.805
K.1. GDP at mp (curr. mill. US$)	213072	257161	298498	280065	273948	292745	298466	290794	281492	305134	372318	413395

Source: CHINA Statistical year book 1988 pp.26, 44, 493, and 643 and IMF Recent Economic Developments 01/17/90.
Exports and Imports of goods and non-factor services are from customs statistics.
See Table 2.1 for explanation.

For 1989 average exchange rate allowing for devaluation in December.

Table 1.2 : CHINA : National Accounts
(in billions of yuan in Constant 1980 prices)

	1978	1979	1980	1981	1982	1983	1984	1985	1986	1987	1988	1989
ORIGIN AND USE OF RESOURCES												
A.1. GDP at market prices	392.76	420.25	447.15	469.06	507.99	557.78	633.08	716.01	773.29	854.48	950.19	987.24
2. Net indirect taxes	..	..	..	..	..	..	..	..	..	..	..	..
3. GDP at factor cost	..	..	..	..	..	..	..	..	..	..	..	..
4. Agriculture	153.85	163.70	160.75	172.16	192.31	208.65	235.78	239.79	248.66	260.59	268.93	277.81
5. Industry	182.39	197.17	218.66	222.37	235.72	258.82	297.38	355.67	389.81	445.55	537.78	582.42
6. Services, etc.	56.52	59.39	67.74	74.52	79.97	90.31	99.92	120.56	134.82	148.34	143.47	127.02
B.1. Resource balance	-0.69	-1.36	-0.12	3.39	9.12	8.01	7.68	-7.14	3.36	13.16	13.27	8.44
2. Exports of GNFS	19.38	24.25	29.77	36.61	38.87	39.08	45.74	50.16	61.92	73.46	86.12	90.05
3. Imports of GNFS	20.07	25.61	29.89	33.22	29.75	31.07	38.05	57.29	58.56	60.31	72.86	81.61
C.1. Domestic absorption	393.46	421.61	447.27	465.67	498.87	549.76	625.39	723.15	769.93	841.33	936.92	978.80
D.1. Total consumption, etc	262.33	274.94	303.29	328.71	348.00	380.05	420.45	445.91	465.84	506.55	567.42	619.68
2. Private, etc	215.11	225.45	251.17	259.02	274.22	299.48	331.31	351.38	367.08	399.16	447.13	488.30
3. General government	47.22	49.49	52.12	69.69	73.78	80.57	89.13	94.53	98.76	107.39	120.29	131.37
E.1. Gross domestic investment	131.13	146.67	143.98	136.97	150.87	169.72	204.95	277.24	304.09	334.78	369.50	359.12
2. Fixed investment	105.38	105.82	107.39	94.40	120.53	137.89	167.57	213.21	240.23	273.93	308.32	251.03
3. Increase in stocks	25.75	40.85	36.60	42.57	30.35	31.82	37.37	64.03	63.85	60.85	61.18	108.09
Memorandum Items:												
G.1. Net factor income	-0.01	-0.07	-0.15	-0.21	0.70	2.34	3.41	2.22	0.47	-0.45	-0.31	-3.34
2. Net current transfers	1.10	1.07	0.98	0.78	0.98	0.83	0.64	0.41	0.68	0.69	-0.83	-0.50
3. Gross national product	392.75	420.18	447.00	468.85	508.69	560.12	636.48	718.23	773.76	854.03	949.87	983.90
H.1. Gross domestic saving	130.44	145.31	143.86	140.40	159.06	174.31	206.54	260.57	291.83	334.38	365.09	355.04
2. Gross national saving	131.52	146.31	144.67	140.97	160.74	177.48	210.59	263.20	292.98	334.62	363.95	351.20
I.1. Capacity to import	19.38	24.25	29.77	36.65	37.93	35.67	39.65	40.62	46.31	59.91	68.44	77.53
2. Terms of trade adjustment	-0.00	0.00	0.00	0.05	-0.94	-3.42	-6.09	-9.53	-15.61	-13.55	-17.68	-12.53
3. Gross domestic income	392.76	420.25	447.15	469.11	507.05	554.36	626.99	706.47	757.68	840.93	932.51	974.72
4. Gross national income	392.75	420.18	447.00	468.90	507.76	556.70	630.39	708.70	758.14	840.48	932.20	971.38
J.1. GDP at current mp	358.81	399.87	447.15	477.51	518.58	578.46	692.44	854.06	971.99	1135.71	1385.77	1573.11

Source: CHINA Statistical Year Book 1988, and Statistical Abstract 1989.

Table 1.3 : CHINA: National Accounts
(Implicit price deflators 1980=100)

	1978	1979	1980	1981	1982	1983	1984	1985	1986	1987	1988	1989
ORIGIN AND USE OF RESOURCES												
A.1. GDP at market prices	91.4	95.1	100.0	101.8	102.1	103.7	109.4	119.3	125.7	132.9	145.8	159.3
2. Net indirect taxes	..	..	..	..	..	..	..	..	..	..	..	..
3. GDP at factor cost	..	..	..	..	..	..	..	..	..	..	..	..
4. Agriculture	76.4	89.4	100.0	106.2	109.1	112.6	117.0	126.2	134.8	147.5	167.2	..
5. Industry	97.2	98.6	100.0	100.3	100.6	100.9	103.7	108.0	113.0	116.6	118.9	..
6. Services, etc.	113.3	99.6	100.0	96.1	89.7	91.2	108.2	138.7	146.7	156.4	206.8	..
B.1. Terms of Trade (Px/Pm)	100.0	100.0	100.0	100.1	97.6	91.3	86.7	81.0	74.8	81.6	79.5	86.1
2. Exports of GNFS	91.4	95.1	100.0	113.1	119.7	124.1	144.9	175.4	189.2	217.5	224.3	237.4
3. Imports of GNFS	91.4	95.1	100.0	113.0	122.7	136.0	167.1	216.6	253.0	266.7	282.3	275.8
C.1. Domestic absorption	91.4	95.1	100.0	101.7	101.9	104.1	110.3	123.1	130.3	135.1	149.2	161.9
D.1. Total consumption, etc	91.4	95.1	100.0	101.7	101.9	104.2	110.7	125.5	133.3	136.6	151.4	163.3
2. Private, etc	87.8	95.5	100.0	107.8	110.9	111.2	115.6	136.2	148.2	155.8	174.8	..
3. General government	107.6	93.3	100.0	78.7	68.4	78.5	92.6	85.6	77.7	65.1	64.6	..
E.1. Gross domestic investment	91.4	95.1	100.0	101.8	102.1	103.7	109.4	119.3	125.7	132.9	145.8	159.3
2. Fixed investment	91.4	95.1	100.0	101.8	102.1	103.7	109.4	119.3	125.7	132.9	145.8	159.3
3. Increase in stocks	91.4	95.1	100.0	101.8	102.1	103.7	109.4	119.3	125.7	132.9	145.8	159.3
Memorandum Items:												
F.1. Net factor income	91.4	95.1	100.0	101.7	101.9	104.1	110.3	123.1	130.3	135.1	149.2	161.9
2. Net current transfers	91.4	95.1	100.0	101.7	101.9	104.1	110.3	123.1	130.3	135.1	149.2	161.9
3. Gross national product	91.4	95.1	100.0	101.8	102.1	103.7	109.4	119.3	125.7	132.9	145.8	159.3
G.1. Gross domestic saving	91.4	95.1	100.0	102.1	103.1	104.6	109.8	113.1	120.4	132.8	144.2	158.0
2. Gross national saving	91.4	95.1	100.0	102.1	103.1	104.6	109.8	113.2	120.4	132.8	144.2	158.0

Source: Table 1.1 divided by Table 1.2.

Table 1.4 : CHINA : National Accounts
(Percentage GROWTH RATES in Current prices)

	1978	1979	1980	1981	1982	1983	1984	1985	1986	1987	1988	1989
ORIGIN AND USE OF RESOURCES												
A.1. GDP at market prices		11.4	11.8	6.8	8.6	11.5	19.7	23.3	13.8	16.8	22.0	13.5
2. Net indirect taxes		..	..	..	..	..	..	..	..	..	..	..
3. GDP at factor cost												
4. Agriculture		24.5	9.8	13.8	14.7	12.0	17.5	9.7	10.8	14.6	17.0	..
5. Industry		9.6	12.5	2.0	6.3	10.2	18.0	24.6	14.6	18.0	23.1	..
6. Services, etc.		-7.5	14.5	5.7	0.2	14.7	31.4	54.6	17.5	18.1	27.9	..
B.1. Resource balance												
2. Exports of GNFS		30.3	29.0	39.1	12.4	4.3	36.5	32.8	33.2	36.4	20.9	10.7
3. Imports of GNFS		32.9	22.6	25.8	-2.8	15.8	50.4	95.1	19.4	8.6	27.8	9.4
C.1. Domestic absorption		11.6	11.5	5.9	7.4	12.5	20.5	29.1	12.7	13.3	23.0	13.3
D.1. Total consumption, etc		9.2	15.9	10.2	6.1	11.8	17.5	20.2	11.0	11.4	24.2	17.8
2. Private, etc		14.1	16.8	11.2	8.9	9.5	15.1	24.9	13.7	14.3	25.7	..
3. General government		-9.1	12.8	5.3	-8.1	25.4	30.4	-1.9	-5.2	-8.8	11.0	..
E.1. Gross domestic investment		16.5	3.2	-3.2	10.5	14.3	27.4	47.5	15.6	16.4	21.1	6.2
2. Fixed investment		..	..	..	28.0	16.2	28.2	38.8	18.7	20.6	23.5	-11.0
3. Increase in stocks		..	..	..	-28.5	6.5	23.9	86.9	5.1	0.8	10.3	93.0
Memorandum Items:												
G.1. Net factor income		..	..	..	..	..	..	..	..	..	..	..
2. Net current transfers		..	..	..	..	..	..	..	..	..	..	..
3. Gross national product		11.4	11.8	6.8	8.8	11.9	19.8	23.1	13.5	16.7	22.0	13.2
H.1. Gross domestic saving		16.0	4.1	-0.4	14.5	11.1	24.5	29.9	19.2	26.4	18.6	6.6
2. Gross national saving		15.9	3.9	-0.5	15.2	11.9	24.6	28.8	18.4	25.9	18.1	5.7
J.1. IFS conversion factor		-7.7	-3.7	13.8	11.0	4.4	17.4	26.6	17.6	7.8	0.0	2.2
K.1. GDP at mp (curr. mill. US$)		20.7	16.1	-6.2	-2.2	6.9	2.0	-2.6	-3.2	8.4	22.0	11.0

Source: Table 1.1.

Table 1.5 : CHINA: National Accounts
(Percentage GROWTH RATES in Constant 1980 prices)

ORIGIN AND USE OF RESOURCES	1978	1979	1980	1981	1982	1983	1984	1985	1986	1987	1988	1989
A.1. GDP at market prices		7.0	6.4	4.9	8.3	9.8	13.5	13.1	8.0	10.5	11.2	3.9
2. Net indirect taxes		..	..	..	..	..	..	..	..	..	..	..
3. GDP at factor cost		..	..	..	..	..	..	..	..	..	..	..
4. Agriculture		6.4	-1.8	7.1	11.7	8.5	13.0	1.7	3.7	4.8	3.2	3.3
5. Industry		8.1	10.9	1.7	6.0	9.8	14.9	19.6	9.6	14.3	20.7	8.3
6. Services, etc.		5.1	14.1	10.0	7.3	12.9	10.6	20.7	11.8	10.0	-3.3	-11.5
B.1. Resource balance		..	..	..	..	..	..	..	..	..	..	..
2. Exports of GNFS		25.1	22.7	23.0	6.2	0.6	17.0	9.7	23.5	18.6	17.2	4.6
3. Imports of GNFS		27.6	16.7	11.1	-10.4	4.5	22.5	50.6	2.2	3.0	20.8	12.0
C.1. Domestic absorption		7.2	6.1	4.1	7.1	10.2	13.8	15.6	6.5	9.3	11.4	4.5
D.1. Total consumption, etc		4.8	10.3	8.4	5.9	9.2	10.6	6.1	4.5	8.7	12.0	9.2
2. Private, etc		4.8	11.4	3.1	5.9	9.2	10.6	6.1	4.5	8.7	12.0	9.2
3. General government		4.8	5.3	33.7	5.9	9.2	10.6	6.1	4.5	8.7	12.0	9.2
E.1. Gross domestic investment		11.8	-1.8	-4.9	10.2	12.5	20.8	35.3	9.7	10.1	10.4	-2.8
2. Fixed investment		..	..	..	27.7	14.4	21.5	27.2	12.7	14.0	12.6	-18.6
3. Increase in stocks		..	..	..	-28.7	4.9	17.4	71.3	-0.3	-4.7	0.5	76.7
Memorandum Items:												
G.1. Net factor income		..	..	..	..	..	..	..	..	..	..	..
2. Net current transfers		..	..	..	..	..	..	..	..	..	..	..
3. Gross national product		7.0	6.4	4.9	8.5	10.1	13.8	12.8	7.7	10.4	11.2	3.6
H.1. Gross domestic saving		11.4	-1.0	-2.4	13.3	9.6	18.5	26.2	12.0	14.6	9.2	-2.8
2. Gross national saving		11.2	-1.1	-2.6	14.0	10.4	18.7	25.0	11.3	14.2	8.8	-3.5
I.1. Capacity to import		..	..	..	..	..	..	..	..	..	..	..
2. Terms of trade adjustment		7.0	6.4	4.9	8.1	9.3	13.1	12.7	7.2	11.0	10.9	4.5
3. Gross domestic income		7.0	6.4	4.9	8.1	9.3	13.1	12.7	7.2	11.0	10.9	4.5
4. Gross national income		7.0	6.4	4.9	8.3	9.6	13.2	12.4	7.0	10.9	10.9	4.2
J.1. GDP at current mp		11.4	11.8	6.8	8.6	11.5	19.7	23.3	13.8	16.8	22.0	13.5

Source: Table 1.2.

Table 1.6 : CHINA: National Accounts
(Percentage GROWTH RATES of Implicit price deflators)

ORIGIN AND USE OF RESOURCES	1978	1979	1980	1981	1982	1983	1984	1985	1986	1987	1988	1989
A.1. GDP at market prices		4.2	5.1	1.8	0.3	1.6	5.5	9.1	5.4	5.7	9.7	9.3
2. Net indirect taxes		..	..	..	..	..	..	..	..	..	..	..
3. GDP at factor cost		..	..	..	..	..	..	..	..	..	..	..
4. Agriculture		17.0	11.9	6.2	2.7	3.2	3.9	7.9	6.8	9.4	13.3	..
5. Industry		1.4	1.5	0.3	0.3	0.3	2.7	4.2	4.6	3.2	2.0	..
6. Services, etc.		-12.0	0.4	-3.9	-6.6	1.6	18.8	28.1	5.0	7.4	32.2	..
B.1. Terms of Trade (Px/Pm)		0.0	0.0	0.1	-2.5	-6.5	-5.0	-6.6	-7.7	9.0	-2.5	8.3
2. Exports of GNFS		4.2	5.1	13.1	5.8	3.7	16.7	21.1	7.9	15.0	3.1	5.8
3. Imports of GNFS		4.2	5.1	13.0	8.6	10.9	22.8	29.6	16.8	5.4	5.8	-2.3
C.1. Domestic absorption		4.2	5.1	1.7	0.2	2.1	6.0	11.6	5.8	3.7	10.4	8.5
D.1. Total consumption, etc		4.2	5.1	1.7	0.2	2.3	6.2	13.3	6.2	2.5	10.9	7.9
2. Private, etc		8.8	4.7	7.8	2.8	0.3	4.0	17.8	8.8	5.1	12.2	..
3. General government		-13.2	7.1	-21.3	-13.1	14.8	17.9	-7.5	-9.3	-16.1	-0.9	..
E.1. Gross domestic investment		4.1	5.1	1.8	0.3	1.6	5.5	9.1	5.4	5.7	9.7	9.3
2. Fixed investment		..	..	..	0.3	1.6	5.5	9.1	5.4	5.7	9.7	9.3
3. Increase in stocks		..	..	..	0.3	1.6	5.5	9.1	5.3	5.7	9.7	9.2
Memorandum Items:												
F.1. Net factor income		4.2	5.1	1.7	0.2	2.1	6.0	11.6	5.8	3.7	10.4	8.5
2. Net current transfers		..	5.1	1.7	0.2	2.1	6.0	11.6	5.8	3.7	10.4	8.5
3. Gross national product		4.2	5.1	1.8	0.3	1.6	5.5	9.1	5.4	5.7	9.7	9.3
G.1. Gross domestic saving		4.1	5.1	2.1	1.0	1.4	5.0	3.0	6.4	10.3	8.6	9.6
2. Gross national saving		4.1	5.1	2.1	1.0	1.4	5.1	3.0	6.4	10.3	8.6	9.6

Source: Table 1.3.

Table 1.7: CHINA: Sources of Growth (in Constant 1980 Prices)

	1978	1979	1980	1981	1982	1983	1984	1985	1986	1987	1988	1989
GDP growth rate (actual)	..	7.00	6.40	4.90	8.30	9.80	13.50	13.10	8.00	10.50	11.20	3.90
SUPPLY SIDE												
Agriculture growth rate	..	6.40	-1.80	7.10	11.70	8.50	13.00	1.70	3.70	4.80	3.20	3.30
Industry growth rate	..	8.10	10.90	1.70	6.00	9.80	14.90	19.60	9.60	14.30	20.70	8.30
Services growth rate	..	5.08	14.08	10.01	7.31	12.93	10.64	20.66	11.83	10.03	-3.28	-11.47
Agriculture Share into GDP	39.17	38.95	35.95	36.70	37.86	37.41	37.24	33.49	32.16	30.50	28.30	28.14
Industry Share into GDP	46.44	46.92	48.90	47.41	46.40	46.40	46.97	49.67	50.41	52.14	56.60	58.99
Services Share into GDP	14.39	14.13	15.15	15.89	15.74	16.19	15.78	16.84	17.43	17.36	15.10	12.87
Total Share	100.00	100.00	100.00	100.00	100.00	100.00	100.00	100.00	100.00	100.00	100.00	100.00
Agr. Share of last year * Weight	..	2.51	-0.70	2.55	4.29	3.22	4.86	0.63	1.24	1.54	0.98	0.93
Ind. Share of last year * Weight	..	3.76	5.11	0.83	2.84	4.55	6.91	9.21	4.77	7.21	10.79	4.70
Ser. Share of last year * Weight	..	0.73	1.99	1.52	1.16	2.03	1.72	3.26	1.99	1.75	-0.57	-1.73
Weighted Average Growth rate	..	7.00	6.40	4.90	8.30	9.80	13.50	13.10	8.00	10.50	11.20	3.90
DEMAND SIDE												
Total Consumption growth rate	..	4.81	10.31	8.38	5.87	9.21	10.63	6.06	4.47	8.74	12.02	9.21
Gross Domestic Investment gr. rate	..	11.85	-1.83	-4.87	10.15	12.49	20.76	35.27	9.68	10.09	10.37	-2.81
Exports of goods & NFS growth rate	..	25.13	22.75	22.98	6.18	0.55	17.02	9.67	23.46	18.64	17.23	4.57
Imports of goods & NFS growth rate	..	27.57	16.70	11.15	-10.44	4.45	22.47	50.56	2.21	2.98	20.80	12.02
C Share into GDP	66.79	65.42	67.83	70.08	68.50	68.14	66.41	62.28	60.24	59.28	59.72	62.77
GDI Share into GDP	33.39	34.90	32.20	29.20	29.70	30.43	32.37	38.72	39.32	39.18	38.89	36.38
EXPGNFS Share into GDP	4.93	5.77	6.66	7.80	7.65	7.01	7.22	7.00	8.01	8.60	9.06	9.12
IMPGNFS Share into GDP	-5.11	-6.09	-6.68	-7.08	-5.86	-5.57	-6.01	-8.00	-7.57	-7.06	-7.67	-8.27
Total Share	100.00	100.00	100.00	100.00	100.00	100.00	100.00	100.00	100.00	100.00	100.00	100.00
C Share(-1) * Weight	..	3.21	6.74	5.68	4.11	6.31	7.24	4.02	2.78	5.26	7.12	5.50
GDI Share(-1)* Weight	..	3.96	-0.64	-1.57	2.97	3.71	6.32	11.42	3.75	3.97	4.08	-1.09
EXPGNFS Share(-1) * Weight	..	1.24	1.31	1.53	0.48	0.04	1.19	0.70	1.64	1.49	1.48	0.41
IMPGNFS Share(-1) * Weight	..	-1.41	-1.02	-0.74	0.74	-0.26	-1.25	-3.04	-0.18	-0.23	-1.47	-0.92
Weighted Average Growth rate	..	7.00	6.40	4.90	8.30	9.80	13.50	13.10	8.00	10.50	11.20	3.9
Contribution to GDP growth in percent												
SUPPLY SIDE												
Agriculture	..	35.81	-10.96	52.09	51.74	32.83	36.02	4.83	15.49	14.70	8.71	23.95
Industry	..	53.74	79.90	16.97	34.27	46.40	51.21	70.28	59.61	68.65	96.37	120.45
Services	..	10.45	31.05	30.94	13.99	20.76	12.76	24.89	24.90	16.65	-5.08	-44.40
Total	..	100.00	100.00	100.00	100.00	100.00	100.00	100.00	100.00	100.00	100.00	100.00
DEMAND SIDE												
Total consumption	..	45.90	105.38	116.01	49.55	64.38	53.65	30.70	34.80	50.13	63.61	141.01
Gross domestic investment	..	56.52	-9.99	-32.02	35.72	37.85	46.79	87.17	46.87	37.80	36.28	-28.00
Exports of goods & NFS	..	17.71	20.51	31.22	5.82	0.43	8.83	5.33	20.54	14.21	13.23	10.61
Imports of goods & NFS	..	-20.13	-15.90	-15.20	8.91	-2.66	-9.27	-23.20	-2.21	-2.15	-13.11	-23.63
Total	..	100.00	100.00	100.00	100.00	100.00	100.00	100.00	100.00	100.00	100.00	100.00

Source: Table 1.2.

Table 1.8: CHINA: GROWTH RATES of Provincial Output
(in Constant Prices)

	1982	1983	1984	1985	1986	1987	Avg. 84-8	Coeff. Variation
1 Beijing	6.2	11.2	16.2	15.0	1.6	8.2	10.3	1.8
2 Tianjing	6.9	8.2	11.9	16.0	5.1	7.2	10.1	2.4
3 Hebei	10.0	12.6	15.4	13.3	5.2	10.4	11.0	2.9
4 Shanxi	14.6	11.0	21.1	8.1	4.1	3.1	9.1	1.3
5 Mongolia	14.8	8.7	15.5	14.1	1.5	6.3	9.4	1.6
6 Liaoning	5.9	10.6	15.8	12.3	7.9	9.9	11.5	3.9
7 Jilin	7.1	18.4	12.1	7.5	6.6	16.3	10.6	2.7
8 Heilongjiang	6.8	10.0	8.5	4.7	8.4	7.9	7.4	4.7
9 Shanghai	5.2	6.5	13.2	13.2	3.6	7.0	9.3	2.2
10 Jiangsu	9.4	11.9	19.5	16.9	10.2	10.4	14.3	3.5
11 Zhejiang	11.3	11.2	23.1	25.3	13.5	12.7	18.7	3.3
12 Anhui	9.8	6.6	19.7	16.2	10.3	8.2	13.6	3.0
13 Fujian	7.1	8.4	17.8	17.9	5.9	12.1	13.4	2.7
14 Jiangxi	9.7	6.1	11.5	14.5	6.2	9.6	10.5	3.5
15 Shandong	9.3	12.3	18.7	10.2	7.6	16.8	13.3	2.9
16 Henan	5.1	13.9	11.1	12.6	4.9	15.4	11.0	2.9
17 Hubei	13.8	10.5	20.5	16.6	4.8	7.8	12.4	2.0
18 Hunan	10.5	6.7	9.7	11.5	7.8	9.2	9.5	7.2
19 Guangdong	12.2	9.7	15.6	18.7	9.0	16.1	14.9	4.2
20 Guangxi	12.9	3.8	4.5	10.4	8.2	9.5	8.2	3.6
21 Sichuan	14.5	11.0	14.2	14.1	5.8	9.3	10.9	3.1
22 Guizhou	19.9	12.1	13.6	7.7	7.6	10.4	9.8	4.0
23 Yunnan	11.5	9.5	13.5	11.5	3.5	11.7	10.1	2.6
24 Tibet	0.3	-5.4	62.2	11.8	-9.2	11.4	19.1	0.7
25 Shanxi	13.7	9.3	17.1	15.5	6.3	9.0	12.0	2.7
26 Gansu	10.5	10.2	13.3	15.1	12.4	6.2	11.8	3.5
27 Qinghai	14.5	1.8	15.3	20.8	7.6	6.4	12.5	2.1
28 Ninghai	9.4	14.1	15.5	15.4	9.8	6.1	11.7	2.9
29 Xinjiang	11.1	12.8	12.9	14.3	9.1	9.1	11.4	4.9
Average growth rate of all Provinces	10.1	9.4	16.5	13.8	6.4	9.8		
Coefficient of Variation	2.6	2.2	1.7	3.3	1.6	3.0		

Source: CHINA: Statistical Year Book 1989 (Chinese) pp.34 for 1987; 1988 pp.46 for 1986; 1987 pp.42 for 1985; 1986 pp.46 for 1984; 1984 pp.28 for 1983; 1983 pp.23 for 1982; 1981 pp.19 for 1981.

NOTE: Used growth rates of GVAIO in Constant 1980 Prices for 1982-83; and growth rates of National Income for 1984-88.

Table 1.9: CHINA: Savings

(As a Percent of GNP)

	1980	1981	1982	1983	1984	1985	1986	1987	1988
Gross National Savings	..	30.1	31.0	31.3	36.5	36.0	37.8	39.3	37.9
State budget (Current Account Surplus)	..	7.0	5.6	5.8	6.5	7.0	5.8	4.5	3.1
Enterprises and other	..	..	14.1	14.3	15.7	15.6	17.6	18.5	18.0
Household	..	..	11.4	11.2	14.3	13.4	14.4	16.3	16.8
of which: Financial Savings	..	3.7	7.8	5.5	8.5	7.2	7.7	9.2	9.5

Source: IMF Recent Economic Developments 01/17/90 pp.41 for 1983-88, 01/30/89 pp.61 for 1983, 01/29/88 pp.6 for 1982, 10/21/86 pp.8 for 1981.

Table 2.1 : CHINA : Balance of Payments
(billions of US dollars)

	1978	1979	1980	1981	1982	1983	1984	1985	1986	1987	1988	1989
A.1. Exports of GNFS	10.513	14.838	19.952	24.290	24.574	24.554	28.567	29.957	33.926	42.934	51.905	56.183
2. Merchandise (FOB)	9.750	13.660	18.270	22.010	22.320	22.230	26.140	27.350	30.940	39.440	47.540	52.486
3. Non-factor services	0.763	1.178	1.682	2.280	2.254	2.324	2.427	2.607	2.986	3.494	4.365	3.697
B.1. Imports of GNFS	10.890	15.670	19.550	22.010	19.280	21.390	27.410	42.250	42.910	43.210	55.250	59.142
2. Merchandise (FOB)	9.986	14.369	17.927	20.183	17.680	19.615	25.135	38.743	39.348	39.624	50.664	54.233
3. Non-factor services	0.904	1.301	1.623	1.827	1.600	1.775	2.275	3.507	3.562	3.586	4.586	4.909
C.1. Resource balance	-0.377	-0.832	0.402	2.280	5.294	3.164	1.157	-12.293	-8.984	-0.276	-3.345	-2.959
D.1. Net factor income	-0.008	-0.045	-0.100	-0.124	0.378	1.233	1.620	0.932	0.176	-0.164	-0.126	-1.421
2. Factor receipts	0.236	0.305	0.512	0.697	1.017	1.528	2.008	1.478	1.100	1.027	1.504	1.876
a. of which labor income	..	..	..	..	..	0.075	0.086	0.091	0.199	0.051	0.035	0.044
3. Factor payments	0.244	0.350	0.612	0.821	0.639	0.295	0.388	0.546	0.924	1.191	1.630	3.097
a. of wh. LT interest (DRS)	..	..	0.317	0.519	0.543	0.525	0.611	0.588	0.646	1.117	1.593	2.267
E.1. Net current transfers (prv)	0.597	0.656	0.640	0.464	0.530	0.438	0.305	0.171	0.255	0.249	-0.331	-0.211
2. Transfer receipts	..	..	0.640	0.464	0.543	0.446	0.317	0.180	0.266	0.260	0.200	0.214
a. of wh. workers remit.	..	..	..	..	0.541	0.446	0.317	0.180	0.208	0.166	0.129	0.138
3. Transfer payments	..	..	..	..	0.013	0.010	0.012	0.009	0.011	0.011	0.531	0.425
F.1. Curr.Acct.Bal exc.off.trans	0.212	-0.221	0.942	2.620	6.202	4.833	3.082	-11.190	-8.553	-0.191	-3.802	-4.591
G.1. Long-term capital inflow	-0.830	0.822	1.760	0.631	0.409	1.172	1.608	4.337	7.058	5.790	7.056	3.383
2. Net direct investment	-0.069	-0.030	0.057	0.285	0.430	0.636	1.124	1.030	1.425	1.669	2.344	1.400
3. Net official transfers	..	..	-0.070	0.108	-0.044	0.075	0.137	0.072	0.124	-0.025	0.042	0.042
4. Net LT loans (DRS)	..	..	1.926	0.596	0.535	0.986	1.070	4.005	4.851	6.238	6.771	0.771
a. disbursements	..	..	2.539	1.800	1.837	2.375	2.357	5.302	6.725	8.152	8.868	2.908
b. repayments	..	..	0.613	1.204	1.302	1.389	1.287	1.297	1.874	1.914	2.097	2.137
5. Other LT inflows (net)	..	..	-0.153	-0.338	-0.512	-0.525	-0.723	-0.770	0.658	-2.092	-2.101	1.170
H.1. Other items (Net)	-0.130	0.002	-2.330	-1.326	-0.336	-1.912	-2.874	2.215	-0.496	-0.747	-1.018	-0.412
2. Net short-term capital	-1.231	-0.452	-4.001	-2.088	-0.821	-1.362	-1.942	1.650	-1.076	0.703	0.076	-0.010
3. Capital flows n.e.i.	0.000	0.000	0.000	0.000	0.000	0.000	0.000	0.000	0.000	0.000	0.000	0.000
4. Errors and omissions	1.101	0.454	1.671	0.762	0.485	-0.550	-0.932	0.565	0.580	-1.450	-1.094	-0.402
I.1. Changes in net reserves	0.748	-0.603	-0.372	-1.925	-6.275	-4.093	-1.816	4.638	1.991	-4.852	-2.236	1.620
2. Use of IMF credit	0.000	0.000	0.000	0.524	-0.027	-0.496	0.000	0.000	0.731	0.000	0.000	0.079
3. Other reserve changes	0.748	-0.603	-0.372	-2.449	-6.248	-3.597	-1.816	4.638	1.260	-4.852	-2.236	1.541

Source: CHINA Statistical year book 1988 pp.643 and IMF. Merchandise exports (fob), and merchandise imports (cif) are from Statistical year book of 1988 pp.643 (which are identical to customs statistics). Exports of non-factor services are from IMF recent economic developments 01/30/89. Merchandise fob imports are calculated by multiplying cif imports by a constant factor 0.917 (from IFS). Imports of non-factor services are calculated as the difference between CIF and FOB imports.

Table 2.2 : CHINA : Balance of Payments
(Percentage GROWTH RATES)

	1978	1979	1980	1981	1982	1983	1984	1985	1986	1987	1988	1989
A.1. Exports of GNFS	..	41.1	33.9	22.2	1.2	-0.1	16.3	4.9	13.3	26.5	20.9	8.2
2. Merchandise (FOB)		40.1	33.1	21.0	1.5	-0.4	17.5	4.7	13.1	27.5	20.5	10.4
3. Non-factor services		54.4	42.8	35.6	-1.1	3.1	4.4	7.4	14.5	17.0	24.9	-15.3
B.1. Imports of GNFS		43.9	27.3	10.3	-12.4	10.9	28.1	54.1	1.5	0.7	27.8	7.0
2. Merchandise (FOB)		43.9	27.3	10.3	-12.4	10.9	28.1	54.1	1.5	0.7	27.8	7.0
3. Non-factor services		43.9	27.3	10.3	-12.4	10.9	28.1	54.1	1.5	0.7	27.8	7.0
C.1. Resource balance	..	..	..	..	..	..	..	..	..	..	..	..
D.1. Net factor income		29.2	67.9	36.1	45.9	50.2	31.4	-26.4	-25.6	-6.6	46.4	11.5
2. Factor receipts		..	..	..	..	..	14.7	5.8	118.7	-74.4	-31.4	25.0
a. of which labor income		..	..	..	..	..	..	..	..	..	..	..
3. Factor payments		43.4	74.9	34.2	-22.2	-53.8	31.5	40.7	69.2	28.9	36.8	90.0
a. of wh. LT interest (DRS)		..	..	63.7	4.6	-3.3	16.4	-3.8	9.9	72.9	42.6	41.1
E.1. Net current transfers (prv)		..	..	..	..	..	..	..	..	..	..	..
2. Transfer receipts		..	..	..	..	..	..	..	..	..	..	..
a. of wh. workers remit.		..	..	..	..	..	..	..	..	..	..	..
3. Transfer payments		..	..	..	..	..	..	..	..	..	..	..
F.1. Curr.Acct.Bal exc.off.trans		..	..	..	..	..	..	..	..	..	..	..
G.1. Long-term capital inflow		..	114.1	-84.1	-35.2	186.6	37.2	169.7	62.7	-18.0	21.9	-52.1
2. Net direct investment		..	..	364.9	62.3	47.9	76.7	-8.4	38.3	17.1	40.4	-40.3
3. Net official transfers		..	..	-69.1	-10.2	84.3	8.5	274.3	21.1	28.6	8.6	-51.5
4. Net LT loans (DRS)		..	..	-29.1	2.1	29.3	-0.8	124.9	26.8	21.2	8.8	-38.9
a. disbursements		..	..	96.4	8.1	6.7	-7.3	0.8	44.5	2.1	9.5	1.9
b. repayments		..	..	..	..	..	..	..	..	..	..	..
5. Other LT inflows (net)		..	..	..	..	..	..	..	..	..	..	..
H.1. Other items (Net)		..	..	..	..	..	..	..	..	..	..	..
2. Net short-term capital		..	..	..	..	..	..	..	..	..	..	..
3. Capital flows n.e.i.		..	..	..	..	..	..	..	..	..	..	..
4. Errors and omissions		..	..	..	..	..	..	..	..	..	..	..
I.1. Changes in net reserves		..	..	..	..	..	..	..	..	..	..	..
2. Use of IMF credit		..	..	..	..	..	..	..	..	..	..	..
3. Other reserve changes		..	..	..	..	..	..	..	..	..	..	..

Source: Table 2.1.

Table 2.3: CHINA : Services
(In millions of U.S. Dollars)

	1979	1980	1981	1982	1983	1984	1985	1986	1987	1988	1989
A. Shipment of freight											
Credit	348	553	848	785	786	668	671	705	904	1308	1313
Debit	-906	-1187	-1181	-635	-739	-761	-1224	-850	-1186	-1387	-2493
B. Insurance											
Credit	68	127	225	202	203	224	196	229	252	345	180
Debit	-32	-66	176	89	110	-121	-69	-82	-142	-214	-195
C. Other transportation											
Credit	33	106	113	140	174	209	271	304	152	169	160
Debit	-12	..	..	..	..	..	..	..	..	..	..
D. Port expenses											
Credit	316	385	422	388	381	378	360	306	289	304	298
Debit	-376	-566	-710	-612	-614	-560	-300	-670	-456	-889	-835
E. Travel receipts											
Credit	413	511	672	703	767	922	979	1227	1693	2078	2016
Debit	..	..	-69	-66	-53	-150	-314	-308	-387	-633	-572
F. Profits											
Credit	..	..	..	20	31	2	6	..	10	..	..
Debit	..	..	..	1	..	..	-14	-15	-2	-8	-4
G. Interest											
Credit	..	..	..	5	707	925	484	216	177	427	906
Debit	..	..	..	-16	-41	-92	-68	-298	-457	-644	-1762
H. Bank interest and charges											
Credit	305	512	697	992	715	995	897	685	789	1042	2086
Debit	-350	-612	-821	-824	-254	-296	-464	-611	-732	-978	-1969
I. Posts											
Credit	..	..	..	..	..	..	..	..	..	24	24
Debit	..	..	..	..	..	..	..	..	..	11	4
J. Interofficial											
Credit	..	..	..	36	13	28	130	215	204	137	141
Debit	..	..	..	-159	-154	-223	-263	-251	-150	-277	-418
K. Labor income											
Credit	..	..	..	..	75	86	91	199	51	35	44
Debit	..	..	..	..	..	..	..	..	..	..	..
L. Other services											
Credit	210	215	123	482	423	384	448	841	892	458	652
Debit	-316	-272	-376	-643	-544	-563	-354	-115	-164	-193	-136
M. Total services											
Credit	1693	2409	3100	3753	4275	4819	4533	4927	5413	6327	7819
Debit	-1992	-2703	-2981	-2665	-2289	-2766	-3070	-3200	-3676	-5211	-8379
N. Factor Services (F+G+H+K)											
Receipts (Credit)	305	512	697	1017	1528	2008	1478	1100	1027	1504	3035
Payments (Debit)	-350	-612	-821	-639	-296	-388	-546	-924	-1191	-1630	-3735
O. Non-Factor Services (M-N-L)											
Receipts (Credit)	1178	1682	2280	2254	2324	2427	2607	2986	3494	4365	4132
Payments (Debit) (IMF def.)	-1326	-1819	-1784	-1383	-1450	-1815	-2170	-2161	-2321	-3389	-4508
Payments (Debit) (IFS def.)	-1301	-1623	-1827	-1600	-1775	-2275	-3507	-3562	-3586	-4586	-4586
(Imports cif customs basis * 0.083)											

Source: IMF Recent Economic Developments 01/17/90 pp.69 for 1984-89, 10/24/85 pp.115 for 1981-83, 11/03/83 pp.100 for 1979-80; and BESD data base file IMFBOPFC (which is identical to the data in IMF Recent Developments).

Table 2.4: CHINA : Transfers
(In millions of U.S. Dollars)

	1979	1980	1981	1982	1983	1984	1985	1986	1987	1988	1989
Private unrequited transfers (net)	656	840	464	530	436	305	171	255	249	416	279
Credit	..	..	..	..	..	..	180	266	260	428	293
Debit	..	..	..	..	..	..	-9	-11	-11	-12	-15
Nonresident remittances											
Credit	..	..	..	..	..	..	180	208	166	129	66
Debit	..	..	..	..	..	..	-3	-3	-3	-4	-3
Migrants' transfers											
Credit	..	..	..	..	..	..	..	58	94	299	227
Debit	..	..	..	..	..	..	-6	-8	-8	-8	-12
Public unrequited transfers (net)	-30	-70	108	-44	75	137	73	124	-25	3	171
International organizations											
Credit	..	..	..	..	..	..	63	140	58	61	181
Debit	..	..	..	..	..	..	-42	-44	-34	-19	-24
Grants and aid											
Credit	..	..	..	..	..	..	197	110	71	79	121
Debit	..	..	..	..	..	..	-145	-82	-120	-118	-107

Source: IMF Recent Economic Developments 01/17/90 pp.70 for 1985-9, 01/30/89 pp.89 for 84, 10/24/85 pp.115 for 1981-3,
11/03/83 pp.100 for 1979-80.

Table 3.1 : CHINA : Commodity Composition of Merchandise Exports
(US $ million)

		1980	1981	1982	1983	1984	1985	1986	1987	1988	198
PRIMARY GOODS	S0+S1+S2+S3+S4	9137	10251	10033	9623	11934	13828	11272	13231	14430	15026
FOOD	S0	2999	2925	2909	2854	3232	3803	4448	4781	5891	6145
of which											
Live animals chiefly for food	D00	:	:	:	:	326	304	338	348	386	395
Meat and meat products	D01	:	:	:	:	456	448	483	520	585	657
Fishes,shell-fish,molluscs etc.	D03	:	:	:	:	305	283	491	721	969	1039
Grain and grain products	D04	:	:	:	:	444	1065	898	579	682	719
Vegetables and fruits	D05	:	:	:	:	829	825	1092	1290	1674	1623
Coffee, tea,cocoa etc.	D07	:	:	:	:	449	435	466	488	524	568
NON-FOOD	S2	1728	2098	1810	2102	2421	2653	2908	3650	4257	4211
of which											
Oil seeds & oil-containing fruits	D22	:	:	:	:	505	487	580	674	684	645
Textile fibers etc.	D26	:	:	:	:	929	1145	1160	1508	1672	1546
Animal and vegetable raw materials	D29	60	89	78	105	442	398	486	645	724	844
MINERAL FUELS	S3	4273	5228	5314	4667	6027	7132	3683	4544	3972	4270
of which											
Coal, coke and briquettes	D32	:	:	:	:	322	349	455	536	594	680
Petroleum,petroleum products etc.	D33	:	:	:	:	5701	6777	3224	4003	3372	3581
OTHER	S1+S4	139	0	0	0	254	240	233	256	310	400
MANUFACTURED GOODS	S5+S6+S7+S8+S9	9051	11759	12297	12607	14195	13522	19670	26206	33111	37460
CHEMICALS & RELATED PRODUCTS	S5	1125	1342	1196	1251	1364	1358	1733	2235	2897	3201
of which											
Organic	D51	:	:	:	:	294	309	411	500	575	690
Inorganic	D52	:	:	:	:	283	287	379	553	762	794
LIGHT INDUSTRY	S6	4019	4706	4302	4366	5054	4493	5886	8570	10491	10897
of which											
Yarn,fabrics,manuf. goods etc.	D65	:	:	:	:	3093	3243	4220	5790	6458	6994
Non-metallic minerals	D66	:	:	:	:	260	227	317	439	579	793
Metal products	D67	:	:	:	:	477	426	553	797	1008	709
MACHINERY & TRANSPORT EQUIPMENT	S7	846	1087	1263	1220	1493	772	1094	1741	2769	3874
OTHER	S8	2850	3725	3702	3805	4687	3486	4948	6273	8268	10755
Clothing and garments	D84	:	:	:	:	2653	2050	2913	3749	4872	6130
PRODUCTS NOT CLASSIFIED ELSEWHERE	S9	210	899	1834	1965	1597	3413	6009	7387	8685	8734
TOTAL		18188	22010	22330	22230	26129	27350	30942	39437	47541	52486

Source: CHINA Customs Statistics 1990.1 pp.13 for 1989; 1989.1 pp.17 for 1988; CHINA Statistical Year Book 1988 pp.644 for 1987, 1986;
1987 pp.520 for 1985; 1986 pp.482 for 1984; 1985 pp.494 for 1983; 1984 pp.381 for 1982;
1983 pp.405 for 1981; 1981 pp.73 for 1980.

Table 3.2 : CHINA : Commodity Composition of Merchandise Exports
(Percentage Shares)

		1980	1981	1982	1983	1984	1985	1986	1987	1988	1989
PRIMARY GOODS	S0+S1+S2+S3+S4	50.2	46.6	44.9	43.3	45.7	50.6	36.4	33.5	30.4	28.6
FOOD	S0	16.5	13.3	13.0	12.8	12.4	13.9	14.4	12.1	12.4	11.7
of which											
Live animals chiefly for food	D00	..	..	..	..	1.2	1.1	1.1	0.9	0.8	0.8
Meat and meat products	D01	..	..	..	..	1.7	1.6	1.6	1.3	1.2	1.3
Fishes,shell-fish,molluscs etc.	D03	..	..	..	..	1.2	1.0	1.6	1.8	2.0	2.0
Grain and grain products	D04	..	..	..	..	1.7	3.9	2.9	1.5	1.4	1.4
Vegetables and fruits	D05	..	..	..	..	3.2	3.0	3.5	3.3	3.5	3.1
Coffee, tea,cocoa etc.	D07	..	..	..	..	1.7	1.6	1.5	1.2	1.1	1.1
NON-FOOD	S2	9.5	9.5	8.1	9.5	9.3	9.7	9.4	9.3	9.0	8.0
of which											
Oil seeds & oil-containing fruits	D22	..	..	..	..	1.9	1.8	1.9	1.7	1.4	1.2
Textile fibers etc.	D26	..	..	..	..	3.6	4.2	3.7	3.8	3.5	2.9
Animal and vegetable raw materials	D29	0.3	0.4	0.3	0.5	1.7	1.5	1.6	1.6	1.5	1.6
MINERAL FUELS	S3	23.5	23.8	23.8	21.0	23.1	26.1	11.9	11.5	8.4	8.1
of which											
Coal, coke and briquettes	D32	..	..	..	..	1.2	1.3	1.5	1.4	1.2	1.3
Petroleum,petroleum products etc.	D33	..	..	..	..	21.8	24.8	10.4	10.2	7.1	6.8
OTHER	S1+S4	0.8	0.0	0.0	0.0	1.0	0.9	0.8	0.6	0.7	0.8
MANUFACTURED GOODS	S5+S6+S7+S8+S9	49.8	53.4	55.1	56.7	54.3	49.4	63.6	66.5	69.6	71.4
CHEMICALS & RELATED PRODUCTS	S5	6.2	6.1	5.4	5.6	6.2	5.0	5.8	5.7	6.1	6.1
of which											
Organic	D51	..	..	..	..	1.1	1.1	1.3	1.3	1.2	1.3
Inorganic	D52	..	..	..	..	1.1	1.0	1.2	1.4	1.6	1.5
LIGHT INDUSTRY	S6	22.1	21.4	19.3	19.6	19.3	16.4	19.0	21.7	22.1	20.8
of which											
Yarn,fabrics,manuf. goods etc.	D65	..	..	..	..	11.8	11.9	13.6	14.7	13.6	13.3
Non-ferrous metals	D68	..	..	..	..	1.0	0.8	1.0	1.1	1.2	1.5
Metal products	D67	..	..	..	..	1.8	1.6	1.8	2.0	2.1	1.4
MACHINERY & TRANSPORT EQUIPMENT	S7	4.7	4.9	5.7	5.5	5.7	2.8	3.5	4.4	5.8	7.4
OTHER	S8	16.7	16.9	16.6	17.1	17.9	12.7	16.0	15.9	17.4	20.5
Clothing and garments	D84	..	..	..	..	10.2	7.5	9.4	9.5	10.2	11.7
PRODUCTS NOT CLASSIFIED ELSEWHERE	S9	1.2	4.1	8.2	8.8	6.1	12.5	19.4	18.7	18.3	16.6
TOTAL		100.0	100.0	100.0	100.0	100.0	100.0	100.0	100.0	100.0	100.0

Source: Table 3.1.

Table 3.3 : CHINA : Commodity Composition of Merchandise Exports
(Percentage Growth Rates)

		1980	1981	1982	1983	1984	1985	1986	1987	1988	1989
PRIMARY GOODS	S0+S1+S2+S3+S4	..	12.2	-2.1	-4.1	24.0	15.9	-18.5	17.4	9.1	4.1
FOOD	S0	..	-2.5	-0.5	-1.9	13.2	17.7	17.0	7.5	23.2	4.3
of which											
Live animals chiefly for food	D00	..	..	..	..	..	-6.7	11.2	3.0	11.0	2.3
Meat and meat products	D01	..	..	..	..	..	-1.8	7.8	7.7	12.5	12.2
Fishes,shell-fish,molluscs etc.	D03	..	..	..	..	..	-7.2	73.5	46.8	34.3	7.3
Grain and grain products	D04	..	..	..	..	..	139.9	-15.7	-35.5	17.7	5.5
Vegetables and fruits	D05	..	..	..	..	..	-0.5	32.4	18.1	29.8	-3.0
Coffee, tea,cocoa etc.	D07	..	..	..	..	..	-3.1	7.1	4.7	7.4	8.3
NON-FOOD	S2	..	21.5	-13.7	16.1	15.2	9.6	9.6	25.5	16.6	-1.1
of which											
Oil seeds & oil-containing fruits	D22	..	..	..	..	..	-3.6	19.1	16.2	1.4	-5.6
Textile fibers etc.	D26	..	..	..	..	..	23.3	1.3	30.0	10.9	-7.5
Animal and vegetable raw materials	D29	..	49.1	-12.4	34.6	321.0	-10.0	22.1	32.7	12.3	16.6
MINERAL FUELS	S3	..	22.4	1.6	-12.2	29.1	18.3	-48.4	23.4	-12.6	7.5
of which											
Coal, coke and briquettes	D32	..	..	..	..	..	8.4	30.4	17.8	10.8	14.6
Petroleum,petroleum products etc.	D33	..	..	..	..	..	18.9	-52.4	24.2	-15.8	6.2
OTHER	S1+S4	..	..	..	..	..	-5.5	-2.9	9.9	21.3	28.8
MANUFACTURED GOODS	S5+S6+S7+S8+S9	..	29.9	4.6	2.5	12.6	-4.7	45.5	33.2	26.3	13.1
CHEMICALS & RELATED PRODUCTS	S5	..	19.3	-10.9	4.6	9.0	-0.4	27.6	29.0	29.6	10.5
of which											
Organic	D51	..	..	..	..	..	5.1	33.0	21.7	15.1	19.9
Inorganic	D52	..	..	..	..	..	1.4	32.1	45.9	37.8	4.2
LIGHT INDUSTRY	S6	..	17.1	-8.6	1.5	15.8	-11.1	31.0	45.6	22.4	3.9
of which											
Yarn,fabrics,manuf. goods etc.	D65	..	..	..	..	..	4.8	30.1	37.2	11.5	8.3
Non-ferrous metals	D68	..	..	..	..	..	-12.7	39.6	38.5	31.9	36.8
Metal products	D67	..	..	..	..	..	-10.7	29.8	44.1	26.2	-29.5
MACHINERY & TRANSPORT EQUIPMENT	S7	..	28.4	16.2	-3.4	22.4	-48.3	41.7	59.1	59.1	39.9
OTHER	S8	..	30.7	-0.6	2.8	23.2	-25.6	41.9	26.8	31.8	30.1
Clothing and garments	D84	..	..	..	..	..	-22.7	42.1	28.7	..	..
PRODUCTS NOT CLASSIFIED ELSEWHERE	S9	..	..	104.0	7.1	-18.7	113.7	76.1	22.9	17.6	0.6
TOTAL		..	21.0	1.5	-0.4	17.5	4.7	13.1	27.5	20.5	10.4

Source: Table 3.1.

Table 3.4: CHINA: Exports in Current Prices and Constant (1980) Prices

Merchandise Exports in Current Prices
(US$ million)

		1980	1981	1982	1983	1984	1985	1986	1987	1988	1989
Food	(S0+S1+S4)	3138	2925	2909	2854	3486	4043	4681	5037	6201	6544
Petroleum	(S3)	4273	5228	5314	4667	6027	7132	3683	4544	3972	4270
Manufacturing	(S5+S6+S7+S8+S9)	9051	11759	12297	12607	14195	13522	19670	26206	33111	37460
Other	(S2)	1726	2098	1810	2102	2421	2653	2908	3650	4257	4211
Total		18188	22010	22330	22230	26129	27350	30942	39437	47541	52486

Source: Table 3.1.

Price Indices (in US dollars)

		1980	1981	1982	1983	1984	1985	1986	1987	1988	1989
Food	(S0+S1+S4)	100.00	86.91	77.86	84.70	91.82	79.88	72.18	55.34	61.02	57.36
Petroleum	(S3)	100.00	111.81	102.44	95.41	95.03	91.28	39.36	45.74	33.65	40.77
Manufacturing	muv	100.00	100.53	99.14	96.55	94.87	95.87	112.53	123.41	132.37	131.91
Other	non-food	100.00	86.37	77.16	88.91	84.30	70.11	54.23	61.47	59.02	59.87

Source: World Bank Commodity Projections; IECCM 02/08/90

Merchandise Exports in 1980 Constant Prices
(US$ million)

		1980	1981	1982	1983	1984	1985	1986	1987	1988	1989
Food	(S0+S1+S4)	3138	3366	3736	3370	3797	5061	6485	9102	10162	11409
Petroleum	(S3)	4273	4676	5188	4892	6342	7813	9357	9935	11805	10473
Manufacturing	(S5+S6+S7+S8+S9)	9051	11697	12404	13058	14962	14105	17480	21235	25013	28398
Other	(S2)	1726	2429	2346	2364	2872	3784	5362	5938	7212	7035
Total		18188	22168	23673	23683	27973	30763	38684	46210	54193	57314

Table 3.5: CHINA: Total Exports of Goods and Services
(in million US$ and Yuan)

Total Exports
(US$ million)

	1980	1981	1982	1983	1984	1985	1986	1987	1988	1989
MERCHANDISE										
Current Prices	18188	22010	22330	22230	26129	27350	30942	39437	47541	52486
Constant Prices	18188	22168	23673	23683	27973	30763	38684	46210	54193	57314
SERVICES (use muv index)										
Current Prices	1682	2280	2254	2324	2427	2607	2986	3494	4365	3697
Constant Prices	1682	2268	2274	2407	2558	2719	2654	2831	3297	2803
Total										
Current Prices	19870	24290	24584	24554	28556	29957	33928	42931	51906	56183
Constant Prices	19870	24436	25947	26090	30531	33482	41337	49041	57490	60116

Source: Table 3.4.

	1980	1981	1982	1983	1984	1985	1986	1987	1988	1989
Exchange Rate	1.498	1.705	1.893	1.976	2.320	2.937	3.453	3.722	3.722	3.805

Total Exports
(Yuan million)

	1980	1981	1982	1983	1984	1985	1986	1987	1988	1989
GOODS										
in Current Prices	27246	37527	42271	43926	60619	80327	106843	146785	176946	199726
in Constant Prices	27246	33207	35463	35477	41903	48083	57948	69223	81181	85856
SERVICES										
in Current Prices	2520	3887	4267	4592	5631	7657	10311	13005	16247	14068
in Constant Prices	2520	3398	3406	3606	3832	4074	3975	4241	4940	4198
Total										
Current Prices	29766	41414	46538	48519	66250	87984	117153	159789	193193	213795
Constant Prices	29766	36605	38869	39083	45735	50156	61923	73464	86121	90054

Source: Table above.

Table 3.6: CHINA: Price Indices of Exports of Goods and Services (1980=100)

in US dollars

	1980	1981	1982	1983	1984	1985	1986	1987	1988	1989
MERCHANDISE	100.0	99.3	94.3	93.9	93.4	88.9	80.0	85.3	87.7	91.6
SERVICES	100.0	100.5	99.1	96.5	94.9	95.9	112.5	123.4	132.4	131.9
TOTAL	100.0	99.4	94.7	94.1	93.5	89.5	82.1	87.5	90.3	93.5

in Yuan

	1980	1981	1982	1983	1984	1985	1986	1987	1988	1989
MERCHANDISE	100.0	113.0	119.2	123.8	144.7	174.3	184.4	212.0	218.0	232.6
SERVICES	100.0	114.4	125.3	127.4	146.9	188.0	259.4	306.6	328.9	335.1
TOTAL	100.0	113.1	119.7	124.1	144.9	175.4	189.2	217.5	224.3	237.4

Source: Table 3.4.

Table 3.7 : CHINA: Total Exports and its Relative Share in the World Exports

	1978	1979	1980	1981	1982	1983	1984	1985	1986	1987	1988	1989
(million US$ in Current Prices)												
China Exports	9750	13660	18188	22010	22330	22230	26129	27350	30942	39437	47541	52486
World Exports	1227170	1566610	1892520	1861440	1724730	1674610	1775830	1800080	1981390	2333200	2679560	3090000
(Growth Rate)												
China Exports	..	40.1	33.2	21.0	1.5	-0.4	17.5	4.7	13.1	27.5	20.5	10.4
World Exports	..	27.7	20.8	-1.6	-7.3	-2.9	6.0	1.4	10.1	17.8	14.8	15.3
(Percentage Share)												
China Exports into World Exports	0.8	0.9	1.0	1.2	1.3	1.3	1.5	1.5	1.6	1.7	1.8	1.7
China Exports into China GDP	4.6	5.3	6.1	7.9	8.2	7.6	8.8	9.4	11.0	12.9	12.8	12.7
Memo Items:												
China GDP in Current Prices (million Yuan)	358810	399870	447150	477510	518580	578460	692440	854060	971990	1135710	1385770	1573110
Exchange Rate (Yuan per US$)	1.684	1.555	1.498	1.705	1.893	1.976	2.320	2.937	3.453	3.722	3.722	3.805
China GDP in Current Prices (US$ million)	213070	257151	298498	280065	273946	292743	298466	290793	281491	305134	372319	413396

Source: CHINA Statistical Year Book 1988 pp.643 for 1978-87 and Statistical Abstract 1989 pp.82 for 1988.
International Financial Statistics for World Exports and Exchange rate.

Table 3.8: CHINA: Summary of Composition of Exports
(Percentage Growth Rates)

		1986	1987	1988	1988		1989	
					Q 1-2	Q 3-4	Q 1-2	Q 3
PRIMARY GOODS	S0+S1+S2+S3+S4	-18.5	17.4	9.1	11.8	6.7	-0.7	13.0
FOOD	S0	17.0	7.5	23.2	21.2	24.8	5.9	4.4
NON-FOOD (Crude materials)	S2	9.6	25.5	16.6	13.8	19.3	-3.9	14.0
MINERAL FUELS	S3	-48.4	23.4	-12.6	0.3	-22.8	-8.9	27.4
MANUFACTURED GOODS	S5+S6+S7+S8+S9	45.5	33.2	26.3	34.5	20.8	9.7	21.8
CHEMICALS & RELATED PRODUCTS	S5	27.6	29.0	29.6	36.1	25.2	16.0	17.3
LIGHT INDUSTRY	S6	31.0	45.6	22.4	26.9	19.3	4.9	7.9
MACHINERY & TRANSPORT EQUIPMENT	S7	41.7	59.1	59.0	75.0	48.9	38.6	61.6
OTHER	S8	41.9	26.8	31.8	30.1	32.6	23.8	38.8
PRODUCTS NOT CLASSIFIED ELSEWHERE	S9	76.1	22.9	17.6	37.9	4.6	-6.4	11.1
TOTAL		13.1	27.5	20.5	26.3	16.3	6.4	19.5

Source: CHINA Customs Statistics 1988 and 1989; and Table 3.3.

Table 4.1: CHINA : Imports (CIF) Customs basis
(US $ million)

	Code	1980	1981	1982	1983	1984	1985	1986	1987	1988	1989
FOOD	SO+S1+S4	3211	3932	4437	3238	2527	1881	2002	3055	4191	5269
Food	SO	2934	3620	4200	3122	2331	1553	1625	2443	3476	4193
Beverages	S1	36	213	130	46	116	206	172	263	346	201
Animal fat	S4	241	99	107	70	80	122	205	349	369	875
PETROLEUM (Mineral Fuels)	S3	203	83	183	111	139	172	504	539	787	1650
INTERMEDIATE	S5+S2+D61+D63+D65 to D68	10639	10980	10091	12047	13856	19175	17552	16769	23392	23415
Chemicals and related products	S5	2899	2617	2936	3183	4237	4469	3771	5008	9139	7556
Crude materials (non-food)	S2	3574	4328	3250	2575	2542	3236	3143	3321	5090	4835
Leather+Cork=D61+D63=Light In.-D64	to D68	4165	4035	3905	6289	415	770	851	728	842	747
Leather	D61	..	..	..	..	..	..	..	184	224	280
Cork	D63	..	..	..	..	..	..	..	544	618	467
Textile Yarn (yarn, fabrics etc.)	D65	..	..	..	..	953	1607	1632	1848	2388	2845
Non metallic minerals	D66	..	..	..	..	225	325	363	342	430	520
Iron and Steel	D67	..	..	..	..	4361	7120	6741	4787	4625	5797
Non-ferrous metals	D68	..	..	..	..	1123	1848	1051	735	878	1114
CONSUMER GOODS	D84+D62+D82 to D89	544	557	486	782	1423	2330	2431	1743	1757	1866
Paper (Paper and related products)	D64	..	..	..	..	241	428	554	727	610	634
D62+D82+D83+D84+D85		544	557	486	782	1182	1902	1877	108	150	165
Rubber	D62	..	..	..	..	..	..	..	45	51	50
Furniture	D82	..	..	..	..	..	..	..	42	61	68
Travel goods	D83	..	..	..	..	..	..	..	3	8	6
Clothing	D84	..	..	..	..	..	..	..	17	28	38
Footwear	D85	..	..	..	..	..	..	..	1	2	3
Photo supplies	D88	..	..	..	..	..	..	..	432	365	398
Miscellaneous	D89	..	..	..	..	..	..	..	476	632	669
MANUFACTURED	(Residual)	5353	6461	4083	5213	9465	18694	20415	21110	25125	26942
Total		19950	22012	19280	21391	27410	42252	42904	43216	55251	59142

Source: CHINA Customs Statistics 1990.1 PP.13 FOR 1989; 1989.1 pp.17 for 1988; CHINA Statistical Year Book 1988 pp.645 for 1987,1986;
1987 pp.521 for 1985; 1986 pp.483 for 1984; 1985 pp.495 for 1983; 1984 pp.382 for 1982;
1983 pp.406 for 1981; 1981 pp.73 for 1980 (in yuan).

Table 4.2: CHINA : Imports (CIF) Customs basis
(Percentage Shares)

		1980	1981	1982	1983	1984	1985	1986	1987	1988	1989
FOOD	SO+S1+S4	16.1	17.9	23.0	15.1	9.2	4.5	4.7	7.1	7.6	8.9
Food	SO	14.7	16.4	21.8	14.6	8.5	3.7	3.8	5.7	6.3	7.1
Beverages	S1	0.2	1.0	0.7	0.2	0.4	0.5	0.4	0.6	0.6	0.3
Animal fat	S4	1.2	0.4	0.6	0.3	0.3	0.3	0.5	0.8	0.7	1.5
PETROLEUM (Mineral Fuels)	S3	1.0	0.4	0.9	0.5	0.5	0.4	1.2	1.2	1.4	2.8
INTERMEDIATE	S5+S2 +D61+D63+D65 to D68	53.3	49.9	52.3	56.3	50.6	45.4	40.9	38.8	42.3	39.6
Chemicals and related products	S5	14.5	11.9	15.2	14.9	15.5	10.6	8.8	11.6	16.5	12.8
Crude materials (non-food)	S2	17.9	19.7	16.9	12.0	9.3	7.7	7.3	7.7	9.2	8.2
Leather+Cork=D61+D63=Light In.-D64 to D68		20.9	18.3	20.3	29.4	1.5	1.8	2.0	1.7	1.5	1.3
Leather	D61	..	..	..	..	..	..	..	0.4	0.4	0.5
Cork	D63	..	..	..	..	..	..	..	1.3	1.1	0.8
Textile Yarn (yarn, fabrics etc.)	D65	..	..	..	..	3.5	3.8	3.8	4.3	4.3	4.8
Non metallic minerals	D66	..	..	..	..	0.8	0.8	0.8	0.8	0.8	0.9
Iron and Steel	D67	..	..	..	..	15.9	16.9	15.7	11.1	8.4	9.8
Non-ferrous metals	D68	..	..	..	..	4.1	3.9	2.4	1.7	1.6	1.9
CONSUMER GOODS	D64+D62+D82 to D89	2.7	2.5	2.5	3.7	5.2	5.5	5.7	4.0	3.2	3.2
Paper (Paper and related products)	D64	..	..	..	..	0.9	1.0	1.3	1.7	1.1	1.1
D62+D82+D83+D84+D85		2.7	2.5	2.5	3.7	4.3	4.5	4.4	0.2	0.3	0.3
Rubber	D62	..	..	..	..	..	..	..	0.1	0.1	0.1
Furniture	D82	..	..	..	..	..	..	..	0.0	0.0	0.0
Travel goods	D83	..	..	..	..	..	..	..	0.0	0.0	0.1
Clothing	D84	..	..	..	..	..	..	..	0.0	0.1	0.0
Footwear	D85	..	..	..	..	..	..	..	0.0	0.0	0.0
Photo supplies	D88	..	..	..	..	..	..	..	1.0	0.7	0.7
Miscellaneous	D89	..	..	..	..	..	..	..	1.1	1.1	1.1
MANUFACTURED	(Residual)	26.8	29.3	21.2	24.4	34.5	44.2	47.6	48.8	45.5	45.6
Total		100.0	100.0	100.0	100.0	100.0	100.0	100.0	100.0	100.0	100.0

Source: Table 4.1.

Table 4.3: CHINA : Imports (CIF) Customs basis
(Percentage Growth Rates)

		1980	1981	1982	1983	1984	1985	1986	1987	1988	1989
FOOD	SO+S1+S4	..	22.4	12.9	-27.0	-21.9	-25.6	6.4	52.6	37.2	25.7
Food	SO	..	23.4	16.0	-25.7	-25.3	-33.4	4.6	50.3	42.3	20.6
Beverages	S1	..	486.3	-38.8	-64.9	154.4	77.6	-16.5	52.9	31.6	-41.8
Animal fat	S4	..	-58.9	8.1	-34.6	14.3	52.5	68.0	70.2	5.7	137.2
PETROLEUM (Mineral Fuels)	S3	..	-59.0	120.5	-39.3	25.2	23.7	193.0	6.9	46.0	109.8
INTERMEDIATE S5+S2+D61+D63+D65 to D68		..	3.2	-8.1	19.4	15.0	38.4	-8.5	-4.5	39.5	0.1
Chemicals and related products	S5	..	-9.7	12.2	8.4	33.1	5.5	-15.6	32.8	82.5	-17.3
Crude materials (non-food)	S2	..	21.1	-24.9	-20.8	-1.3	27.3	-2.9	5.7	53.3	-5.0
Leather+Cork=D61+D63=Light In.-D64 to D68		..	-3.1	-3.2	61.0	-93.4	85.5	10.5	-14.5	15.7	-11.3
Leather	D61	..	:	:	:	:	:	:	:	21.7	25.1
Cork	D63	..	:	:	:	:	:	:	:	13.6	-24.4
Textile Yarn (yarn, fabrics etc.)	D65	..	:	:	:	:	68.6	1.6	13.2	29.2	19.1
Non metallic minerals	D66	..	:	:	:	:	44.4	11.7	-5.8	25.7	21.0
Iron and Steel	D67	..	:	:	:	:	63.3	-5.3	-29.0	-3.4	25.3
Non-ferrous metals	D68	..	:	:	:	:	46.7	-36.2	-30.1	19.4	26.9
CONSUMER GOODS D64+D62+D82 to D89	D89	..	2.5	-12.7	60.9	82.0	63.7	4.3	-28.3	0.8	6.2
Paper (Paper and related products)	D64	..	2.5	-12.7	60.9	51.2	77.6	29.4	31.2	-16.1	4.0
D82+D82+D83+D84+D85		..	:	:	:	:	60.9	-1.3	-94.2	38.9	9.8
Rubber	D62	..	:	:	:	:	:	:	:	13.3	-2.9
Furniture	D82	..	:	:	:	:	:	:	:	45.2	10.8
Travel goods	D83	..	:	:	:	:	:	:	:	166.7	-27.2
Clothing	D84	..	:	:	:	:	:	:	:	64.7	37.0
Footwear	D85	..	:	:	:	:	:	:	:	100.0	68.0
Photo supplies	D88	..	:	:	:	:	:	:	:	-15.5	9.1
Miscellaneous	D89	..	:	:	:	:	:	:	:	32.8	5.8
MANUFACTURED	(Residual)	..	20.7	-36.8	27.7	81.6	97.5	9.2	3.4	19.0	7.2
Total		..	10.3	-12.4	10.9	28.1	54.1	1.5	0.7	27.8	7.0

Source: Table 4.1.

Table 4.4: CHINA: Imports in Current Prices and Constant (1980) Prices

Imports (CIF) in Current Prices
(US $ million)

	1980	1981	1982	1983	1984	1985	1986	1987	1988	1989
FOOD S0+S1+S4	3211	3932	4437	3238	2527	1881	2002	3055	4191	5269
PETROLEUM (Mineral Fuels) S3	203	83	183	111	139	172	504	539	787	1650
INTERMEDIATE S5+S2 +D61+D63+D65 to D68	10639	10980	10091	12047	13856	19175	17552	16769	23392	23415
CONSUMER GOODS D64+D62+D82 to D89	544	557	486	782	1423	2330	2431	1743	1757	1866
MANUFACTURED (Residual)	5353	6461	4083	5213	9465	18694	20415	21110	25125	26942
Total	19950	22012	19280	21391	27410	42252	42904	43216	55251	59142

Source: Table 4.1.

Price Indices (in US dollars)

	1980	1981	1982	1983	1984	1985	1986	1987	1988	1989
FOOD	100.00	86.91	77.86	84.70	91.82	79.88	72.18	55.34	61.02	57.36
PETROLEUM	100.00	111.81	102.44	95.41	95.03	91.28	39.36	45.74	33.65	40.77
INTERMEDIATE (Imports MUV)	100.00	102.40	104.86	107.37	109.95	112.59	115.29	118.06	127.50	126.61
CONSUMER GOODS (Imports MUV)	100.00	102.40	104.86	107.37	109.95	112.59	115.29	118.06	127.50	126.61
MANUFACTURED (Imports MUV)	100.00	102.40	104.86	107.37	109.95	112.59	115.29	118.06	127.50	126.61

Source: World Bank Commodity Projections; IECCM 02/08/90

Imports (CIF) in 1980 Constant Prices
(US $ million)

	1980	1981	1982	1983	1984	1985	1986	1987	1988	1989
FOOD S0+S1+S4	3211	4524	5698	3823	2752	2365	2773	5520	6868	9186
PETROLEUM (Mineral Fuels) S3	203	74	179	116	146	188	1280	1179	2338	4048
INTERMEDIATE S5+S2 +D61+D63+D65 to D68	10639	10723	9624	11220	12602	17031	15224	14204	18346	18493
CONSUMER GOODS D64+D62+D82 to D89	544	544	463	728	1294	2069	2109	1476	1378	1474
MANUFACTURED (Residual)	5353	6309	3894	4855	8608	18604	17707	17881	19705	21279
Total	19950	22174	19858	20742	25403	38247	39094	40260	48635	54480

Table 4.5: CHINA: Total Imports of Goods and Services
(in million US$ and Yuan)

Total Imports
(US$ million)

	1980	1981	1982	1983	1984	1985	1986	1987	1988	1989
MERCHANDISE (91.7% of Total)										
Current Prices	18294	20185	17680	19616	25135	38745	39343	39629	50665	54233
Constant Prices	18294	20333	18210	19021	23295	35072	35849	36918	44598	49958
SERVICES (8.3% of Total)										
Current Prices	1656	1827	1600	1775	2275	3507	3561	3587	4586	4909
Constant Prices	1656	1840	1648	1722	2108	3174	3245	3342	4037	4522
TOTAL										
Current Prices	19950	22012	19280	21391	27410	42252	42904	43216	55251	59142
Constant Prices	19950	22174	19858	20742	25403	38247	39094	40260	48635	54480

Source: Table 4.4.

| Exchange Rate | 1.498 | 1.705 | 1.893 | 1.976 | 2.320 | 2.937 | 3.453 | 3.722 | 3.722 | 3.805 |

Total Imports
(Yuan million)

	1980	1981	1982	1983	1984	1985	1986	1987	1988	1989
MERCHANDISE										
Current Prices	27405	34415	33468	38760	58313	113794	135851	147499	188575	206374
Constant Prices	27405	30459	27278	28493	34895	52539	53701	55304	66808	74837
SERVICES										
Current Prices	2480	3115	3029	3508	5278	10300	12296	13351	17068	18679
Constant Prices	2480	2757	2489	2579	3158	4755	4861	5006	6047	6774
TOTAL										
Current Prices	29885	37530	36497	42269	63591	124094	148148	160850	205643	225054
Constant Prices	29885	33216	29747	31072	38054	57294	58562	60309	72855	81611

Source: Table above.

Table 4.6: CHINA: Price Indices of Imports of Goods and Services (1980=100)

in US dollars

	1980	1981	1982	1983	1984	1985	1986	1987	1988	1989
MERCHANDISE	100.0	99.3	97.1	103.1	107.9	110.5	109.7	107.3	113.6	108.6
SERVICES	100.0	99.3	97.1	103.1	107.9	110.5	109.7	107.3	113.6	108.6
TOTAL	100.0	99.3	97.1	103.1	107.9	110.5	109.7	107.3	113.6	108.6

in Yuan

	1980	1981	1982	1983	1984	1985	1986	1987	1988	1989
MERCHANDISE	100.0	113.0	122.7	136.0	167.1	216.6	253.0	266.7	282.3	275.8
SERVICES	100.0	113.0	122.7	136.0	167.1	216.6	253.0	266.7	282.3	275.8
TOTAL	100.0	113.0	122.7	136.0	167.1	216.6	253.0	266.7	282.3	275.8

Source: Table 4.5.

Table 5.1 : CHINA: External Debt
Disbursements and Repayments
(in US$ million)

	1978	1979	1980	1981	1982	1983	1984	1985	1986	1987	1988
DISBURSEMENTS											
A. Public & Publicly Guar. LT	583	1779	2540	1800	1837	2375	2357	5302	6725	8104	8868
1. Official Creditors	27	199	244	573	665	609	844	1132	1437	1193	1922
a. Multilateral	0	0	0	0	1	78	208	599	620	722	1122
aa of which IBRD	0	0	0	0	0	0	73	354	324	306	553
ab of which IDA	0	0	0	0	1	67	124	212	282	394	557
b. Bilateral	27	199	244	573	664	531	636	533	817	471	800
2. Private Creditors	556	1580	2295	1227	1173	1766	1513	4171	5288	6911	6946
a. Suppliers	77	531	671	560	664	1038	882	486	370	215	637
b. Commercial Banks	480	965	159	97	90	269	303	610	1439	4563	4308
c. Other Private	0	83	1465	571	419	462	328	3076	3479	2133	2001
B. Private Non-Guaranteed LT	0	0	0	0	0	0	0	0	0	0	0
C. Total LT Disbursements (A+B)	583	1779	2540	1800	1837	2375	2357	5302	6725	8104	8868
D. IMF Purchases	..	0	0	896	0	0	0	0	701	0	0
E. Net Short-Term Capital	..	..	..	..	..	..	..	..	..	..	..
F. Total Disbursements (C+D+E)	..	..	..	..	..	..	..	..	..	..	..
REPAYMENTS											
A. Public & Publicly Guar. LT	0	0	613	1205	1302	1389	1287	1297	1874	1894	2097
1. Official Creditors	0	0	50	78	77	56	57	43	263	475	478
a. Multilateral	0	0	0	0	0	0	0	0	2	99	41
aa of which IBRD	0	0	0	0	0	0	0	0	0	97	39
ab of which IDA	0	0	0	0	0	0	0	0	0	0	0
b. Bilateral	0	0	50	78	77	56	57	43	261	378	437
2. Private Creditors	0	0	563	1127	1226	1334	1230	1253	1611	1419	1619
a. Suppliers	0	0	294	475	399	475	585	696	323	459	320
b. Commercial Banks	0	0	161	333	313	168	125	77	105	275	481
c. Other Private	0	0	107	318	513	691	519	480	1184	685	817
B. Private Non-Guranteed LT	0	0	0	0	0	0	0	0	0	0	0
C. Total LT Repayments (A+B)	0	0	613	1205	1302	1389	1287	1297	1874	1894	2097
D. IMF Repurchases	0	0	0	0	0	481	0	0	36	80	83
E. Total LT Repay + IMF Repur.	0	0	613	1205	1302	1870	1287	1297	1910	1974	2180
Memorandum Item:											
Arrears (Principal)	..	..	..	..	..	..	..	..	..	..	..
COMMITMENTS											
IBRD commitments	0	0	0	100	165	299	616	660	672	692	856
of which fast Disbursing	0	0	0	0	0	0	0	0	0	0	200
IDA commitments	0	0	0	96	165	139	343	433	448	606	576
of which fast Disbursing	0	0	0	0	0	0	0	0	0	0	97

Source: World Bank Debt and International Finance division. IECDI 01/17/90

Table 5.2 : CHINA: External Debt
Interest and Debt outstanding
(in US$ million)

	1978	1979	1980	1981	1982	1983	1984	1985	1986	1987	1988
INTEREST											
A. Public & Publicly Guar. LT	0	61	318	518	541	523	610	586	644	1116	1593
1. Official Creditors	0	5	17	55	78	98	122	164	275	387	421
a. Multilateral	0	0	0	0	0	3	9	30	76	126	143
aa of which IBRD	0	0	0	0	0	3	6	28	66	111	126
ab of which IDA	0	0	0	0	0	1	4	4	8	12	15
b. Bilateral	0	5	17	55	78	95	113	134	199	261	278
2. Private Creditors	0	56	301	463	463	425	487	423	370	729	1172
a. Suppliers	0	0	82	118	140	170	209	208	96	113	110
b. Commercial Banks	0	56	140	110	72	47	40	54	45	146	455
c. Other Private	0	0	79	235	250	208	239	161	229	470	606
B. Private Non-Guaranteed LT	0	0	0	0	0	0	0	0	0	0	0
C. Total LT Interest (A+B)	0	61	318	518	541	523	610	586	644	1116	1593
D. IMF Service Charges	0	0	0	21	34	21	2	2	2	49	51
E. Interest Paid on ST Debt	0	0	0	0	248	277	386	594	417	640	534
F. Total Interest Paid (C+D+E)	0	61	318	539	823	821	998	1182	1063	1805	2178
Memorandum Item:											
Arrears (Interest)	..	..	..	..	..	..	..	..	..	..	..
DEBT OUTSTANDING & DISB. (DOD)											
A. Public & Publicly Guar. LT	623	2183	4504	4913	5221	5301	6179	9963	16598	26051	32196
1. Official Creditors	27	226	446	919	1453	2028	2627	4478	6753	9275	10406
a. Multilateral	0	0	0	0	1	77	271	984	1810	2860	3758
aa of which IBRD	0	0	0	0	0	4	73	498	965	1427	1832
ab of which IDA	0	0	0	0	1	67	181	431	774	1330	1819
b. Bilateral	27	226	446	919	1452	1951	2356	3495	4943	6415	6648
2. Private Creditors	596	1957	4058	3994	3768	3273	3552	5485	9845	16777	21790
a. Suppliers	82	572	1037	1041	1580	1700	1817	1303	1587	1615	1849
b. Commercial Banks	514	131	1514	632	369	405	546	444	1843	6338	10061
c. Other Private	0	84	1506	2321	1820	1168	1189	3738	6416	8824	9880
B. Private Non-Guaranteed LT	0	0	0	0	0	0	0	0	0	0	0
C. Total LT DOD (A+B)	623	2183	4504	4913	5221	5301	6179	9963	16598	26051	32196
D. Use of IMF Credit	0	0	0	884	838	324	303	340	1072	1155	1013
E. Short-Term Debt	0	0	0	0	2300	3984	5600	6419	6076	8221	8806
F. Total External Debt (C+D+E)	623	2183	4504	5798	8359	9609	12082	16722	23746	35428	42015
G. Principal Reduction Due to:											
1. Debt-Equity Swaps+Buybacks	..	..	..	..	..	..	..	..	..	..	..
2. Debt Exchanges	..	..	..	..	..	..	..	..	..	..	..
3. Debt Forgiveness	..	..	..	..	..	..	..	..	..	..	..
Memorandum Item:											
% Debt on Concessional Terms	0	0	1	1	8	15	21	23	21	20	19
% Debt at Variable Int. Rates	83	60	59	54	38	28	22	28	28	36	39

Source: World Bank Debt and International Finance division. IECDI 01/17/90

Table 5.3 : CHINA: Terms of External Borrowing

	1981	1982	1983	1984	1985	1986	1987	1988
Concessional loans as % of long-term debt	1.1	8.1	15.1	20.5	22.7	20.8	19.5	19.4
Variable-rate loans as % of long-term debt	53.8	37.7	27.6	21.7	27.8	27.6	36.0	38.7
Average terms of new borrowing								
All Creditors								
Interest (%)	8.2	6.9	7.2	7.5	7.5	6.4	6.6	7.1
Maturity (years)	13.0	18.5	16.8	18.2	12.0	13.8	14.7	12.7
Grace Period (years)	3.6	5.5	4.3	4.7	3.9	5.0	4.0	3.7
Official Creditors								
Interest (%)	5.2	4.3	5.7	5.9	5.8	5.5	4.7	4.3
Maturity (years)	22.8	28.1	26.4	28.3	26.6	27.1	28.3	22.7
Grace Period (years)	7.0	8.5	7.1	7.1	6.8	6.6	6.8	7.1
Private Creditors								
Interest (%)	9.9	10.1	8.7	8.9	8.1	6.7	7.0	8.0
Maturity (years)	7.5	7.0	7.8	9.1	7.2	9.8	11.5	9.7
Grace Period (years)	1.7	2.0	1.6	2.6	3.0	4.6	3.4	2.7

Source: World Debt Tables 1989.

Table 6.1: CHINA : Monetary Survey, 1984-89 1/

	1984	1985	1986	1987	1988 March	1988 June	1988 Sept.	1988 Dec.	1989 March	1989 June	1989 Sept.	1989 Dec.	1990 March
					(in billions of yuan; end of period)								
Net foreign assets	35.1	20.8	3.9	23.0	32.0	34.2	31.3	30.3	27.5	23.0	24.0	37.7	57.0
Net domestic assets	408.9	499.3	668.3	812.0	835.0	891.3	940.1	979.7	991.8	1033.6	1075.9	1157.3	1191.9
Loans to enterprises and individuals	509.9	628.9	814.5	980.3	1003.2	1057.5	1102.6	1141.8	1151.4	1180.2	1223.2	1347.0	1378.6
Budget (net) 2/	9.5	-9.3	5.8	20.8	9.6	10.3	17.1	30.5	24.3	30.2	23.7	30.5	26.6
Other assets (net) 3/	-110.4	-120.4	-152.1	-189.1	-177.8	-176.4	-179.6	-192.7	-183.9	-176.7	-170.9	-220.2	-213.3
Money and quasi-money	444.0	520.0	672.2	835.0	867.0	925.5	971.3	1009.9	1019.2	1056.6	1099.9	1194.9	1248.9
Money	340.0	374.0	474.1	568.5	575.3	623.8	669.9	695.0	668.5	672.0	676.5	744.2	714.3
Currency in circulation	79.2	98.8	121.8	145.4	144.2	154.2	184.9	213.3	209.7	207.9	208.1	234.4	215.2
Household demand deposits	31.4	39.7	50.6	70.8	75.6	80.8	86.5	94.8	91.5	93.3	92.9	..	..
Enterprise deposits	197.0	203.0	262.1	307.3	315.9	348.9	359.2	347.7	329.4	332.0	333.5	..	..
Official institutions & Org.	32.4	32.6	39.6	44.9	39.6	39.9	39.4	39.3	37.9	38.8	42.0	..	..
Quasi-money	104.1	145.9	198.0	266.5	291.6	301.7	301.4	314.9	350.7	384.7	423.5	450.7	534.6
Capital construction deposits	14.0	23.5	25.1	30.9	33.0	34.3	34.5	31.2	31.9	35.1	38.0	41.1	53.0
Household term deposits	90.1	122.4	172.9	235.6	258.7	267.4	267.0	283.7	318.8	349.6	385.4	409.6	481.7
					(Percent change from same period of the preceding year)								
Net domestic assets	31.1	22.1	33.9	21.5	22.2	26.0	23.8	20.7	18.8	16.0	14.4	18.2	20.2
Of which: Loans to enterprises and individuals	33.5	22.3	29.5	20.3	22.7	23.8	21.1	16.5	14.8	11.6	10.9	18.0	19.7
Money and quasi-money	..	17.1	29.3	24.2	25.7	28.4	25.5	21.0	17.6	14.2	13.2	18.3	22.5
Of which: Currency	..	24.7	23.3	19.4	26.3	35.8	45.6	46.6	45.4	34.8	12.5	9.8	2.6
Memorandum Item:													
Currency/deposit ratio (percent)	21.9	23.5	22.1	21.1	20.0	20.0	23.5	26.8	25.9	24.5	23.3	52.0	40.3
(seasonally adjusted)	20.4	21.8	20.5	19.5	20.1	21.4	23.8	24.7	26.1	26.2	23.6	..	..

Source:IMF Recent Economic Developments 01/17/90 pp.17.

1/ Covers operations of the People's Bank, four specialized banks, two universal banks, and rural credit cooperatives.
2/ Claims related to state budget operations less government deposits, which include extrabudgetary deposits of local governments.
3/ Includes financial bonds issued by banks.

Table 6.2: CHINA : Operations of the People's Bank, 1985-89   1/

(in billions of yuan; end of period)

	1985	1986	1987	1988				1989			
				March	June	Sept.	Dec.	March	June	Sept.	
Net foreign assets	12.4	3.7	15.0	23.9	23.9	22.5	20.9	22.9	24.7	31.1	
Claims on financial institutions	224.9	269.4	277.4	270.3	270.3	292.0	338.8	332.9	331.6	348.5	
Other domestic assets (net)	-8.7	9.6	29.9	16.8	16.8	39.0	45.8	46.9	51.2	46.4	
Loans	8.6	13.0	22.7	23.3	23.3	26.4	30.6	30.2	31.4	33.0	
Budgetary borrowing, net 2/	-9.3	5.8	20.8	9.6	9.6	17.1	30.5	24.3	30.2	23.7	
Other items, net	-7.9	-9.3	-13.6	-16.1	-16.1	-4.5	-15.3	-7.6	-10.4	-10.3	
Reserve Money	228.6	282.7	322.3	311.0	311.0	353.5	405.5	402.7	407.5	426.0	
Liabilities to banks	96.4	120.1	127.4	121.3	121.3	122.1	145.4	147.0	152.8	167.1	
Required deposits	42.0	56.5	67.0	70.8	70.8	85.6	84.1	87.2	92.0	96.8	
Other deposits	47.0	55.8	52.8	43.5	43.5	27.4	50.9	47.8	49.0	58.9	
Cash in vault	7.3	7.8	7.6	7.0	7.0	9.1	10.4	11.9	11.8	11.4	
Liabilities to nonbanks	132.2	162.6	194.8	189.7	189.7	231.3	260.1	255.7	254.7	258.9	
Currency in circulation	98.8	121.8	145.4	144.2	144.2	184.9	213.3	209.7	207.9	208.1	
Deposits	33.4	40.8	49.4	45.5	45.5	46.4	46.9	46.0	46.8	50.8	
Total Liabilities	228.6	282.7	322.2	311.0	311.0	353.4	405.5	402.7	407.5	426.0	
Memorandum Item:											
Money multiplier 3/	2.27	2.38	2.59	2.79	2.82	2.75	2.49	2.53	2.59	2.58	
(seasonally adjusted)	2.40	2.51	2.73	2.75	2.76	2.70	2.63	2.50	2.54	2.53	
Excess reserves to deposit (percent)	12.1	11.0	8.2	6.4	6.0	3.7	6.8	6.3	6.1	7.0	
(seasonally adjusted) 4/	11.1	10.0	7.5	6.6	6.0	4.1	6.2	6.4	6.0	7.8	

Source:IMF Recent Economic Developments 01/17/90 pp.21.

1/ Balance sheet data on the People's Bank as a separate central bank are available from June 1985.
2/ Claims related to state budget operations less government deposits, which include extrabudgetary deposits of local governments.
3/ The ratio of money and quasi-money to reserve money.
4/ Deposits exclude deposits with PBC.

Table 6.3: CHINA : Monetary and Velocity Developments, 1984-1989

(Percentage fourth quarter to fourth quarter)

	1984	1985	1986	1987	1988	1989
Money and quasi-money	42.4	17.1	29.3	24.2	21.0	18.3
Currency	49.4	24.7	23.3	19.4	46.6	5.7
Household deposits	32.6	33.4	38.0	37.4	23.7	35.3
Demand	44.0	26.4	28.1	41.0	34.5	7.6
Time	29.1	35.9	41.3	36.3	20.4	44.4
Enterprise deposits 1/	62.9	7.3	29.2	17.2	13.1	-7.2
Other deposits 2/	-14.3	0.6	21.5	13.4	-12.6	6.7
Velocity (ratio) 3/	1.52	1.60	1.41	1.34	1.39	1.38 /4
(percent change)	-16.5	5.3	-11.9	-5.0	3.7	-0.7
Memorandum item:						
Augmented money and quasi-money 5/	..	..	32.3	26.8	23.2	14.8 /6

Source: IMF Recent Economic Developments 01/17/90 pp.19.

1/ Includes deposits with the People's Construction Bank of China (PCBC).
2/ Deposits of official institutions.
3/ Ratio of GNP to the end-year money and quasi-money.
4/ Adjusted for seasonal factors.
5/ Includes deposits held at trust and investment companies and urban credit cooperatives.
6/ June 1989 over June 1988.

Table 6.4: CHINA : Specialized and Universal Banks'
Domestic Currency Assets and Liabilities,1986-89

(billions of yuan; end of period)

	1986 Dec.	1987 Dec.	1988 March	1988 June	1988 Sept.	1988 Dec.	1989 March	1989 June	1989 Sept.
Total deposits	463.5	573.9	595.9	636.9	650.2	668.6	672.7	706.8	742.1
Enterprises	223.9	268.8	273.7	303.7	311.3	293.2	281.1	286.6	289.7
Sight	198.8	237.9	240.7	269.4	276.9	262.0	249.2	251.6	251.7
Term	25.1	30.9	33.0	34.3	34.4	31.2	31.9	35.0	38.0
Saving	146.4	202.8	220.8	233.2	239.9	258.9	284.0	312.3	340.1
Sight	28.0	41.0	44.7	49.6	54.2	59.7	58.8	61.3	61.1
Term	118.4	161.8	176.1	183.6	185.7	199.2	225.2	251.0	279.0
Township enterprises	4.6	5.6	4.9	6.4	6.6	6.2	5.4	5.4	5.2
Agricultural collectives	1.1	1.2	1.4	1.6	1.8	1.8	1.4	1.4	1.4
Rural credit cooperatives	50.2	56.3	47.6	44.8	43.1	58.8	50.7	51.3	53.9
Other deposits	37.3	39.2	47.5	47.2	47.5	49.7	50.1	49.8	51.8
Liabilities to the PBC	268.4	275.0	266.8	265.3	289.1	336.1	329.8	328.7	344.4
Self-owned funds of banks	74.1	81.5	81.5	81.5	81.5	91.4	91.4	91.4	91.4
Other liabilities, net	51.6	62.7	51.7	61.8	61.8	56.7	57.5	52.8	51.9
Total Liabilities	857.6	993.1	995.9	1045.5	1082.6	1152.8	1151.4	1179.7	1229.8
Loans	749.0	884.3	889.8	936.0	974.2	1023.7	1022.7	1045.0	1082.4
Industrial	189.4	221.2	226.7	241.3	248.8	260.4	264.7	275.5	289.4
Commercial	308.4	350.0	336.2	343.0	362.0	409.5	405.0	406.5	420.4
Construction	36.9	46.7	50.4	54.9	50.0	49.5	48.1	50.4	53.0
Urban collectives	41.5	53.6	57.0	62.9	65.7	63.6	64.0	65.2	65.8
Business loans to individuals	1.1	1.5	1.9	2.4	2.7	1.9	1.9	1.9	1.9
Agricultural loans	52.8	65.4	71.1	78.5	81.7	77.9	79.1	82.3	83.6
Loans to rural credit coops.	4.3	3.8	4.7	5.7	5.2	3.5	3.7	4.4	4.1
Fixed investment loans	88.6	111.9	111.5	120.3	131.2	138.7	137.1	139.0	143.3
Other loans	26.0	30.2	30.3	27.0	26.9	18.7	19.1	19.8	20.9
Cash in vault	7.8	7.8	7.0	7.8	9.1	10.4	11.9	11.8	11.4
Required deposits	56.3	65.8	69.3	73.8	82.6	80.9	84.0	88.7	93.3
Other deposits at the PBC	47.5	40.5	29.8	28.2	16.8	37.6	32.9	34.3	42.6
Total Assets	860.6	998.2	995.9	1045.8	1082.7	1152.6	1151.5	1179.8	1229.7

Source: IMF Recent Economic Developments 01/17/90 pp.58.

Table 6.5: CHINA : Rural Credit Cooperatives, 1986-89

(in billions of yuan; end of period)

	1986	1987	1988				1989		
	Dec.	Dec.	March	June	Sept.	Dec.	March	June	Sept.
Deposits	75.5	103.9	129.0	132.5	132.7	140.0	141.5	146.4	153.0
Rural collective enterprises	5.8	7.1	7.8	8.3	8.6	9.8	7.8	7.8	7.3
Township enterprises	5.9	8.1	9.5	11.5	12.6	12.8	10.4	10.8	10.6
Individual deposits	62.0	86.7	109.3	110.1	108.6	114.3	120.5	124.8	131.8
Sight	17.8	24.5	30.9	31.2	32.3	35.1	32.7	32.0	31.8
Term	44.2	62.2	78.4	78.9	76.3	79.2	87.8	92.8	100.0
Other deposits	1.8	2.0	2.4	2.6	2.9	3.1	2.8	3.0	3.3
Loans from banks	4.1	5.4	4.7	5.9	5.5	3.6	4.0	4.8	4.5
Other liabilities, net	5.2	8.8	11.8	14.7	14.4	5.3	5.5	6.2	6.8
Total liabilities	84.8	118.1	145.5	153.1	152.6	148.9	151.0	157.4	164.3
Domestic credit	49.1	75.6	94.8	105.6	107.3	90.8	102.1	108.2	112.0
Loans to collective enterprises	4.1	5.5	8.8	8.4	8.8	8.0	8.6	9.2	9.8
Loans to township enterprises	19.9	32.9	41.1	46.3	47.4	45.6	49.4	51.2	53.7
Loans to individuals	25.1	37.2	44.9	50.9	51.1	37.2	44.1	47.8	48.5
Redeposits at banks	35.7	42.4	50.7	47.6	45.5	58.0	48.8	49.1	52.4
Total assets	84.8	118.0	145.5	153.2	152.8	148.8	150.9	157.3	164.4

Source: IMF Recent Economic Developments 01/17/90 pp.59.

Table 6.6: CHINA : Percentage Increase of Credit

	1988 Entire	1989 Jan-Sept.
Total Credit	15.8	5.7
Agriculture	20.2	16.3
State Industry	17.7	11.1
of which: Large Enterprises	19.3	14.9
Foreign trade	17.7	11.4
Rural Enterprises	21.6	5.9
Urban Collectives	18.8	3.4
Fixed Investment	24.0	3.3

Table 6.7: CHINA : Credit to Rural Enterprises

	1988 End	1989 September	Increment
State Banks	41.1	38.0	-3.1
Rural Credit Cooperatives	45.6	53.7	8.1
Total	86.7	91.7	5.0

Table 7.1: CHINA: Structure of Consolidated Government Revenue, 1978-88

(as a % of Total Revenue)

	1978	1979	1980	1981	1982	1983	1984	1985	1986	1987	1988
Tax Revenue	42.2	42.6	43.5	45.5	49.6	54.5	58.2	95.8	92.0	90.4	89.9
Taxes on income and profits	6.9	6.1	5.7	5.5	5.8	7.4	8.4	32.4	30.2	27.9	25.4
Profit tax	4.4	3.6	3.4	3.2	3.4	3.8	5.1	30.5	28.4	24.0	23.6
Agricultural tax	2.5	2.3	2.1	2.0	2.1	2.1	1.9	1.8	1.8	2.0	1.8
Other	0.0	0.2	0.2	0.3	0.4	1.6	1.4	0.0	0.0	2.0	0.0
Taxes on goods and services	32.9	34.4	35.2	36.1	39.4	35.7	37.0	42.2	43.0	42.6	44.4
Product tax	0.0	0.0	0.0	0.0	0.0	0.0	0.0	28.0	22.4	20.9	16.8
VAT	0.0	0.0	0.0	0.0	0.0	0.0	0.0	6.5	9.5	9.8	13.4
Business tax	0.0	0.0	0.0	0.0	0.0	0.0	0.0	9.2	10.7	11.7	13.9
Taxes on international trade	2.4	2.1	2.6	3.9	3.3	3.4	5.6	9.0	6.2	5.9	5.4
Other taxes	0.0	0.0	0.0	0.1	1.0	8.0	7.2	12.3	12.6	14.1	14.6
Nontax revenue	57.8	57.4	56.5	54.5	50.4	45.5	41.8	4.2	8.0	9.6	10.1
of which: Profit remittances	55.6	54.6	53.9	52.2	47.3	41.8	37.4	1.9	1.7	1.6	1.8
Memorandum items:											
Revenue from enterprises	60.0	58.1	57.3	55.3	50.7	45.5	42.5	32.5	30.1	25.6	25.4
Profit tax	4.4	3.6	3.4	3.2	3.4	3.8	5.1	30.5	28.4	24.0	23.6
Profit remittances	55.6	54.6	53.9	52.2	47.3	41.8	37.4	1.9	1.7	1.6	1.8
Extrabudgetary receipts	0.0	0.0	0.0	0.0	0.0	1.0	1.0	0.9	0.8	0.7	0.5
Total Revenue	100.0	100.0	100.0	100.0	100.0	100.0	100.0	100.0	100.0	100.0	100.0

Source: Ministry of Finance.

Table 7.2: CHINA: Developments in Government Revenue 1978-88

(as a % of GNP)

	1978	1979	1980	1981	1982	1983	1984	1985	1986	1987	1988
Total Revenue	34.4	31.8	29.4	29.0	27.2	27.4	26.4	26.6	25.1	22.6	20.7
Taxes on income and profits	2.4	1.9	1.7	1.6	1.6	2.0	2.2	8.6	7.6	6.3	5.3
Profit tax	1.5	1.1	1.0	0.9	0.9	1.0	1.3	8.1	7.1	5.4	4.9
Agricultural tax	0.9	0.7	0.6	0.6	0.8	0.6	0.5	0.5	0.5	0.4	0.4
Other	0.0	0.1	0.0	0.1	0.1	0.4	0.4	0.0	0.0	0.4	0.0
Taxes on goods and services	11.3	10.9	10.4	10.5	10.7	9.8	9.8	11.2	10.8	9.6	9.2
Product tax	0.0	0.0	0.0	0.0	0.0	0.0	0.0	6.9	5.6	4.7	3.5
VAT	0.0	0.0	0.0	0.0	0.0	0.0	0.0	1.7	2.4	2.2	2.8
Business tax	0.0	0.0	0.0	0.0	0.0	0.0	0.0	2.5	2.7	2.7	2.9
Taxes on international trade	0.8	0.7	0.8	1.1	0.9	0.9	1.5	2.4	1.6	1.3	1.1
Other taxes	0.0	0.0	0.0	0.0	0.3	2.2	1.9	3.3	3.2	3.2	3.0
Nontax revenue	19.9	18.1	16.6	15.8	13.7	12.5	11.0	1.1	2.0	2.2	2.1
of which: Profit remittances	19.1	17.2	15.9	15.1	12.9	11.5	9.9	0.5	0.4	0.4	0.4
Memorandum items:											
Revenue from enterprises	20.6	18.4	16.9	16.1	13.8	12.5	11.2	8.6	7.6	5.8	5.2
Profit tax	1.5	1.1	1.0	0.9	0.9	1.0	1.3	8.1	7.1	5.4	4.9
Profit remittances	19.1	17.2	15.9	15.1	12.9	11.5	9.9	0.5	0.4	0.4	0.4
Extrabudgetary receipts	0.0	0.0	0.0	0.0	0.0	0.3	0.3	0.2	0.2	0.2	0.1

Source: Ministry of Finance.

Table 7.3: CHINA: Structure of Government Expenditure, 1978-88
(In percent of total expenditure)

	1978	1979	1980	1981	1982	1983	1984	1985	1986	1987	1988
Total Expenditure and net lending	100.0	100.0	100.0	100.0	100.0	100.0	100.0	100.0	100.0	100.0	100.0
Current expenditure	56.5	58.7	67.7	74.2	76.3	74.8	71.2	72.3	71.4	72.6	74.6
Administrative	4.0	3.9	4.6	4.9	5.5	6.0	7.1	6.2	6.4	6.4	6.9
Defense	13.7	15.2	13.3	11.6	11.9	10.5	9.3	8.3	7.6	7.5	6.8
Culture, education, public health	9.2	9.0	10.7	11.8	13.3	13.2	13.6	13.6	14.4	14.3	15.1
Economic services	14.6	12.7	13.1	11.6	11.9	11.1	10.5	9.6	9.6	9.3	9.0
Subsidies	9.3	13.3	18.7	25.5	25.1	25.2	21.1	21.8	22.1	23.9	23.7
Daily necessities	6.4	10.9	16.4	21.1	20.2	18.3	16.2	13.5	9.8	10.5	9.9
Agricultural inputs	0.0	0.0	0.0	1.5	1.4	0.8	0.5	0.6	0.0	0.0	0.0
Enterprise losses	2.9	2.4	2.3	2.9	3.5	6.1	4.4	7.7	12.3	13.3	13.9
Other	5.6	4.6	7.3	8.7	8.6	8.9	9.6	12.8	11.3	11.2	13.1
Developmental expenditure	43.5	41.3	32.3	25.8	23.7	25.2	28.8	27.7	28.6	27.4	25.4

Source: Ministry of Finance.

Table 7.4: CHINA: Developments in Government Expenditure, 1978-88
(In percent of GNP)

	1978	1979	1980	1981	1982	1983	1984	1985	1986	1987	1988
Total Expenditure and net lending	34.1	36.7	32.8	30.2	28.6	29.1	27.9	27.1	27.1	24.7	23.2
Current expenditure	19.3	21.6	22.2	22.4	21.8	21.8	19.8	19.6	19.3	18.0	17.3
Administrative	1.4	1.4	1.5	1.5	1.6	1.7	2.0	1.7	1.7	1.6	1.6
Defense	4.7	5.6	4.4	3.5	3.4	3.1	2.6	2.2	2.1	1.9	1.6
Culture, education, public health	3.1	3.3	3.5	3.6	3.8	3.8	3.8	3.7	3.9	3.6	3.5
Economic services	5.0	4.7	4.3	3.5	3.4	3.2	2.9	2.6	2.6	2.3	2.1
Subsidies	3.2	4.9	6.1	7.7	7.2	7.3	5.9	5.9	6.0	5.9	5.5
Daily necessities	2.2	4.0	5.4	6.4	5.8	5.3	4.5	3.7	2.6	2.6	2.3
Agricultural inputs	0.0	0.0	0.0	0.5	0.4	0.2	0.1	0.2	0.0	0.0	0.0
Enterprise losses	1.0	0.9	0.8	0.9	1.0	1.8	1.2	2.1	3.3	3.3	3.2
Other	1.9	1.7	2.4	2.6	2.5	2.6	2.7	3.5	3.1	2.8	3.0
Developmental expenditure	14.9	15.2	10.6	7.8	6.8	7.3	8.0	7.5	7.7	6.8	5.9
GNP in Current Prices (billion yuan)	358.8	399.8	447.0	477.3	519.3	580.9	696.2	856.8	972.6	1135.1	1385.3

Source: Ministry of Finance.

Table 7.5: CHINA: Budget and Its Financing 1978-88

	1978	1979	1980	1981	1982	1983	1984	1985	1986	1987	1988
	(In billions of yuan)										
Revenue	123.3	126.3	131.6	138.6	141.2	159.4	183.5	228.3	244.3	256.2	286.7
Expenditure	122.4	146.9	146.4	144.3	148.3	169.2	193.9	232.4	263.3	280.9	321.3
Deficit	0.9	-20.6	-14.8	-5.7	-7.1	-9.8	-10.4	-4.1	-19.0	-24.7	-34.6
Financing	-0.9	20.6	14.8	5.7	7.1	9.8	10.4	4.1	19.0	24.7	34.6
Domestic	-1.2	17.0	12.6	2.5	7.3	8.7	8.6	4.0	13.4	17.8	23.2
PBC	-1.2	17.0	12.6	-2.2	2.9	4.4	4.5	-2.1	7.5	6.4	7.8
Nonbank	0.0	0.0	0.0	4.8	4.4	4.3	4.2	6.1	5.8	11.4	15.4
Foreign	0.2	3.8	2.2	3.1	-0.2	1.1	1.8	0.1	5.6	6.9	11.4
	(In percent of GNP)										
Revenue	34.4	31.6	29.4	29.0	27.2	27.4	26.4	26.6	25.1	22.6	20.7
Expenditure	34.1	36.7	32.8	30.2	28.6	29.1	27.9	27.1	27.1	24.7	23.2
Deficit	0.3	-5.2	-3.3	-1.2	-1.4	-1.7	-1.5	-0.5	-2.0	-2.2	-2.5
Financing	-0.3	5.2	3.3	1.2	1.4	1.7	1.5	0.5	2.0	2.2	2.5
Domestic	-0.3	4.3	2.8	0.5	1.4	1.5	1.2	0.5	1.4	1.6	1.7
PBC	-0.3	4.3	2.8	-0.5	0.6	0.8	0.6	-0.2	0.8	0.6	0.6
Nonbank	0.0	0.0	0.0	1.0	0.8	0.7	0.6	0.7	0.6	1.0	1.1
Foreign	0.1	0.9	0.5	0.7	-0.0	0.2	0.3	0.0	0.6	0.6	0.8
	(As a percent of total deficit)										
Financing	100.0	100.0	100.0	100.0	100.0	100.0	100.0	100.0	100.0	100.0	100.0
Domestic	125.0	82.5	84.9	44.8	102.8	88.6	82.9	97.6	70.4	72.0	67.1
PBC	125.0	82.5	84.9	-39.7	40.8	44.8	42.9	-51.2	39.7	26.0	22.6
Nonbank	0.0	0.0	0.0	84.5	62.0	43.8	40.0	148.8	30.7	46.0	44.5
Foreign	-25.0	17.5	15.1	55.2	-2.8	11.4	17.1	2.4	29.6	28.0	32.9

Source: Ministry of Finance.

Table 7.6: CHINA : Evolution of Expenditures
(Percent of GNP)

	1978	1988
Capital	14.4	5.4
Working Capital	1.9	0.1
Military	4.7	1.6
Civilian, Current	10.4	9.2
Subsidies	5.2	5.4
Total Outlays	36.6	21.7
Deficit	0.0	1.9

Table 7.7: CHINA : Central and Local Government Budgets
(Billion Yuan and Percent of Outlays)

	1987	%	1989 (Budget)	%
Central Government				
Total Revenue	95.5		114.7	
Total Expenditure	126.0	100	138.1	100
of which				
Capital outlay	51.9	41	54.3	39
Current outlay	47.8	38	58.3	42
Subsidies	26.3	21	25.5	18
Local Governments				
Total Revenue	161.1		195.5	
Total Expenditure	156.4	100	207.1	100
of which				
Capital outlay	27.9	18	21.1	10
Current outlay	87.7	56	118.3	57
Subsidies	40.8	26	67.7	33

Table 7.8: CHINA : Fixed Investment: Central Government Plan and Funding
(Percent of GNP)

	1978	1979	1980	1981	1982	1983	1984	1985	1986	1987	1988
Total Fixed Investment in State Units	19.2	18.0	17.2	14.4	16.8	16.9	17.5	20.2	20.9	20.8	19.5
of which											
In Central Plan	9.0	8.3	7.9	6.5	7.2	7.6	7.6	8.2	8.3	8.5	7.5
Funded by Central Budget (estimate)	8.7	8.0	5.6	4.1	4.2	4.7	4.6	3.7	3.5	3.2	2.3
Central Govt. Borrowing Requirements	0.3	0.3	2.3	2.4	3.0	3.0	3.0	4.4	4.8	5.4	5.2

Table 7.9: CHINA : Loss Making Enterprises by Region in 1987

	EAST			MIDDLE			WEST		
	Proportion of loss making enterprises	Loss (million)	Loss as a Proportion of net income	Proportion of loss making enterprises	Loss (million)	Loss as a Proportion of net income	Proportion of loss making enterprises	Loss (million)	Loss as a Proportion of net income
Coal	24.50	9.15	33.40	29.50	9.73	17.60	27.90	7.35	38.80
Food	14.70	3.32	2.10	16.00	3.74	2.80	16.70	1.54	2.00
Machine Building	9.10	2.87	1.20	11.30	3.05	3.30	10.20	2.20	4.20
Mining and preparation of building materials	15.40	2.78	2.30	14.90	2.23	3.40	19.90	1.64	5.80
Textiles	16.70	2.73	1.30	17.60	1.67	2.30	14.40	0.44	1.20
Chemicals	13.50	1.44	1.00	16.20	1.21	2.00	18.60	0.64	2.20
Transport equipment	10.20	1.09	1.90	15.30	0.73	1.70	15.80	0.71	4.20
Power generation	12.30	0.69	0.01	9.20	1.48	2.70	15.20	0.53	1.60
Electronics	13.00	1.31	2.00	17.00	0.58	4.80	12.80	0.41	3.50
Petrol and gas	25.00	1.74	2.50	37.50	0.05	..	7.70	0.20	0.01
Electrical equipment	14.10	1.17	1.30	14.30	0.49	0.02	13.50	0.19	1.30
Total LOSS for the Product group		28.29			24.98			15.85	
Loss as a proportion of net industrial income in region			1.34			2.30			3.13

Source: CHINA: Industrial Yearbook 1988.

Table 7.10: CHINA : State Budget 1989-90

(billion Yuan)

	1989 Budget	1989 Actual	Actual 89 / Budget 89 %	1990 Budget	Budget 90 / Actual 89 %
REVENUE					
Total	285.680	294.800	3.2	323.653	9.8
Domestic	269.180	280.000	4.0	307.210	9.7
Tax	255.714	273.059	8.8	299.899	9.8
Bonds	11.100	14.010	26.2	17.000	21.3
Construction/Energy tax	20.500	19.812	-3.4	21.500	8.5
Other	12.730	17.402	36.7	17.160	-1.4
Enterprise revenue	4.004	6.099	52.3	4.909	-19.5
Enterprise losses	52.148	59.976	15.0	65.758	9.8
Foreign exchange loans	16.500	14.000	-15.2	18.443	17.5
Special Projects	5.280	..	..	12.500	54.4
Regulatory fund	12.000	8.094	-32.6		
EXPENDITURE					
Total	293.080	304.000	3.7	332.545	9.4
Capital construction	62.792	61.258	-2.4	65.945	7.7
Technology transfer	12.583	15.005	19.2	14.912	-0.6
Agriculture/Rural support	17.396	19.907	14.4	21.481	7.9
Urban construction	10.300	11.860	15.1	11.856	-0.0
Culture, Education & Health	51.388	55.868	8.7	59.745	6.9
Defence	24.550	25.146	2.4	28.970	15.2
Administration	22.664	26.708	17.8	27.234	2.0
Price Subsidies	40.989	37.043	-9.6	40.558	9.5
Domestic debt	2.548	2.673	4.9	12.400	363.9
Foreign exchange debt	7.020	4.583	-34.7	7.000	52.7
Other	40.870	41.404	1.3	42.444	2.5
DEFICIT					
Chinese definition	-7.400	-9.200		-8.892	
% of GNP	-0.530	-0.585		-0.500	
IMF definition	-35.000	-36.665		-42.335	
% of GNP	-2.230	2.340		-2.390	

Source: Ministry of Finance, and China daily 08/26/90.

Table 8.1 : CHINA : Production of Major Crops
(million tons)

	1978	1979	1980	1981	1982	1983	1984	1985	1986	1987	1988	1989
Total Food Grains	305	332	321	325	355	387	407	379	392	403	394	407
Rice	137	144	140	144	162	169	178	169	172	174	169	
Wheat	54	63	55	70	68	81	88	86	90	86	85	
Corn	56	60	63	59	61	68	73	64	71	79	77	
Soybeans	8	7	8	9	9	10	10	11	12	12	12	
Tuber	32	28	29	26	27	29	28	26	25	28	27	
Total Oil Seeds	5	6	8	10	12	11	12	16	15	15	13	13
Peanuts	2	3	4	4	4	4	5	7	6	6	6	
Rapeseed	2	2	2	4	6	4	4	6	6	7	5	5
Cotton	2	2	3	3	4	5	6	4	4	4	4	4
Sugarcane	21	22	23	30	37	31	40	52	50	47	49	49
Beetroots	3	3	6	6	7	9	8	9	8	8	13	9
Cured Tobacco	1	1	1	1	2	1	2	2	1	2	2	2
Fruits	7	7	7	8	8	9	10	12	13	17	17	18
Apples	2	3	2	3	2	4	3	4	3	4	4	
Citrus	0	1	1	1	1	1	1	2	3	3	3	
Pears	2	1	1	2	2	2	2	2	2	2	3	
Bananas	0	0	0	0	0	0	0	1	1	2	2	

Source: CHINA Statistical Year Book 1989 (Chinese) pp.198-201 and 1988 pp.212-3 for 1978-87.

Table 8.2 : CHINA : Production of Major Crops
(Percentage GROWTH RATES)

	1978	1979	1980	1981	1982	1983	1984	1985	1986	1987	1988	1989
Total Food Grains	::	9.0	-3.5	1.4	9.1	9.2	5.2	-6.9	3.3	2.9	-2.2	3.4
Rice	::	5.0	-2.7	2.9	12.3	4.5	5.6	-5.4	2.2	1.2	-3.0	
Wheat	::	16.5	-12.0	26.1	-1.7	18.9	7.9	-2.3	4.9	-4.6	-0.5	
Corn	::	7.3	4.3	-5.4	2.3	12.6	7.6	-13.0	10.9	11.8	-2.4	
Soybeans	::	-1.5	6.4	17.5	-3.2	8.1	-0.6	8.2	10.6	7.4	-6.6	
Tuber	::	-10.3	0.9	-9.6	4.2	8.1	-2.6	-8.6	-2.7	11.3	-4.4	
Total Oil Seeds	::	23.3	19.5	32.7	15.8	-10.7	12.9	32.5	-6.6	3.7	-13.6	-2.2
Peanuts	::	18.7	27.6	6.3	2.4	0.9	21.9	38.4	-11.7	4.9	-7.7	
Rapeseed	::	28.6	-0.7	70.5	39.1	-24.2	-1.9	33.3	4.9	12.3	-23.6	7.9
Cotton	::	1.8	22.7	9.6	21.2	28.9	35.0	-33.7	-14.6	19.9	-2.3	-8.7
Sugarcane	::	1.9	6.0	30.1	24.3	-15.6	26.9	30.4	-2.6	-5.7	3.6	-1.0
Beetroots	::	15.0	103.0	0.9	5.5	36.8	-9.8	7.7	-6.9	-2.0	57.4	-26.9
Cured Tobacco	::	-23.4	-11.0	78.4	44.5	-37.7	34.1	34.5	-33.8	19.1	42.8	3.1
Fruits	::	6.8	-3.2	14.8	-1.1	23.0	3.8	18.2	15.8	23.8	-0.1	10.3
Apples	::	28.1	-17.6	27.2	-19.2	45.7	-16.9	22.9	-7.7	27.8	1.9	
Citrus	::	44.9	28.5	11.9	17.7	38.0	15.7	20.6	40.9	26.5	-20.6	
Pears	::	-5.2	1.9	8.7	10.2	2.3	17.0	1.8	9.9	6.0	9.3	
Bananas	::	-12.9	-17.6	106.6	59.5	3.0	44.9	110.3	98.3	62.2	-9.8	

Source: Table 8.1.

Table 8.3 : CHINA : Total Sown Area
(million hectares)

	1978	1979	1980	1981	1982	1983	1984	1985	1986	1987	1988	1989
Total Food Grains	121	119	117	115	114	114	113	109	111	111	110	
of which												
Rice	34	34	34	33	33	33	33	32	32	32	32	
Wheat	29	29	29	28	28	29	30	29	30	29	29	
Corn	20	20	20	19	19	19	19	18	19	20	20	
Soybeans	7	7	7	8	8	8	7	8	8	8	8	
Tuber	12	11	10	10	9	9	9	9	9	9	9	
Peanuts	2	2	2	2	2	2	2	3	3	3	3	
Rapeseed	3	3	3	4	4	4	3	4	5	5	5	
Cotton	5	5	5	5	6	6	7	5	4	5	6	
Sugarcane	1	1	0	1	1	1	1	1	1	1	1	
Beetroots	0	0	0	0	0	1	1	1	1	0	1	
Cured Tobacco	1	1	0	1	1	1	1	1	1	1	1	
Fruits	..	..	..	..	..	..	..	3	4	5	5	
of which												
Apples	..	..	..	..	..	..	..	1	1	1	2	
Citrus	..	..	..	..	..	..	..	1	1	1	1	
Pears	..	..	..	..	..	..	..	0	0	0	0	
Bananas	..	..	..	..	..	..	..	0	0	0	0	
Total Sown Area	150	149	146	145	145	144	144	144	144	145	145	
Total Irrigated Area	..	45	45	45	44	45	44	44	44	44	44	45

Percentage to Total Sown Area

	1978	1979	1980	1981	1982	1983	1984	1985	1986	1987	1988	1989
Grain Crops	80.3	80.3	80.1	79.2	78.4	79.2	79.3	75.8	76.9	76.8	76.0	
Total Industrial Crops	9.6	10.0	10.9	12.1	13.0	12.3	13.4	15.6	14.1	14.3	14.8	

Source: CHINA Statistical Year Book 1989 (Chinese) pp.183, 192, and 197 for 1988; 1988 pp.197, 206 and 211 for 1978-87.
(converted into hectares with 1 mu=0.0667 ha).

Table 8.4 : CHINA : Total Sown Area
(Percentage GROWTH RATES)

	1978	1979	1980	1981	1982	1983	1984	1985	1986	1987	1988	1989
Total Food Grains	..	-1.1	-1.7	-1.9	-1.3	0.5	-1.0	-3.6	1.9	0.3	-1.0	
of which												
Rice	..	-1.8	0.0	-1.7	-0.7	0.2	0.1	-3.3	0.6	-0.2	-0.6	
Wheat	..	0.6	-0.4	-3.2	-1.2	3.9	1.8	-1.2	1.4	-2.8	-0.0	
Corn	..	0.9	1.1	-4.6	-4.5	1.5	-1.5	-4.5	8.1	5.7	-2.6	
Soybeans	..	1.4	-0.3	11.0	4.9	-10.1	-3.7	5.9	7.5	1.8	-3.8	
Tuber	..	-7.2	-7.3	-5.2	-2.6	0.3	-4.4	-4.6	1.3	2.1	2.1	
Peanuts	..	17.3	12.8	5.7	-2.3	-8.9	10.0	37.1	-2.0	-7.1	-1.5	
Rapeseed	..	7.0	3.0	33.6	8.5	-11.0	-7.0	31.7	9.4	7.1	-6.3	
Cotton	..	-7.3	9.0	5.4	12.4	4.3	13.9	-25.7	-16.2	12.5	14.3	
Sugarcane	..	-6.7	-6.4	15.0	18.5	0.1	11.3	32.5	-1.5	-9.6	7.6	
Beetroots	..	-1.6	36.1	-1.5	6.0	17.7	-7.7	11.7	-7.1	-4.4	49.5	
Cured Tobacco	..	-17.0	-22.0	47.9	51.5	-35.6	25.1	50.6	-17.0	2.1	42.8	
Fruits	..	..	..	..	..	..	..	..	34.2	22.8	12.4	
of which												
Apples	..	..	..	..	..	..	..	..	35.6	22.8	15.2	
Citrus	..	..	..	..	..	..	..	..	32.6	28.5	10.6	
Pears	..	..	..	..	..	..	..	..	16.7	11.9	10.4	
Bananas	..	..	..	..	..	..	..	..	51.3	113.2	-7.1	
Total Sown Area	..	-1.1	-1.4	-0.8	-0.3	-0.5	0.2	-0.4	0.4	0.5	-0.1	
Total Irrigated Area	..	..	-0.3	-0.7	-0.9	1.1	-0.4	-0.9	0.4	0.4	-0.1	0.8

GROWTH RATE of Percentage to Total Sown Area

	1978	1979	1980	1981	1982	1983	1984	1985	1986	1987	1988	1989
Grain Crops	..	0.0	-0.2	-1.1	-1.0	1.0	0.1	-4.4	1.5	-0.1	-1.0	
Total Industrial Crops	..	4.2	9.0	11.0	7.4	-5.4	8.9	16.4	-9.6	1.4	3.5	

Source: Table 8.3.

- 156 -

Table 8.5 : CHINA : Average Unit Area Yield of Major Crops
(At sown area   kg/hectare)

	1978	1979	1980	1981	1982	1983	1984	1985	1986	1987	1988
Total Food Grains	2534	2834	2744	2834	3133	3403	3613	3478	3523	3613	3583
Rice	3973	4243	4138	4318	4888	5097	5367	5247	5337	5412	5277
Wheat	1844	2144	1889	2114	2444	2804	2969	2939	3043	2984	2969
Corn	2804	2984	3073	3043	3268	3628	3958	3598	3703	3913	3928
Soybeans	1064	1034	1094	1169	1079	1289	1334	1364	1394	1469	1439
Tuber	2699	2594	2834	2699	2894	3118	3163	3028	2909	3178	2984
Peanuts	1349	1364	1544	1544	1619	1799	1799	2009	1814	2039	1904
Rapeseed	720	870	840	1079	1379	1169	1229	1244	1199	1259	1019
Cotton	450	495	555	570	615	765	915	810	825	870	750
Sugarcane	38486	42009	47541	53793	56432	47586	54258	53403	52834	55112	53088
Beetroots	8171	9550	14243	14588	14513	16882	16492	15907	15952	16342	17181
Cured Tobacco	1724	1589	1814	2189	2084	2009	2159	1919	1529	1784	1799

Source: CHINA Statistical Year Book 1989 (Chinese) pp.205 for 1988 and 1988 pp.217 for 1978-87.
(converted into hectares with 1 mu=0.0667 ha).

Table 8.6 : CHINA : Average Unit Area Yield of Major Crops
(Percentage GROWTH RATES)

	1978	1979	1980	1981	1982	1983	1984	1985	1986	1987	1988
Total Food Grains	..	11.8	-3.2	3.3	10.6	8.6	6.2	-3.7	1.3	2.6	-0.8
Rice	..	6.8	-2.5	4.3	13.2	4.3	5.3	-2.2	1.7	1.4	-2.5
Wheat	..	16.3	-11.9	11.9	15.6	14.7	5.9	-1.0	3.6	-2.0	-0.5
Corn	..	6.4	3.0	-1.0	7.4	11.0	9.1	-9.1	2.9	5.7	0.4
Soybeans	..	-2.8	5.8	6.8	-7.7	19.4	3.5	2.2	2.2	5.4	-2.0
Tuber	..	-3.9	9.2	-4.8	7.2	7.8	1.4	-4.3	-4.0	9.3	-6.1
Peanuts	..	1.1	13.2	0.0	4.9	11.1	0.0	11.7	-9.7	12.4	-6.6
Rapeseed	..	20.8	-3.4	28.6	27.8	-15.2	5.1	1.2	-3.6	5.0	-19.0
Cotton	..	10.0	12.1	2.7	7.9	24.4	19.6	-11.5	1.9	5.5	-13.8
Sugarcane	..	9.2	13.2	13.2	4.9	-15.7	14.0	-1.6	-1.1	4.3	-3.7
Beetroots	..	16.9	49.1	2.4	-0.5	16.3	-2.3	-3.5	0.3	2.4	5.1
Cured Tobacco	..	-7.8	14.2	20.7	-4.8	-3.6	7.5	-11.1	-20.3	16.7	0.8

Source: Table 8.5.

Table 9.1: CHINA: Gross Output Value of Industry

(million yuan)

	1985	1986	1987	1988	1989
Total	971647	1119426	1381299	1822458	2188000
By Type of ownership					
State-owned	630212	697112	825009	1035128	1824200
Collective-owned	311719	375154	478174	658749	
of which: Township	76055	98108	128419	184669	
Village	66272	83849	116535	170363	
Individual	17975	30854	50239	79049	
Urban	3339	2913	5027	6848	
Rural	14636	27941	45212	72200	
Other	11741	16306	27877	49532	
By Type of industry					
Light	457532	533035	665643	897924	1070000
Heavy	514115	586391	715656	924534	1118000

Source: CHINA Statistical Year book 1989 pp. 263 for 1988 and 1988 pp.267 for 1985-7.

Table 9.2: CHINA: Gross Output Value of Industry

(in percentages)

	1985	1986	1987	1988	1989
Total	100.0	100.0	100.0	100.0	100.0
By Type of ownership					
State-owned	64.9	62.3	59.7	56.8	83.4
Collective-owned	32.1	33.5	34.6	36.1	
of which: Township	7.8	8.8	9.3	10.1	
Village	6.8	7.5	8.4	9.3	
Individual	1.8	2.8	3.6	4.3	
Urban	0.3	0.3	0.4	0.4	
Rural	1.5	2.5	3.3	4.0	
Other	1.2	1.5	2.0	2.7	
By Type of industry					
Light	47.1	47.6	48.2	49.3	48.9
Heavy	52.9	52.4	51.8	50.7	51.1

Source: Table 9.1

Table 9.3: CHINA: Output of Major Industrial Products

Product	Unit	1979	1980	1981	1982	1983	1984	1985	1986	1987	1988	1989
Coal	million tons	635	620	622	666	715	789	872	894	928	947	1040
Crude Oil	million tons	108	106	101	102	106	115	125	131	134	137	137
Natural Gas	billion cu m	15	14	13	12	12	12	13	13	14	14	..
Electricity	billion kWh	282	301	309	328	351	377	411	450	497	539	582
Hydro power	billion kWh	50	58	66	74	86	87	92	95	100	107	118
Steel	million tons	34	37	36	37	40	43	47	52	56	59	61
Rolled Steel	million tons	25	27	37	29	31	34	37	41	44	47	49
Cement	million tons	74	80	83	95	108	123	146	166	186	203	207
Timber	million cu m	54	54	49	50	52	64	63	65	64	62	61
Railway Freight Cars	1000 units	16	11	9	11	16	18	19	21	22	23	..

Source: CHINA Statistical Abstract 1989 pp.42-4.

Table 9.4: CHINA: Percentage Growth Rates of Output of Major Industrial Products

Product	1980	1981	1982	1983	1984	1985	1986	1987	1988	1989	1980-5	1986-9	1980-9
Coal	-2.4	0.3	7.1	7.4	10.3	10.5	2.5	3.8	2.0	9.8	5.5	4.5	5.1
Crude Oil	-0.2	-4.5	0.9	3.9	8.1	9.0	4.6	2.6	2.0	0.1	2.9	2.4	2.7
Natural Gas	-1.7	-10.7	-6.4	2.3	1.8	4.0	3.5	3.8	2.9	..	-1.8	3.4	-0.0
Electricity	6.6	2.9	5.9	7.2	7.3	8.9	9.4	10.6	8.4	8.0	6.5	9.1	7.5
Hydro power	16.2	12.5	13.6	16.1	0.5	6.5	2.5	5.6	6.7	10.8	10.9	6.4	9.1
Steel	7.7	-4.1	4.4	7.7	8.6	7.6	11.6	7.8	5.2	3.5	5.3	7.0	8.0
Rolled Steel	8.8	35.1	-20.9	5.9	9.8	9.5	9.9	8.1	7.1	3.6	8.0	7.2	7.7
Cement	8.1	3.8	14.8	13.7	13.6	18.6	13.8	12.2	9.2	1.8	12.1	9.2	11.0
Timber	-1.5	-7.8	2.0	3.8	22.0	-1.0	2.8	-1.4	-3.0	-1.8	2.9	-0.9	1.4
Railway Freight Cars	-33.8	-17.0	20.5	49.1	14.6	6.6	6.7	4.9	7.9	..	6.7	6.5	6.6

Source: Table 9.3.

Table 9.5: CHINA: Shares by Industrial Sectors
(in Percent)

	Shares of Gross Outputs				Shares of Employment				Shares of Investment		
	1971	1978	1981	1987	1978	1981	1984	1987	1981	1984	1987
Metallurgy	11.1	8.7	8.8	8.0	7.1	6.4	6.3	6.3	11.5	11.9	12.2
Power	3.7	3.8	3.8	3.1	1.7	1.8	1.8	2.0	12.0	12.9	15.3
Coal and Coke	3.3	2.8	2.8	2.2	8.8	8.2	8.2	7.4	10.3	12.5	7.2
Petroleum	4.6	5.5	5.4	4.2	1.0	1.0	1.1	1.3	14.3	15.0	12.5
Chemical	10.9	12.4	11.4	11.8	9.0	8.8	8.8	9.1	9.7	10.6	12.0
Machinery	25.3	27.3	20.9	28.0	30.6	30.0	29.0	27.2	13.3	12.8	13.5
Building materials	2.8	3.6	3.8	4.5	9.3	9.0	9.6	10.9	3.9	4.9	5.8
Forest	1.9	1.8	2.0	1.5	3.9	3.9	3.7	3.5	2.6	2.0	1.2
Food	11.9	11.1	13.3	11.1	5.8	6.2	6.5	6.8	5.7	5.3	7.2
Textile, clothing & leather	..	15.3	20.4	18.1	14.9	16.0	16.2	17.3	12.2	8.0	8.6
Papermaking and cultural articles	..	3.3	3.7	5.1	5.0	5.1	4.9	5.7	2.1	1.5	2.0
Others	..	3.9	3.3	3.5	3.0	3.7	4.0	2.6	2.3	2.6	2.5
TOTAL	100.0	100.0	100.0	100.0	100.0	100.0	100.0	100.0	100.0	100.0	100.0

Source: (a) Shares of gross outpus are from: CHINA Statistics Press, "Zhongguo gongye jingji tongji nianjian 1988" (Industrial
Statistics Yearbook of China 1988), pp.54-57;
(b) Shares of employment and investment are estimated based on data from CHINA Statistical Yearbook , various years.

Table 11.1: CHINA: Labor force by Sector
(million)

	1978	1979	1980	1981	1982	1983	1984	1985	1986	1987	1988
Farming forestry, animal husbandry, fishery & water conservency	284	287	292	298	309	312	309	312	313	317	323
Industry	61	63	67	70	72	74	79	83	90	93	97
Geological survey & exploration	1	1	1	1	1	1	1	1	1	1	1
Construction	9	9	10	11	12	13	17	21	23	24	25
Transportation, posts & telecommunications	7	8	8	8	9	9	11	12	13	14	14
Commerce, catering trade, supply & marketing of materials and warehouses	12	12	14	15	16	18	20	24	25	27	28
Real estate administration, public utilities, residential & consultancy services	2	2	3	3	4	4	5	4	5	5	6
Public health, sports and social welfare	4	4	4	4	4	4	4	5	5	5	5
Education, culture, art, radio and television broadcasting	11	11	11	11	11	12	12	13	13	14	14
Scientific research, technical service	1	1	1	1	1	1	1	1	2	2	2
Banking and insurance	1	1	1	1	1	1	1	1	2	2	2
Governments, parties and organizations	5	5	5	6	6	6	7	8	9	9	10
Others	5	5	6	8	7	9	13	13	13	15	17
TOTAL	402	410	424	437	453	464	482	499	513	528	543

Source: CHINA Statistical Year book 1989 (Chinese) pp.102 for 1988 and 1988 pp.124 for 1978-87.

Table 12.1 : CHINA : General Price Indices
(1980=100)

	1978	1979	1980	1981	1982	1983	1984	1985	1986	1987	1988	1989
Retail Prices	92.5	94.3	100.0	102.4	104.4	105.9	108.9	118.5	125.6	134.8	159.7	188.1
Cost of Living of Staff & Workers	91.3	93.0	100.0	102.5	104.6	106.7	109.6	122.6	131.2	142.8	172.3	
Purchasing Price of Farm & Sideline Products	76.4	93.4	100.0	105.9	108.2	113.0	117.5	127.6	135.8	152.0	187.0	
Retail Prices of Industrial Products in Rural Areas	99.1	99.2	100.0	101.0	102.6	103.6	106.9	110.3	113.8	119.3	137.5	
Price Parity between Industrial & Agricultural Products	129.5	106.2	100.0	95.4	94.6	91.5	90.8	86.4	83.8	78.5	73.3	
Market Price of Consumer goods	102.7	98.0	100.0	105.8	109.3	113.9	113.4	132.9	143.7	167.1	217.7	244.0

Source: CHINA Statistical Year Book 1988 pp.692, 700 for 1978-87 and (Chinese) 1989 pp.688, 703 for 1988.

Percentage GROWTH RATES over last year

	1978	1979	1980	1981	1982	1983	1984	1985	1986	1987	1988	1989
Retail Prices	..	2.0	6.0	2.4	1.9	1.5	2.8	8.8	6.0	7.3	18.5	17.8
Cost of Living of Staff & Workers	..	1.9	7.5	2.5	2.0	2.0	2.7	11.9	7.0	8.8	20.7	
Purchasing Price of Farm & Sideline Products	..	22.1	7.1	5.9	2.2	4.4	4.0	8.6	6.4	12.0	23.0	
Retail Prices of Industrial Products in Rural Areas	..	0.1	0.8	1.0	1.6	1.0	3.1	3.2	3.2	4.8	15.2	
Price Parity between Industrial & Agricultural Products	..	-18.0	-5.8	-4.6	-0.8	-3.3	-0.8	-4.8	-3.0	-6.4	-6.5	
Market Price of Consumer goods	..	-4.5	2.0	5.8	3.3	4.2	-0.4	17.2	8.1	16.3	30.3	12.1

Source: CHINA Statistical Year Book 1988 pp.692, 700 for 1978-87 and (Chinese) 1989 pp.688, 703 for 1988.

Table 12.2: CHINA: Growth Rate of Overall Retail Sales Price Index

Whole Nation

(Growth rate over same month last year)

	Food	Grain	Non Staple Food	Fresh Vegeta-bles	Dried Vegeta-bles	Meat Poultry & Eggs	Aquatic Products	Fresh Fruit	Dried Fruit	Garments	Daily Use Articles	Overall
1988												
January	..	..	..	..	..	..	..	..	..	..	..	..
February	15.3	6.2	23.9	48.3	13.6	27.6	25.5	7.7	17.6	5.6	3.3	11.2
March	15.8	5.7	24.3	30.2	12.7	30.3	26.3	13.7	16.6	6.8	4.8	11.6
April	16.1	7.4	24.7	16.0	14.7	35.4	27.1	7.5	16.2	8.6	6.5	12.6
May	17.7	8.9	26.9	17.8	15.6	37.7	26.5	6.0	17.4	10.1	8.4	14.7
June	20.2	13.5	29.5	13.2	15.0	40.3	33.0	8.7	17.6	11.0	10.7	16.5
July	23.6	12.3	32.3	30.3	16.6	41.0	31.6	29.0	16.5	12.5	12.8	19.3
August	28.9	18.6	37.4	47.8	19.1	42.6	37.1	18.2	17.6	15.2	15.6	23.2
September	..	..	..	..	..	..	..	..	..	..	..	..
October	30.4	12.3	39.0	42.0	23.9	43.8	38.7	32.2	28.8	18.7	19.3	26.1
November	31.9	26.0	35.6	30.5	23.5	38.8	36.5	45.0	30.8	19.8	21.4	26.0
December	30.5	29.2	31.2	16.8	25.6	33.8	32.9	44.0	32.1	21.2	21.8	26.7
Average 1988												
1989												
January	29.2	29.8	29.5	16.5	27.4	30.4	34.3	45.0	36.1	20.8	22.2	27.0
February	29.3	29.8	30.1	14.7	29.5	31.7	33.7	37.8	35.8	22.8	23.0	27.9
March	27.2	33.3	26.2	-3.7	27.5	30.7	28.9	24.9	37.9	23.4	22.6	26.2
April	26.6	33.6	25.0	6.2	26.5	26.5	27.4	22.4	38.3	22.7	21.4	25.8
May	24.4	32.8	21.1	15.4	25.3	19.7	25.2	28.8	36.8	22.4	20.4	24.4
June	..	..	..	..	..	..	..	..	..	..	..	..
July	17.8	26.8	13.8	8.1	21.7	12.3	18.7	21.1	35.8	20.0	16.8	19.0
August	12.3	19.6	9.6	0.3	19.8	9.1	18.9	11.7	35.5	17.9	14.0	15.2
September	8.0	15.8	5.1	-6.3	15.0	4.3	7.2	2.9	29.5	15.1	13.4	11.4
October	4.6	9.9	2.2	-4.6	11.2	0.2	4.7	-2.1	17.7	13.5	0.3	8.7

Source: China Statistics Monthly, University of Illinois, Chicago.

Table 12.3: CHINA: Growth Rate of Overall Retail Price Index

(same month last year = 100)

	Beijing	Tianjin	Shenyang	Shanghai	Nanjing	Wuhan	Guangzhou	Chengdu	Xian	Urban Total
1988										
January	10.2	6.5	7.9	15.4	16.0	13.7	15.5	14.4	13.0	11.7
February	10.0	9.9	15.5	15.6	16.9	16.1	20.9	14.5	14.2	13.4
March	10.1	10.7	12.4	15.9	18.2	15.2	20.7	22.0	16.7	14.2
April	12.2	10.2	8.8	13.4	20.8	17.7	20.0	17.7	14.8	14.2
May	12.5	11.5	10.9	19.4	22.7	17.8	23.8	17.6	13.9	16.0
June	22.2	14.8	17.2	23.7	21.9	16.4	20.8	18.4	15.6	18.1
July	25.9	22.6	20.4	24.2	25.3	21.6	27.5	21.6	18.5	22.0
August	30.7	25.1	26.7	24.3	32.2	28.2	35.9	31.7	26.7	27.4
September	29.9	24.0	32.2	25.4	32.0	32.9	44.3	37.8	28.3	29.8
October	33.3	24.9	31.0	28.8	29.4	31.9	41.7	41.1	31.0	30.2
November	29.1	25.1	29.9	27.4	27.5	29.4	43.4	38.4	34.0	30.4
December	30.5	24.9	32.1	25.4	29.2	28.1	38.6	35.0	32.8	28.9
Average 1988	21.4	17.5	20.4	21.6	24.3	22.4	29.4	25.8	21.6	21.4
1989										
January	28.9	24.4	34.1	26.4	27.5	24.5	44.0	32.9	37.9	27.8
February	28.5	22.0	31.3	29.7	30.5	25.3	45.0	32.7	34.9	27.8
March	28.4	20.2	28.9	26.9	25.8	23.9	41.5	23.7	31.0	26.0
April	25.6	19.9	27.4	26.5	21.1	20.0	39.5	26.2	32.8	25.6
May	..	..	..	..	..	..	..	..	..	..
June	14.8	14.6	19.6	21.3	18.4	19.2	40.1	19.8	25.9	21.0
July	16.4	10.3	15.4	16.9	15.9	16.3	21.4	16.7	21.9	17.2
August	12.1	8.4	12.5	14.4	12.7	9.8	12.6	10.5	19.2	12.6
September	10.6	7.6	9.7	12.4	11.8	6.4	10.9	5.7	14.0	8.6

Source: China Statistics Monthly, University of Illinois, Chicago.

Table 12.4: CHINA: Growth Rate of Cost of Living Index of Staff and Workers

(Goods and Services)

(Growth rate over same month last year)

	Beijing	Tianjin	Shenyang	Shanghai	Nanjing	Wuhan	Guangzhou	Chengdu	Xian	Urban Total
1988										
January	9.6	6.1	7.4	13.9	14.7	12.6	13.8	13.4	12.8	11.2
February	9.6	9.3	10.7	14.6	15.6	14.8	19.1	13.5	14.1	12.8
March	9.8	10.2	11.6	15.0	16.7	14.1	19.2	20.2	16.6	13.6
April	11.5	9.7	8.2	13.4	19.2	16.4	18.2	16.5	14.9	13.7
May	12.0	11.0	10.3	18.8	21.0	16.5	17.9	16.5	14.1	15.4
June	20.7	14.0	16.1	22.7	20.4	15.3	19.3	17.7	15.6	17.5
July	24.1	21.4	19.0	23.2	23.6	20.1	25.5	20.5	18.4	21.2
August	28.6	23.8	24.8	23.2	30.1	28.6	33.3	30.1	25.8	26.6
September	27.9	22.9	29.7	24.4	30.1	31.1	42.1	36.6	27.8	29.2
October	31.0	23.8	29.4	26.8	27.3	30.3	39.9	39.9	30.2	29.7
November	27.1	24.0	28.4	25.4	25.8	28.1	41.6	37.5	33.0	29.8
December	28.3	23.8	30.5	23.6	27.3	26.9	37.4	34.4	31.9	28.6
Average 1988	20.0	16.7	18.8	20.4	22.7	21.1	27.3	24.7	21.3	20.8
1989										
January	26.6	23.2	32.6	25.4	26.3	23.5	42.5	32.6	36.1	27.3
February	26.2	21.0	29.1	28.2	29.9	24.3	43.4	32.3	33.3	27.4
March	26.2	19.4	26.9	25.7	25.5	23.0	40.2	24.4	30.3	25.7
April	23.6	19.0	25.5	24.5	21.1	19.3	38.7	26.7	31.7	25.3
May	..	..	18.3	19.7	18.6	18.4	39.1	20.3	..	21.0
June	13.8	14.0	14.4	15.7	16.3	15.7	22.1	17.6	25.9	17.5
July	15.3	9.9	11.9	13.5	13.2	9.3	14.2	11.3	22.2	13.0
August	11.4	8.2	9.6	12.4	13.1	6.4	10.5	5.8	20.0	9.2
September	10.2	7.6							15.2	

Source: China Statistics Monthly, University of Illinois, Chicago.

Table 13.1: CHINA: Total Investment in Fixed Assets

	(million yuan)				(percentages)				GDP (million yuan) (current prices)	% of Total Investment to GDP
	Total Invest-ment	State Owned	Collec-tive	Indivi-dual	Total Invest-ment	State Owned	Collec-tive	Indivi-dual		
1981	96101	66751	11524	17826	100.0	69.5	12.0	18.5	477510	20.1
1982	123040	84531	17428	21081	100.0	68.7	14.2	17.1	518580	23.7
1983	143006	95196	15633	32177	100.0	66.6	10.9	22.5	578460	24.7
1984	183287	118518	23869	40900	100.0	64.7	13.0	22.3	692240	26.5
1985	254319	168051	32746	53522	100.0	66.1	12.9	21.0	854060	29.8
1986	301982	197850	39174	64938	100.0	65.5	13.0	21.5	971990	31.1
1987	364086	229799	54701	79586	100.0	63.1	15.0	21.9	1135710	32.1
1988	449654	276276	71171	102208	100.0	61.4	15.8	22.7	1388770	32.4
1989	400000	251000	51200	98700	100.2	62.8	12.8	24.7	1578110	25.4

Source: Statistical Year Book of China 1988 pp.493 for 1981-87 and
Statistical Year Book of China (in Chinese) 1989 pp.477 for 1988.

Table 13.2: CHINA: Total Investment in Fixed Assets

State-Owned Enterprises

(million yuan)

	Total Invest-ment	Capital constr-uction	Techni-cal updating	Other
1978	66872	50099	16773	0
1979	69936	52348	17588	0
1980	74590	55889	18701	0
1981	66751	44291	19530	2930
1982	84531	55553	25037	3941
1983	95196	59413	29113	6670
1984	118518	74315	30928	13275
1985	168051	107437	44914	15700
1986	197850	117611	61921	18318
1987	229799	134310	75859	19630
1988	271280	152579	97951	20751
1989	251000	153800	..	..

(percentages)

	Total Invest-ment	Capital constr-uction	Techni-cal updating	Other
1978	100.0	74.9	25.1	0.0
1979	100.0	74.9	25.1	0.0
1980	100.0	74.9	25.1	0.0
1981	100.0	66.4	29.3	4.4
1982	100.0	65.7	29.6	4.7
1983	100.0	62.4	30.6	7.0
1984	100.0	62.7	26.1	11.2
1985	100.0	63.9	26.7	9.3
1986	100.0	59.4	31.3	9.3
1987	100.0	58.4	33.0	8.5
1988	100.0	56.2	36.1	7.6
1989	100.0	61.3	..	..

Source: Statistical Year Book of China 1988 pp.498 for 1981-87 and
Statistical Year Book of China (in Chinese) 1989 pp.482 for 1988.

Table 13.3 : CHINA: Investment in Capital Construction by Sector of National Economy

State-Owned Enterprises

(in million yuan)

	All Sectors	Agriculture	Industry	Construction	Geology	Transport	Commerce	Research	Utilities	other
1981	44291	2921	21601	909	250	4047	2801	4363	3185	4214
1982	55553	3412	26060	1052	259	5721	3597	5081	4221	6149
1983	59413	3545	28228	1032	336	7804	2893	5944	3802	5830
1984	74315	3712	34159	1124	372	10846	3517	7879	5736	6970
1985	107437	3894	44649	2200	725	17095	7209	12081	9274	10510
1986	117611	3666	53164	1853	711	18081	6891	14028	8301	10914
1987	134310	4282	68279	1554	734	18973	7842	15117	6169	11361
1988	152679	4719	79609	1497	464	20829	9935	15283	7061	13182

Source: Statistical Year Book of China 1988 pp.504 for 1981-87 and
Statistical Year Book of China (in Chinese) 1989 pp.488 for 1988.

Table 13.4 : CHINA: Investment in Capital Construction by Sector of National Economy

State-Owned Enterprises
(in percentages)

	All Sectors	Agricul- ture	Indsutry	Const- ruction	Geology	Trans- port	Commerce	Research	Utili- ties	other
1981	100.0	6.6	48.8	2.1	0.6	9.1	6.3	9.9	7.2	9.5
1982	100.0	6.1	46.9	1.9	0.5	10.3	6.5	9.1	7.6	11.1
1983	100.0	6.0	47.5	1.7	0.6	13.1	4.9	10.0	6.4	9.8
1984	100.0	5.0	46.0	1.5	0.5	14.6	4.7	10.6	7.7	9.4
1985	100.0	3.4	41.6	2.0	0.7	15.9	6.7	11.2	8.6	9.8
1986	100.0	3.1	45.2	1.6	0.6	15.4	5.9	11.9	7.1	9.3
1987	100.0	3.2	50.8	1.2	0.5	14.1	5.8	11.3	4.8	8.5
1988	100.0	3.1	52.2	1.0	0.3	13.7	6.5	10.0	4.6	8.6

Source: Table 13.3.

Table 13.5 : CHINA: Investment in Capital Construction by Sector by Branch of Industry

State-Owned Enterprises
(in million yuan)

	Total Industry	Metallu- rgical	Power	Coal	Petro- leum	Chemical	Machine Building	Forest	Building Materials	Textile	Food	Paper making
1981	21601	2735	4014	2315	2795	1902	2439	663	879	1988	926	191
1982	26060	4300	4623	2985	2530	2578	2712	785	1167	2116	1407	169
1983	28228	4247	5746	4007	2902	3007	2675	642	1400	1708	1128	171
1984	34159	4673	7899	5514	3063	3574	3043	705	1667	1810	1191	207
1985	44649	5203	10786	5511	3317	5380	4748	849	2738	2074	1749	338
1986	53164	5416	15974	5770	3861	5893	4175	743	3188	2687	2231	432
1987	68279	7927	20864	5960	5855	8400	5017	956	3416	3096	3071	536
1988	79609	9543	24432	6350	8645	10131	5682	892	3210	3610	2946	673

Source: Statistical Year Book of China 1988 pp.504 for 1981-87 and
Statistical Year Book of China (in Chinese) 1989 pp.489 for 1988.

Table 13.6 : CHINA: Investment in Capital Construction by Sector by Branch of Industry

State-Owned Enterprises
(in percentages)

	Total Industry	Subtotal	Metallurgical	Power	Coal	Petroleum	Chemical	Machine Building	Forest	Building Materials	Textile	Food	Paper making
1981	100.0	96.5	12.7	18.6	10.7	12.9	8.8	11.3	3.1	4.1	9.2	4.3	0.9
1982	100.0	97.4	16.5	17.7	11.5	9.7	9.9	10.4	3.0	4.5	8.1	5.4	0.6
1983	100.0	97.9	15.0	20.4	14.2	10.3	10.7	9.5	2.3	5.0	6.1	4.0	0.6
1984	100.0	97.0	13.7	22.5	16.1	9.0	10.5	8.9	2.1	4.9	5.3	3.5	0.6
1985	100.0	95.2	11.7	24.2	12.3	7.4	12.0	10.6	1.5	6.1	4.6	3.9	0.8
1986	100.0	94.7	10.2	30.0	10.9	7.3	11.1	7.9	1.4	6.0	5.1	4.2	0.8
1987	100.0	95.3	11.8	30.6	8.7	8.6	12.3	7.3	1.4	5.0	4.5	4.5	0.8
1988	100.0	95.6	12.0	30.7	8.0	10.9	12.7	7.1	1.1	4.0	4.5	3.7	0.8

Source: Statistical Year Book of China 1988 pp.504 for 1981-87 and
Statistical Year Book of China (in Chinese) 1989 pp.489 for 1988.

Table 13.7: CHINA : Sectoral Breakdown of Investment
(Percentage Shares)

	1981	1982	1983	1984	1985	1986	1987	1988
Capital Construction	100.0	100.0	100.0	100.0	100.0	100.0	100.0	100.0
of which								
Agriculture	6.6	6.1	6.0	5.0	3.4	3.0	3.1	4.6
Industry	48.8	46.9	47.5	46.0	41.6	45.2	50.8	..
Energy	21.4	18.4	21.5	22.3	19.0	22.5	24.5	24.0
Communications	9.1	10.3	13.1	14.6	15.9	16.4	14.1	14.1
Technical Updating	100.0	100.0	100.0	100.0	100.0	100.0	100.0	100.0
of which								
Agriculture	2.6	2.2	2.1	1.7	1.4	1.2	1.3	..
Industry	73.2	70.0	71.3	72.9	78.2	77.4	77.1	..
Energy	13.0	12.6	13.0	13.1	10.4	10.3	9.8	..
Communications	11.2	10.9	11.2	11.3	9.0	8.9	8.5	..
Collectives	100.0	100.0	100.0	100.0	100.0	100.0	100.0	100.0
of which								
Agriculture	22.5	20.2	18.5	13.3	9.3	8.4	8.1	..
Industry	72.0	70.2	69.0	67.5	62.1	63.2	63.4	..
Energy	1.0	1.0	1.0	1.0	1.0	1.0	0.9	..
Communications	2.4	2.5	2.3	2.0	1.3	5.2	5.4	..

Source: CHINA Statistical Year book 1988 pp. 258,277,493,503f,543,545f,571,573,579;
State Statistical Bureau, Statistics for 1988 Socioeconomic Development;
Beijing Review, March 6-12, 1989, and World Bank estimates.

Note: Technical updating investment in energy has been calculated by assuming the
.. of energy to transport investment in 1987 throughout. Sectoral investment ratios
for collectives assume that the ratio of sectoral investment to sectoral GVIO is
the same as in 1987 for all years.

Table 13.8: CHINA : Sectoral Allocation of National Capital Construction Investment
(Investment as a Percentage of Total State Investment in all Sectors)

	1953-87	1958-62	1963-65	1966-70	1971-75	1976-80	1958-80	1981-85	1981	1982	1983	1984	1985	1986	1987
Agriculture	7.1	11.3	17.7	10.7	9.8	10.5	12.0	5.1	6.6	6.1	6.0	5.0	3.4	3.0	3.1
Light Industry	6.4	6.4	3.9	4.4	5.8	6.7	5.4	6.9	9.8	8.4	6.5	5.7	5.9	7.0	7.4
Heavy Industry	36.1	54.0	45.9	51.1	49.6	45.9	49.3	38.5	39.0	38.5	41.0	40.3	35.7	38.2	43.5

Source: "Investment Issues in the Chinese Countryside" by Andrew Watson in Australian Journal of Chinese Affairs, No. 22, July 1989.

Table 14.1: CHINA: Total Production and Consumption of Energy and its Composition

	1978	1979	1980	1981	1982	1983	1984	1985	1986	1987	1988
PRODUCTION (millions of standard fuel)	628	646	637	632	668	713	779	855	881	913	958
Proportion (%)											
Coal	70.3	70.2	69.4	70.2	71.2	71.6	72.4	72.8	72.4	72.6	73.1
Crude Oil	23.7	23.5	23.8	22.9	21.9	21.3	21.0	20.9	21.2	21.0	20.4
Natural Gas	2.9	3.0	3.0	2.7	2.4	2.3	2.1	2.0	2.1	2.0	2.0
Hydro Power	3.1	3.3	3.8	4.2	4.5	4.8	4.5	4.3	4.3	4.4	4.5
CONSUMPTION (millions of standard fuel)	571	586	603	594	626	660	709	770	817	859	920
Proportion (%)											
Coal	70.7	71.3	72.5	72.2	73.9	74.2	75.3	75.9	76.1	76.3	76.1
Crude Oil	22.7	21.8	20.7	20.0	18.8	18.1	17.4	17.0	17.0	17.0	17.1
Natural Gas	3.2	3.3	3.1	2.8	2.5	2.4	2.4	2.3	2.2	2.1	2.1
Hydro Power	3.4	3.6	4.0	4.5	4.8	5.3	4.9	4.8	4.7	4.6	4.7
GDP (Constant 1980 Prices in million yuan)	392760	420250	447150	489080	507990	557780	633080	716010	773290	854480	950190
Energy Consumption (million ton per billion yuan)	1.5	1.4	1.3	1.3	1.2	1.2	1.1	1.1	1.1	1.0	1.0

Source: CHINA Statistical Year Book 1988 pp.389 for 1978-87; 1989 (Chinese) pp.351 for 1988.

NOTES:

Excluding bio-energy, solar, geothermal and nuclear energy.
All fuels are converted into standard fuel with thermal
equivalent of 7000 kilocalorie per kilogram. The conversion is
1 kg of coal (5000 kcal)   = 0.714 kg of standard fuel.
1 kg of crude oil (10000 kcal)   = 1.43 kg of standard fuel.
1 cubic metre of natural gas (9310 kcal) = 1.33 kg of standard fuel.
The conversion of hydropower into standard fuel is calculated on
the basis of the consumption quota of standard coal for thermal
power generation of the year.

Table 14.2: CHINA: Share of Fuel Sector in Industrial Investment
in 1976-1980 and 1981-85 in Selected Countries

(Percentage)

	1976-80	1981-85	1986-88
CHINA	10.7	26.9	9.1
CPEs			
Czechoslovakia	11.3	14.6	
Hungary	11.3	17.2	
Poland	13.6	20.9	
Romania	13.1	19.1	
Soviet Union	20.8	26.5	
Mature Industrial Western Countries			
Italy	1.8	5.3	
France	..	6.5	

Source: Economic Survey of Europe in 1986-87 (for CPEs) and Yearbook of Industrial Statistics 1981 & 1985.
CHINA Statistical Year book 1988 pp.505 for 1976-87; 1989 (Chinese) pp.489 for 1988.

ANNEX II

ALPHABETICAL NOTES

CHINA

COUNTRY ECONOMIC MEMORANDUM: BETWEEN PLAN AND MARKET

References

Chapter 1

a/ See "False Starts and Second Wind: Financial Reforms in China's Industrial System" by Barry Naughton, in The Political Economy of Reform in
Post-Mao China, eds. Elizabeth J. Perry and Christine Wong, Harvard
Contemporary, China Series, No. 2, 1985, pp. 223-24; China's Political
Economy, by C. Riskin, Oxford University Press, 1987, pp. 342-46. Cyril
Lin notes that, "Chinese reform debates in 1978-82 focused largely on
enterprise autonomy as the pivot on which related aspects of reform would
or should turn." (p. 103). He also goes on to observe that the 1978
experiments with enterprise autonomy in Sichuan, which were extended to
the whole nation in 1979, were derived from the 1962 "Seventy Articles on
Industry." (p. 110). The continuity of change is remarkable. "Open-
ended Economic Reform in China," by Cyril Lin, in Remaking the Economic
Institutions of Socialism, eds. Victor Nee and David Stark, Stanford
University Press, 1989.

b/ The resources and power gained by local authorities through decentrali-
zation and their strong support for reforms that continue this trend are
discussed in "Material Allocation and Decentralization: Impact of the
Local Sector on Industrial Reform," by Christine Wong, esp. p. 276. in
The Political Economy of Reform in Post-Mao China, eds. Elizabeth J.
Perry and Christine Wong, Harvard Contemporary China Series, No. 2, 1985.

c/ Inflation rose to 6 percent in 1980. Even this was viewed as a grave
development and a policy of freezing prices was introduced in late 1980.
By 1981 prices were rising by 2.4 percent. "The Politics of Price Control," by Dorothy J. Solinger, in Policy Implementation in Post-Mao
China, ed. David M. Lampton, University of California Press, 1987,
pp. 81-82.

d/ The enterprise contract system is described in "Enterprise Management:
Issues and Options," World Bank Report, No. 7773-CHA, July 1989.

e/ Prior to reforms, industrial wages were subject to uniform bureaucratic
guidelines. In the mid-eighties some decision-making autonomy concerning
wages, allowances and bonuses was passed down to enterprises. An
announcement in late 1989 indicated that wage bills in 1988 would be
assessed with reference to actual payments in 1984. This prompted
enterprises to use their newly gained powers and grant workers,
promotions salary increases and generous bonuses. Total wage bills rose
by 75.4 percent in December 1984. The stage was set for the wage-price
cycle. "Macroeconomic Development of China: Overheating in 1984-87 and

Problems for Reform", by R. Komiya, <u>Journal of Japanese and International Economies</u>, Vol. 3, 1989, p. 33.

Chapter 2

<u>a</u>/   "The State Council Issues a Notification Demanding Rectification of All Types of Fixed Investment," <u>Jingji Ribao</u>, October 5, 1989, p. 1; a full elaboration of the policy is in "Fundamentals of This Year's Fixed Investment Policy," <u>Zhongguo Jiben Jianshe</u>, 1989, No. 2, pp. 4-6.

<u>b</u>/   Wei Jing, "Scale, Structure, Efficiency: Analysis of 1988 Fixed Investment," <u>Zhongguo Jiben Jianshe</u>, 1989, No. 3, p. 22; <u>China Investment and Construction</u>, 1989, No. 7, p. 8.

<u>c</u>/   "Price Inspectors to Investigate Markets in Major Cities," <u>Jingji Ribao</u>, October 2, 1989, p. 2.

<u>d</u>/   Current heterodox thinking on stabilization policy supports the use of a price freeze to modify expectations, slow the inflation spiral and win adherence to the government's program. See "Israel's Stabilization" by Michael Bruno and Sylvia Piterman, in <u>Inflation Stabilization</u>, eds. M. Bruno, <u>et al.</u>, MIT Press, 1988, p. 11; "The End of the High Israeli Inflation: An Experiment in Heterodox Stabilization" by Alex Cukierman, p. 65; and "Lessons from Mexico," by Francisco Gil Diaz and Raul R. Tercero, in M. Bruno, <u>et al.</u>, eds., 1988, <u>op. cit.</u>

<u>e</u>/   <u>China: Country Economic Memorandum</u>, 1989, <u>op. cit.</u>, pp. 57-61.

<u>f</u>/   On the importance of the call money market for monetary management in Japan during the sixties and seventies, see "Banking and Finance," by Henry C. and Mabel I. Wallich, in <u>Asia's New Giant</u>, eds. Hugh Patrick and Henry Rosovsky, Brookings Institution, 1976, pp. 312-314.

<u>g</u>/   See "Financial Flows to Developing Countries," March 1990, <u>World Bank</u>, Table 15.A., p. 28.

Chapter 3

<u>a</u>/   See <u>China: Country Economic Memorandum</u>, 1989, <u>op. cit.</u>, p. 13 where the evidence on factor productivity is summarized.

<u>b</u>/   See <u>China: Country Economic Memorandum</u>, 1989, <u>op. cit.</u>, pp. 15-17. Josef Brada's study of the CMEA countries for the 1971-85 period suggests, that macropolicy impinging on growth is the major determinant of efficiency, whereas economic reform influences technical efficiency less strongly and its effects are felt more slowly. "Technological Progress and Factor Utilization in Eastern European Economic Growth," by Josef C. Brada, <u>Economica</u>, vol. 56, November 1989, p. 443.

<u>c</u>/   "What Determines the Rate of Growth and Technological Change?" by Paul M. Romer, <u>World Bank Working Paper Series</u>, No. 279, September 1989, p. 23.

d/   The strength of heavy industry's claim on resources arises from the
     importance it has received since the 1950s, the size and quality of its
     bureaucracy and its contribution to the central government's revenues.
     Opposition from this sector could offset the future of industrial reform
     and distort the choice of strategy. "The Politics of Industrial Reform,"
     by Susan L. Shirk, in The Political Economy of Reform in Post-Mao China,
     op. cit., 1985, pp. 207-208.

e/   Examples are Japan, the United States, the Federal German Republic, and
     Italy among developed countries; South Korea and Brazil among the devel-
     oping nations.

f/   A discussion of current industrial plans and suggestions with regard to
     future policies is contained in a forthcoming Bank report, China:
     Industrial Policies in the Medium Term, World Bank, February 1990.

g/   Automobile production capacity in 1989 was 650,000 vehicles, actual
     output 573,000. "Motor Vehicle Production," Xinhua, September 2, 1989.

h/   See "The Economic Costs of Food Self-Sufficiency in China," by Yang
     Yongzheng and Ronald Tyers, World Development, Vol. 17, No. 2 where the
     costs and implications of self-sufficiency are discussed.

i/   The details of reform are to be found in "Agricultural Organization: New
     Forms, New Contradictions," by Reeitsu Kojima, The China Quarterly,
     No. 116, December 1988; and "The Evolution of Agricultural Policy," by
     Robert F. Ash, The China Quarterly, No. 116, December 1988.

j/   See "Investment Issues in the Chinese Countryside," by Andrew Watson,
     Australian Journal of Chinese Affairs, No. 22, July 1989, pp. 90-94. The
     irrigated area was increased from 20 million hectares in 1950 to 45
     million hectares in 1976, 45 percent of the total cultivated. The mul-
     tiple cropping index also increased from 131 percent to 151 percent,
     which is similar to that of India and among the highest in the world.

k/   According to one estimate, 41 percent of the growth in productivity
     during 1965-87 was because of rising inputs with fertilizers accounting
     for two thirds. "Inhibition of Factor Markets, Institutional Reform and
     Induced Technological Theory and Empirical Evidence," by Justin Yifu Lin,
     UCLA Working Paper No. 576, December 1989.

l/   See R. Ash op. cit., 1988, pp. 346-47; and "Trends in Crop Production,
     1978-86," by Kenneth Walker, The China Quarterly, No. 116, December 1988,
     p. 611.

m/   Andrew Watson, op. cit., 1989.

n/   See "Agricultural Crisis in China," by Joseph Fewsmith, Problems of
     Communism, November/December 1988, p. 91. Further discussion of inter-
     sectoral transfers can be found in "Structure and Motifs in the Food and
     Price Policy Story," by Terry Sicular in Food Price Policy in Asia,
     edited by Terry Sicular, Cornell University Press, 1989, esp. pp. 276-77;

"Intersectoral Resource Flows in China Revisited: Who Provided Industrialization Funds?" by Katsuji Nakagane, The Developing Economies, Vol. 27, No. 2, June 1989, pp. 146-173; "Peasants and Politics," by David Zweig, World Policy Journal, Vol. 6, No. 4, Fall, 1989, pp. 637-41; and "China: Consumer Food Subsidies," by Alan Piazza, World Bank, mimeo, February 1990. One interesting finding reported in this paper is that the total transfer value of all food subsidies to the urban population (including budgetary transfers) was Y 44 billion in 1988.

o/ "China's Energetics: A System Analysis," by Vaclav Smil, in Energy in the Developing World, eds. V. Smil and W.E. Knowland, Oxford University Press, 1980, pp. 135-37.

p/ These choices are analyzed in a forthcoming study by the World Bank entitled Managing Agricultural Transition, June 1990. China and India are the countries which will most profoundly influence the cereals deficit of developing countries (and hence market prices) through the year 2000. See World Agriculture: Toward 2000, ed. by Nikus Alexandratos, FAO, Bellhaven Press, 1988, pp 83-92.

q/ For an analysis of tax incidence in terms of direct and indirect taxes, see China: Revenue Mobilization and Tax Policy, Issues and Options (June 15, 1989), World Bank, Report No. 7605-CHA.

r/ Industrial Yearbook, p. 19; Fiscal Statistics, pp. 126-127.

s/ "Fiscal Reform, Elite Turnover and Central-Provincial Relations in Post-Mao China", by James Tong, The Australian Journal of Chinese Affairs, No. 22, July 1989, pp. 2-7.

t/ See "Regional Economies and Government Finances," by Yuzo Ishikawa, China Newsletter, No. 83, November/December 1989, p. 13.

u/ The issuance of money has also transferred resources equivalent to 3.5 percent of GNP on average (1984-88) per annum to the monetary authorities which are then used to finance state investments. The PBC has directly funded the capital spending of 600 to 800 state owned enterprises and indirectly supported the investment of others through low interest lending to the specialized banks.

v/ Gongye Jingji Guanli Congkan [Industrial Economic Management Digest], 1989:3, pp. 3-4; 1989:5, p. 78; 1989:9, p. 5.

w/ The dispersal of political authority in China, which in a small way resembles that of the US, makes it difficult to introduce broad tax reforms as against incremental changes or changes of a particularistic nature. What Steinmo notes of the US is also true for China, "Because political authority is fragmented, it is exceptionally difficult to change the basic rules of the tax system, but introducing or amending specific measures to adjust the system on behalf of specific groups can be done relatively easy .... Similarly the incentive structure of the [political] system forces interest groups to fight for particularistic tax measures even when the general ideological positions would tend to favor a more neutral tax system." "Political Institutions and Tax Policy in the U.S., Sweden and Britain," by Sven Steinmo, World Politics, Vol. 41, No. 4, July 1989, pp. 512-13.

x/ The evidence on the social costs of taxation and the effects of these "deadweight" losses on national output is summarized in "Do Taxes Matter," by Jonathan Skinner, World Bank, Working Paper Series, No. 48, August 1989, esp. p. 45.

y/ "Intersectoral Financial Flows in Developing Countries," by Patrick Honohan and Izak Atiyas, World Bank Working Paper Series, No. 164, March 1989, pp. 32-33.

z/ High tax/GNP ratios and respectable tax elasticities in Sweden and Britain as compared to the US are traced by Steinmo to the breadth and rate of consumption and not income taxes. Steinmo, op. cit., 1989, pp. 513-18.

aa/ "Issues in Income Tax Reform in Developing Countries, by Cheryl W. Gray, World Bank Working Paper Series, August 1989, pp. 31-39.

ab/ See "Implementing Chinese Tax Policy," by David Bachman, in Policy Implementation in Post-Mao China, ed. David M. Lampton, University of California Press, 1987, pp. 152-53.

ac/ "CPEs' Structural Change and World Market Performance: A Permanently Developing Country Status," by Jan Winiecki, Soviet Studies, Vol. 41, No. 3, July 1989, p. 370.

ad/ The Daqing field, which accounts for 40 percent of output, is 14 years old. Total production was 135 million tons in 1988, rising to 137.5 million tons in 1989. New finds in the northwest (Tarim Basin) have been reported but the target of 200 million tons by the year 2000 seems optimistic. "Chinese Oil Industry Begins to Feel its Age," Financial Times, January 5, 1990.

ae/ Since 1985, coal production has risen by 47 million tons per annum and in 1989 reached 1.04 billion tons. China Daily, December 29, 1989.

af/ "China and Japan in the New Energy Era," by Vaclav Smil, Journal of Business Administration, Vol. 16, Nos. 1 and 2, 1986, p. 229.

ag/ Thirty-two coal faces, each capable of producing 1 million tons per annum were commissioned in 1989. China Daily, December 29, 1989.

ah/ Only about one fifth of all coal is washed to separate ash and mining debris. About 30 percent of raw coal output is made up of rocks, clay and ash, this poses problems for the end-user and places an unnecessary burden on the railway system, 40 percent of whose capacity is devoted to transporting coal. Smil, op. cit., 1986, p. 229; and Coal Strategy Note, World Bank, January 24, 1990, pp. 11-12.

ai/ The scale of returns is noted in "Money to Burn," <u>The Economist</u> (London), January 6, 1990, p. 65.

aj/ "The Energy Impediment to China's Growth," R. Granzer, <u>OECD Observer</u>, April/May 1989, p. 14.

ak/ <u>China: Coal Utilization Study</u>, Report No. 8915-CHA, World Bank, July 9, 1990; see also Smil, <u>op. cit.</u>, 1986, p. 229. Upgrading some of the 300,000 boilers in use, especially the smaller ones, would also contribute significantly to energy efficiency.

al/ "Improving the Efficiency of Electricity Use in Industry," by Marc Ross, <u>Science</u>, April 21, 1989, Vol. 244, pp. 311-17.

am/ The General Logistics Department owns and operates a large number of enterprises that were created to make each province at least militarily self-sufficient in the event of a "people's war". These include coal mines and various service sector agencies. The four main defense industries--aeronautics, space, weapons and nuclear power--comprise some 1,200 enterprises, employing approximately 3 million workers. The total production of the defense sector was valued at Y 18.5 billion in 1988 and Y 20 billion in 1989. Civilian goods, e.g., TV sets, motorbikes and refrigerators, accounted for 60 percent or more of the total. Military enterprises have established numerous joint production arrangements with civilian manufacturers and transferred technology in areas such as energy, integrated circuits, aeronautics, medicine and electrical machinery. See "Civilian Goods Production by the Military Supply Industry," by Seiichi Nakajima, <u>China Newsletter</u>, March-April 1990, No. 85, pp. 10-12; "The Military in China," by Harlan W. Jencks, <u>Current History</u>, September 1989, p. 265; and "Defense Budget Will Rise Over Last Year, <u>China Daily</u>, January 23, 1990; and "China's Drive to Close the Technological Gap: S&T Reform and the Imperative to Catch Up," by Denis Fred Simon, <u>China Quarterly</u>, No. 119, September 1989, pp. 612-613.

an/ "Science, Technology and China's Political Future," by Richard P. Suttmeier in <u>Science and Technology in Post-Mao China</u>, edited by Denis Fred Simon and Merle Goldman, Harvard University Press, 1989, pp. 387-88.

ao/ <u>Asia's New Giant</u>, by Alice H. Amsden, Oxford University Press, 1989, Chs. 11 and 12; "Technology: Concepts, Methods and Issues," by Sanjaya Lall, Oxford University, mimeo, June 1989, p. 23.

ap/ "The Quiet Path to Technological Preeminence," <u>Scientific American</u>, Vol. 261, No. 4, October 1989, p. 43.

aq/ "Jiangsu's New Wave in Foreign Investment," by Richard Pomfret, <u>China Business Review</u>, November/December 1989, p. 15.

ar/ "Joint Ventures in China: Inscrutable, <u>The Economist</u> (London), March 17, 1990, pp. 66-68.

as/ "Foreign Direct Investment in the PRC: Progress, Problems and Proposals," by Jerome A. Cohen and Stuart Valentine, Journal of Chinese Law, Vol. 1, No. 2, 1987, pp. 206-14.

at/ "Foreign Land Leases Will Help Develop Coast, SEZs," China Daily, April 13, 1990, p. 1; and "Bank Ready for Active Role," China Daily, April 1, 1990, p. 1.

au/ Hirschman has labeled this phenomenon the "tunnel effect". See "The Changing Tolerance for Income Inequality in the Course of Economic Development" in Economics to Politics and Beyond by Albert O. Hirschman, Cambridge University Press, 1987.

av/ In 1988, the annual average wage for Party and state employees was at the bottom of the scale for nonagricultural employees (1,708 yuan); commerce workers came next with 1,733 yuan; workers in the education sector 1,764 yuan; health workers 1,793; and at the top were industrial workers with 1,931 yuan. Subsidies to government employees narrowed these differentials but, on the other hand, industrial workers also received in-kind benefits which probably restore the gap in total compensation. Data are from 1989 Statistical Yearbook.

aw/ "Reform Corruption: A Discussion on China's Current Development," by Stephen K. Ma, Pacific Affairs, Vol. 62, No. 1, Spring 1989, pp. 49-51.

ax/ See, for instance, "Pre- and Post-Reform Income Distribution in a Chinese Commune: The Case of Dahe Township in Hebei Province," by Bingyuang Hsiung and Louis Putterman, Journal of Comparative Economics, Vol. 13, September 1989, pp. 439-43; and "Growth Processes and Distributional Change in a South Chinese Province: The Case of Guangdong," by Peter Nolan, Contemporary China Institute, SOAS, Research Study No. 5, 1983, p. 88. Nolan attaches more importance to a widening spread of incomes in rural areas along with a decline in poverty.

Chapter 4

a/ "China's Price Reform in the 1980s," by Thomas M.H. Chan, in China: Modernization in the 1980s, ed. Joseph Y.S. Cheng, Chinese University Press, 1989, pp. 312-20; see also "Planning and the Market in China," by Kyoichi Ishihara, The Developing Economies, Vol. 25, No. 4, December 1987, p. 305.

b/ Domestic prices for raw materials are generally below border prices whereas for intermediates, it is the reverse. China: Industrial Policies for an Economy in Transition, World Bank Report Nos. 8312-CHA, February 1990, p. 66.

c/ For example, even with a commodity such as coal where controls are extensive, many consumers buy on the free market. In 1989, the prices for a ton of steam coal in Shanxi were 120-150 yuan and 200-250 yuan in East China, the latter being equal to or above world market prices. Coal Sector Strategy Note, World Bank, January 24, 1990. However, in certain areas such as transport, the fixity as well as the uniformity of prices introduces important distortions. Even though passenger fares were increased by 120 percent in October 1989, freight rates remained unchanged until March 1990 and did not reflect the route, gradient, equipment and traffic volume. Hence, supply routes for commodities such as coal have not been optimally determined and industries that are heavily transport-intensive, e.g., metallurgical as well as power-generating facilities, may not be sited optimally. "Chinese Experience in the Introduction of a Market Mechanism into a Planned Economy: The Role of Pricing," by Yushi Mao and Paul Hare, Journal of Economic Surveys, Vol. 3, No. 2, 1989, p. 144.

d/ China: Industrial Policies in the Medium Term, World Bank, February 1990.

e/ "Factory and Manager in an Era of Reform," by Andrew Walder, The China Quarterly, No. 118, June 1989, p. 243.

f/ "China's Capital Goods Market," Beijing Review, November 13-19, 1989.

g/ "Price Reform in China: Editor's Introduction," by Chen Shenshen, Chinese Economic Studies, Spring 1989, p. 11.

h/ This structuralist explanation of inflation as a struggle over shares has been frequently advanced to explain the macro problems of Latin America. It seems as valid in China. See Varieties of Stabilization Experience by Lance Taylor, Clarendon Press, Oxford, 1988, pp. 63. On China, see "The Politics of Industrial Reform," by Susan Shirk, in The Political Economy of Reform in Post-Mao China, op. cit., 1985, pp. 199-202; "Open-Ended Economic Reform in China," by Cyril Z. Lin, in Remaking the Economic Institutions of Socialism, op. cit., pp. 107-112; and "The Political Economy of Chinese Industrial Reform," by Susan Shirk, in Remaking the Economic Institutions of Socialism, op. cit., pp. 343-348.

i/ See Flexible Rigidities by Ronald Dore, The Athlone Press, London, 1986; "Employment and Wage Systems in Japan and Their Implications for Productivity," by M. Hashimoto, in Paying for Productivity, ed. by Alan S. Blinder, Brookings Institution, 1990; and "Differences in Economic Fluctuations in Japan and the U.S.: The Role of Nominal Rigidities," by John B. Taylor, Journal of Japanese and International Economics, Vol. 3, June 1989.

j/ "Changing Conceptions of the Socialist Enterprise in China, 1979-88," by Robert C. Hsu, Modern China, Vol. 15, No. 4, October 1989, pp. 508-11.

k/ See Andrew Walder, "Factory and Manager in the Era of Reform," The China Quarterly, No. 118, June 1989, pp. 249-53; Jim Mann, writing on the experience of foreign investors in China notes, "Private Western businessmen discovered that Chinese factory managers spent much of their time on welfare problems and had little independent decision-making authority. The real power lay with cadres in the municipalities, in government ministries or in the Party leadership.... Chinese state enterprises were more willing to tolerate inefficiency for the sake of equality of income, full employment and social order." Beijing Jeep, Jim Mann, Simon and Schuster, 1989, p. 307.

l/   Walder, op. cit., 1989, pp. 246-47.

m/   Hsu, op. cit., 1989, p. 516.

n/   A managerial objective in some Western firms in the past, though perhaps less so in the era of leveraged buy-outs.

o/   "Chinese Experience in the Introduction of a Market Mechanism into a Planned Economy: The Role of Pricing," by Yushi Mao and Paul Hare, Journal of Economic Surveys, Vol. 3, No. 2, 1989, p. 149.

p/   See China: Country Economic Memorandum, 1989, Vol. 2, pp. 116-17.

q/   From Marx to the Market, by W. Brus and K. Laski, Clarendon Press, Oxford, 1989, Ch. 10.

r/   The decision in early 1990 to set up the China National Automotive Industry Corporation, enfolding all of China's auto producers, although it may improve planning and coordination under the existing system, is unlikely to advance the cause of industrial competition. Far Eastern Economic Review, February 22, 1990, p. 67.

s/   Brus and Laski, op. cit., 1989, pp. 141-43.

t/   See Rural Non-Farm Activities in China: Growth and Effects of Township Enterprises, 1978-87, by Yok Shiu Federick Lee, PhD dissertation, MIT, May 1988.

u/   A sample of TVEs in five provinces indicated that workers were frequently exposed to high levels of lead dust, mercury, silica dust and asbestos. See China: Long-Term Issues and Options in the Health Transition, World Bank, May 1990, Chapter 3.

w/   However, recent work by Gary Jefferson shows that scale economies may be important in state and collective sectors. He suggests that it may be advisable to regulate the proliferation of small-scale enterprises. "Potential Sources of Productivity Growth Within Chinese Industry" by Gary H. Jefferson, World Development, Vol. 17, No. 1, p. 54.

x/   The nature of China's private sector, its future role and the problems it has generated have been the subject of much discussion in China. See "The Private Economy," ed. Stanley Rosen (1) and (2), Chinese Economic Studies, Fall and Winter, 1987/88; and "Policy, Practice and the Private Sector in China," by Susan Young, Australian Journal of Chinese Affairs, No. 21, January 1989.

Chapter 5

a/ The importance of the SEZs for China's development strategy and the intention to intensify the export orientation of coastal areas was reaffirmed by Premier Li Deng at a conference convened by the State Council in February 1990. "Li Describes SEZs as Part of Nation's Major Reform Plan," China Daily, February 10, 1990.

b/ Post-1988 reform actions by new FTCs and trading enterprises moved some of China's trading partners to consider antidumping actions and threaten to discontinue trading. As legal and market institutions are still too underdeveloped to exert corrective pressures, action by the center was difficult to avoid. "GATT's Problems with China," Far Eastern Economic Review, January 11, 1990, p. 46.

c/ "Information, Transaction Costs and the Organization of Distribution: The Case of Japan's General Trading Companies," by Kwang-shik Shin, Journal of Japanese and International Economics, Vol. 3, September 1989.

d/ The debt service ratio of 15 percent for end-1989 announced by the Chinese authorities includes the amortization of short-term debt.

e/ "China's Hard Currency Problem," China Newsletter, JETRO, No. 82, September/October 1989, p. 6; and "China's Gold Stocks on Increase," China Daily, November 9, 1989. "Financial Difficulties and Prospects for the Future," by Isao Okubo, China Newsletter, No. 84, May-June 1990, p. 16. During the latter half of 1989, China is believed to have sold between 100 and 120 tons of nonpublic gold ingot reserves valued at about $1.3 billion. See "Prolonged Economic Adjustment," by Satoshi Imai, China Newsletter, March-April 1990, pp. 7-8.

f/ A hint of the trend in future spreads is contained in the syndicated loan of $30 million being arranged by CCIC Finance, Ltd. for China International Iron and Steel Investment Corporation. Four Japanese banks committed themselves to this loan in February 1990. The interest rate spread is reported to be 75 to 100 basis points over LIBOR. Spreads reported by the Chinese in mid-1990 are averaging 70 to 80 basis points. A loan of $126 million by the Mitsubishi Trust and Banking Corporation to Air China in early July 190 was made at 1 percent over LIBOR. "Japanese Bank Loan Agreed for Air China," South China Morning Post, July 1, 1990.

g/ See World Bank, Korea: The Management of External Liabilities, 1988.

Chapter 6

a/ "Reform Economics: The Classification Gap," by Janos M. Kovacs, Daedalus, Winter 1990, pp. 216, 223.

b/ Contradictions and Dilemmas by Janos Kornai, The MIT Press, 1986, p. 216.

c/ Kornai, op. cit., 1986, p. 223.

d/ "Localism, Elitism and Immobilism; Elite Formation and Social Change in Post-Mao China," by Cheng Li and David Bachman, World Politics, Vol. 42, October 1989, No. 1, p. 91.

e/ "Fiscal Reform, Elite Turnover and Central-Provincial Relations in Post-Mao China," by James Tong, Australian Journal of Chinese Affairs, No. 22, July 1989, pp. 7-9.

f/ Cheng Li and David Bachman, op. cit., 1989, p. 73.

g/ Questions regarding ownership rights have been debated in China since the late 1970s, initially in the context of setbacks encountered by earlier efforts at decentralization. In the 1985-88 period, the worry has been over the blurring of authority, responsibility and interests between central and local governments and between government and enterprises. With ownership issues still unsettled, negotiation, which is not governed by widely accepted rules, tends to prevail over market forces in the allocation of resources. One of the earliest articles on ownership matters was by Dong Fureng (1979). His contribution, as well as more recent ones by Chinese authors, are collected in "On the Question of Ownership and Property Rights," Chinese Economic Studies, Fall 1989.

h/ China: Reforming Social Security in a Socialist Economy, World Bank Report No. 8074-CHA, March 1990.

i/ The international experience is summarized by Blinder. See "Introduction," by Alan Blinder in Paying for Productivity, ed. Alan S. Blinder, Brookings Institution, 1990.

j/ On the empirical evidence of links between savings and growth, see "The Economics of Development: A Survey," by N. Stern, Economic Journal, vol. 99, No. 397, September 1989, p. 612.

k/ The relationship between savings and the interest rate is quite uncertain. For a positive marshalling of the evidence, see "Financial Liberalization in Developing Countries," by Bela Balassa, World Bank Working Paper Series, No. 55, September 1989.

l/ China Country Economic Memorandum: Macroeconomic Stability and Industrial Growth Under Decentralized Socialism, World Bank, Report No. 7483-CHA, June 12, 1989, pp. 103-113.

Distributors of World Bank Publications

ARGENTINA
Carlos Hirsch, SRL
Galería Guemes
Florida 165, 4th Floor-Ofc. 453/465
1333 Buenos Aires

**AUSTRALIA, PAPUA NEW GUINEA,
FIJI, SOLOMON ISLANDS,
VANUATU, AND WESTERN SAMOA**
D.A. Books & Journals
648 Whitehorse Road
Mitcham 3132
Victoria

AUSTRIA
Gerold and Co.
Graben 31
A-1011 Wien

BAHRAIN
Bahrain Research and Consultancy
  Associates Ltd.
P.O. Box 22103
Manama Town 317

BANGLADESH
Micro Industries Development
  Assistance Society (MIDAS)
House 5, Road 16
Dhanmondi R/Area
Dhaka 1209

> *Branch offices:*
> 156, Nur Ahmed Sarak
> Chittagong 4000
>
> 76, K.D.A. Avenue
> Kulna

BELGIUM
Publications des Nations Unies
Av. du Roi 202
1060 Brussels

BRAZIL
Publicacoes Tecnicas Internacionais
  Ltda.
Rua Peixoto Gomide, 209
01409 Sao Paulo, SP

CANADA
Le Diffuseur
C.P. 85, 1501B rue Ampère
Boucherville, Québec
J4B 5E6

CHINA
China Financial & Economic Publishing
  House
8, Da Fo Si Dong Jie
Beijing

COLOMBIA
Enlace Ltda.
Apartado Aereo 34270
Bogota D.E.

COTE D'IVOIRE
Centre d'Edition et de Diffusion
  Africaines (CEDA)
04 B.P. 541
Abidjan 04 Plateau

CYPRUS
MEMRB Information Services
P.O. Box 2098
Nicosia

DENMARK
SamfundsLitteratur
Rosenoerns Allé 11
DK-1970 Frederiksberg C

DOMINICAN REPUBLIC
Editora Taller, C. por A.
Restauración e Isabel la Católica 309
Apartado Postal 2190
Santo Domingo

EL SALVADOR
Fusades
Avenida Manuel Enrique Araujo #3530
Edificio SISA, 1er. Piso
San Salvador

EGYPT, ARAB REPUBLIC OF
Al Ahram
Al Galaa Street
Cairo

The Middle East Observer
8 Chawarbi Street
Cairo

FINLAND
Akateeminen Kirjakauppa
P.O. Box 128
SF-00101
Helsinki 10

FRANCE
World Bank Publications
66, avenue d'Iéna
75116 Paris

GERMANY, FEDERAL REPUBLIC OF
UNO-Verlag
Poppelsdorfer Allee 55
D-5300 Bonn 1

GREECE
KEME
24, Ippodamou Street Platia Plastiras
Athens-11635

GUATEMALA
Librerias Piedra Santa
5a. Calle 7-55
Zona 1
Guatemala City

HONG KONG, MACAO
Asia 2000 Ltd.
6 Fl., 146 Prince Edward
  Road, W.
Kowloon
Hong Kong

HUNGARY
Kultura
P.O. Box 149
1389 Budapest 62

INDIA
Allied Publishers Private Ltd.
751 Mount Road
Madras - 600 002

> *Branch offices:*
> 15 J.N. Heredia Marg
> Ballard Estate
> Bombay - 400 038
>
> 13/14 Asaf Ali Road
> New Delhi - 110 002
>
> 17 Chittaranjan Avenue
> Calcutta - 700 072
>
> Jayadeva Hostel Building
> 5th Main Road Gandhinagar
> Bangalore - 560 009
>
> 3-5-1129 Kachiguda Cross Road
> Hyderabad - 500 027
>
> Prarthana Flats, 2nd Floor
> Near Thakore Baug, Navrangpura
> Ahmedabad - 380 009
>
> Patiala House
> 16-A Ashok Marg
> Lucknow - 226 001

INDONESIA
Pt. Indira Limited
Jl. Sam Ratulangi 37
P.O. Box 181
Jakarta Pusat

ITALY
Licosa Commissionaria Sansoni SPA
Via Benedetto Fortini, 120/10
Casella Postale 552
50125 Florence

JAPAN
Eastern Book Service
37-3, Hongo 3-Chome, Bunkyo-ku 113
Tokyo

KENYA
Africa Book Service (E.A.) Ltd.
P.O. Box 45245
Nairobi

KOREA, REPUBLIC OF
Pan Korea Book Corporation
P.O. Box 101, Kwangwhamun
Seoul

KUWAIT
MEMRB Information Services
P.O. Box 5465

MALAYSIA
University of Malaya Cooperative
  Bookshop, Limited
P.O. Box 1127, Jalan Pantai Baru
Kuala Lumpur

MEXICO
INFOTEC
Apartado Postal 22-860
14060 Tlalpan, Mexico D.F.

MOROCCO
Société d'Etudes Marketing Marocaine
12 rue Mozart, Bd. d'Anfa
Casablanca

NETHERLANDS
InOr-Publikaties b.v.
P.O. Box 14
7240 BA Lochem

NEW ZEALAND
Hills Library and Information Service
Private Bag
New Market
Auckland

NIGERIA
University Press Limited
Three Crowns Building Jericho
Private Mail Bag 5095
Ibadan

NORWAY
Narvesen Information Center
Book Department
P.O. Box 6125 Etterstad
N-0602 Oslo 6

OMAN
MEMRB Information Services
P.O. Box 1613, Seeb Airport
Muscat

PAKISTAN
Mirza Book Agency
65, Shahrah-e-Quaid-e-Azam
P.O. Box No. 729
Lahore 3

PERU
Editorial Desarrollo SA
Apartado 3824
Lima

PHILIPPINES
National Book Store
701 Rizal Avenue
P.O. Box 1934
Metro Manila

POLAND
ORPAN
Palac Kultury i Nauki
00-901 Warszawa

PORTUGAL
Livraria Portugal
Rua Do Carmo 70-74
1200 Lisbon

SAUDI ARABIA, QATAR
Jarir Book Store
P.O. Box 3196
Riyadh 11471

MEMRB Information Services
> *Branch offices:*
> Al Alsa Street
> Al Dahna Center
> First Floor
> P.O. Box 7188
> Riyadh
>
> Haji Abdullah Alireza Building
> King Khaled Street
> P.O. Box 3969
> Damman
>
> 33, Mohammed Hassan Awad Street
> P.O. Box 5978
> Jeddah

**SINGAPORE, TAIWAN, MYANMAR,
BRUNEI**
Information Publications
  Private, Ltd.
02-06 1st Fl., Pei-Fu Industrial
  Bldg.
24 New Industrial Road
Singapore 1953

SOUTH AFRICA, BOTSWANA
For single titles:
Oxford University Press Southern
  Africa
P.O. Box 1141
Cape Town 8000

For subscription orders:
International Subscription Service
P.O. Box 41095
Craighall
Johannesburg 2024

SPAIN
Mundi-Prensa Libros, S.A.
Castello 37
28001 Madrid

Librería Internacional AEDOS
Consell de Cent, 391
08009 Barcelona

SRI LANKA AND THE MALDIVES
Lake House Bookshop
P.O. Box 244
100, Sir Chittampalam A. Gardiner
  Mawatha
Colombo 2

SWEDEN
For single titles:
Fritzes Fackboksforetaget
Regeringsgatan 12, Box 16356
S-103 27 Stockholm

For subscription orders:
Wennergren-Williams AB
Box 30004
S-104 25 Stockholm

SWITZERLAND
For single titles:
Librairie Payot
6, rue Grenus
Case postale 381
CH 1211 Geneva 11

For subscription orders:
Librairie Payot
Service des Abonnements
Case postale 3312
CH 1002 Lausanne

TANZANIA
Oxford University Press
P.O. Box 5299
Dar es Salaam

THAILAND
Central Department Store
306 Silom Road
Bangkok

**TRINIDAD & TOBAGO, ANTIGUA
BARBUDA, BARBADOS,
DOMINICA, GRENADA, GUYANA,
JAMAICA, MONTSERRAT, ST.
KITTS & NEVIS, ST. LUCIA,
ST. VINCENT & GRENADINES**
Systematics Studies Unit
#9 Watts Street
Curepe
Trinidad, West Indies

TURKEY
Haset Kitapevi, A.S.
Istiklal Caddesi No. 469
Beyoglu
Istanbul

UGANDA
Uganda Bookshop
P.O. Box 7145
Kampala

UNITED ARAB EMIRATES
MEMRB Gulf Co.
P.O. Box 6097
Sharjah

UNITED KINGDOM
Microinfo Ltd.
P.O. Box 3
Alton, Hampshire GU34 2PG
England

URUGUAY
Instituto Nacional del Libro
San Jose 1116
Montevideo

VENEZUELA
Libreria del Este
Aptdo. 60.337
Caracas 1060-A

YUGOSLAVIA
Jugoslovenska Knjiga
P.O. Box 36
Trg Republike
YU-11000 Belgrade